ANTI-BLACK RACISM STILL INFECTS AMERICAN SOCIETY. African Americans are more likely to be killed by police, to be pulled over, arrested, imprisoned, and executed than whites who commit the same crimes. They are more likely to be turned down for a job or offered a bad home loan than equally qualified whites.

The killing of unarmed black men in Ferguson, Missouri, and Baltimore, Maryland, triggered riots. A white terrorist massacred black worshipers in Charleston, South Carolina. Eight black churches were burned in the South in ten days.

Kansas Citians, like so many others across the nation, wonder, "Could it happen here?" The answer lies in this study of Kansas City's darkest moments—slavery, the border war, the Civil War, bombings of black homes, lynchings, the segregation of neighborhoods and schools, the civil rights struggle, the Black Panther movement, the 1968 race riot, assassinations in the 1970s, the infamous *Missouri v. Jenkins* U.S. Supreme Court case, and the racial inequities that still plague Kansas City today. Threaded throughout *Racism in Kansas City* are stories of Kansas Citians, black and white, who fought ardently against racist policies—and won.

Racism in Kansas City, in the end, offers readers a hopeful message: with awareness comes understanding, then a willingness to push for positive social change.

RACISM
IN KANSAS CITY
A SHORT HISTORY

WITH A FOREWORD BY ALVIN BROOKS

BY G. S. GRIFFIN

CHANDLER LAKE BOOKS

Published by Chandler Lake Books,
an Imprint of Mission Point Press

Readers are encouraged to go to www.MissionPoint-
Press.com to contact the author or to find information
on how to buy this book in bulk at a discounted rate.

Published by Chandler Lake Books, an Imprint of
Mission Point Press
2554 Chandler Lake Rd.
Traverse City, MI 49686
(231) 421-9513
www.MissionPointPress.com

ISBN: 978-1-943338-02-3

Printed in the United States of America.
Library of Congress Control Number: 2015945035

TO GEORGE SAKOULAS, THE GREATEST HISTORIAN I KNOW.

CONTENTS

FOREWORD

As I write this foreword to *Racism in Kansas City: A Short History,* our nation and our president are mourning the domestic terrorist attack on nine African Americans (six women and three men), who were murdered during a prayer meeting at the Emanuel African Methodist Episcopal Church in Charleston, South Carolina. A young white male racist gunned down these people with the intent and mission, in his own words, "to start a race war."

This latest act of hatred based on the race of a people—African Americans—demonstrates that the issue of race in America has to be faced and addressed by all Americans with all deliberate speed.

Garrett S. Griffin, a young white "suburbanite," has written with intelligent research and oral interviews a well-documented history of black-white relations in an urban city, Kansas City, Missouri. *Racism in Kansas City: A Short History,* although written about Kansas City's past, can be fast-forwarded to our nation today. Griffin is skillful enough to integrate in his work the conditions that led up to the modern era of Kansas City. I'm able to identify with much of Griffin's work, from 1950 until the present, and therefore can attest to its clarity and accuracy. Griffin took on the challenge of writing this short history, which I'm sure surprised him as it unfolded before him. In this process, he learned about black-white relations and saw the disparities in Kansas City, which is a microcosm of America.

Racism in Kansas City: A Short History should be mandatory reading beginning with our middle school children and ending with parents and other adults. If together blacks, whites, and all others work toward eliminating those issues that divide us, no longer will so many be kept from benefiting from the "American dream." Griffin has set the stage for us…if not now, then when?

— *Alvin Brooks*

INTRODUCTION

In a time of white denial and ideas of racial transcendence (the notion that racism is a thing of the past), a study of racial animosity and violence in local history is hugely important. That is why I wrote this book. Before Michael Brown's death in Ferguson, Missouri (just 240 miles east of Kansas City), there were many unarmed black males who died in altercations with white policemen in the U.S.—but it was the ensuing riot that garnered national attention and sparked a new dialogue on race relations. When reflecting on police shootings and race riots, many white Americans insisted neither racism, nor the hopelessness of poverty, played any significant role in the conflict. Some went so far as to conclude not that "racism is a problem," but rather "black people are a problem." But other whites came to believe what most black Americans believe: that the black struggle is not over. Certainly, the events in Ferguson got Kansas Citians—just like others across the country—talking more and more about race. Kansas City papers published several articles covering race, while the mayor held a public forum on the topic. People starting asking: What is our racial history? What are present race relations like? Could Ferguson happen here?

Ferguson was a local story, as was Freddie Gray's death in a police van in late April of 2015 and the ensuing riots in Baltimore. Two months later, nine African Americans were killed in a Charleston church during their evening Bible study by a white terrorist. Other terrorists then began burning black churches in the South. The only way to understand these events is to examine local histories of black-white relations. There is much history to uncover. For example, when we think of the civil rights movement, perhaps we remember the great protests in Montgomery, Alabama, or Washington, D.C., yet events in other cities have failed to become part of the national narrative and are largely forgotten, even by their own residents. For example, when Martin Luther King, Jr., was assassinated, race riots erupted in 125 cities from coast to coast. Kansas City was one of them. What a loss for Kansas Citians, and other Americans, who may have never read the accounts of how this city fits into our racial history. Upheavals far away provoked thought and action in Kansas City, and Kansas City, in turn, affected people's struggles in other cities. To fully understand the American story, how progress is not inevitable, how it is won and how it is lost, we must study local history. In this way, we learn who we are as citizens of our city, our nation, and the human race.

This book will explore the entire greater metro area of Kansas City, which spans the state line of Missouri and Kansas; my references to Kansas City usually refer to Kansas City, Missouri, unless otherwise specified. One other note: while hatred greatly affected other minority groups in Kansas City, I feel that each story deserves its own book and hope readers will not be offended that I did not include information on the hardships faced by Russian Jewish Americans, Mexican Americans, Irish Americans, and other residents.

The 400 years of American slavery and segregation were years of unspeakable savagery; the education of American citizens in regards to this history is largely incomplete. This Introduction provides a brief overview of black-white relations in U.S. history to help the reader understand the disadvantages Black America faces in employment, education, housing, healthcare, and politics today. This will serve as an appropriate backdrop for a local study of racism in Kansas City.

Racism is a relatively recent human construct, arising long after slavery. British author Chris Harman writes, "The prevalence of racism today leads people to think it has always existed, arising from an innate aversion of people from one ethnic background for those from another. Slavery is then seen as a by-product of racism, rather than the other way around."[1] Indeed, though the idea of ethnic inferiority existed in ancient times (the Greek philosopher Aristotle was a proponent), it was not universal and was not the basis of ancient slavery. History's first slaves or indentured servants were prisoners of war, individual debtors, and the people of conquered cities. They suffered horribly, but in some places they were given the right to own property (including, sometimes, their own slaves), buy their freedom, or earn it by marrying into the owner's family or fighting in war. Though barbaric, slavery was not a lifelong sentence due to mythical biological inferiority.

Africans were neither prisoners of war nor debtors, and thus European traders and owners were forced to concoct new justifications for their atrocities when the slave trade exploded in the 1600s alongside the cultivation of tobacco and sugar.[2] This is how the idea of black stupidity and laziness emerged, quite incredible considering many African kingdoms were as advanced as European states in many ways (Timbuktu had a university that was an international center of learning). Treating people like animals was easy to justify after dehumanizing them. In pursuit of the massive profits provided by free labor, European whites packed ships with naked Africans, who lay in their own filth for months until reaching the Caribbean or Americas. There they were "sold at auctions and then whipped into working 15, 16 or even 18 hours a day until they died. About 12 million people suffered this fate. A million and a half died while making the passage. The death toll on the planta-tions was horrendous, since the planters found it profitable to work someone to death and then buy a replacement."[3] This was especially true in the British Caribbean islands.[4]

These horrible conditions are not news to anyone who has undertaken serious study of the matter. One only need read the works of historian James W. Loewen to see how school text-books whitewash and omit the true barbarism of slavery and segregation.[5] Americans know of the chains and whippings, the Ku Klux Klan, the separate drinking fountains, theaters, and city buses. But the depths of white hatred are far more dis-turbing. The late historian Howard Zinn, in *A People's History of the United States,* wrote of slavery:

> The system was psychological and physical at the same time. The slaves were taught discipline, were impressed again and again with the idea of their own inferiority to "know their place," to see blackness as a sign of subordi-nation, to be awed by the power of the master, to merge their interest with the master's, destroying their own in-dividual needs. To accomplish this there was the disci-pline of hard labor, the breakup of the slave family, the

lulling effects of religion (which sometimes led to "great mischief," as one slaveholder reported), the creation of disunity among slaves by separating them into field slaves and more privileged house slaves, and finally the power of law and the immediate power of the overseer to invoke whipping, burning, mutilation, and death. Dismemberment was provided for in the Virginia Code of 1705. Maryland passed a law in 1723 providing for cutting off the ears of blacks who struck whites...[6]

John W. Blassingame writes, "Floggings of 50 to 75 lashes were not uncommon. On numerous occasions, planters branded, stabbed, tarred and feathered, burned, shackled, tortured, maimed, crippled, mutilated, and castrated their slaves."[7] Slaves could lose so much blood during a whipping or removal of a body part they would go into shock. Masters used instruments of torture such as heavy iron neck collars, which slaves might wear for weeks or months, making work more painful and sleeping comfortably impossible. Another device was the thumbscrew, used to crush the bones of a disobedient slave's thumbs. Some slaves were locked in metal masks to prevent them from attempting suicide through suffocation.

Owners made religion into a weapon. The Christian Bible was used to breed submissive and obedient slaves. Slavery propagandists pressured their clergymen to uphold slavery as a "divine institution which was a blessing to both master and slave."[8] Blassingame writes:

> Pointing to a long list of Bible verses, white ministers argued that Christianity would make the slaves easier to manage because obedience would be inner-directed rather than based on the whip.... Indeed, the Bible verses

the white ministers quoted frequently admonished slaves to be orderly and dependable workers devoted to their owner's interests, to be satisfied with their station in life, to accept their stripes patiently, and to view their faithful service to earthly masters as a service to God.... White ministers often taught the slaves that they did not deserve freedom, that it was God's will that they were enslaved, that the devil was creating those desires for liberty in their breasts.[9]

Such manipulation was despised and rejected by black adults, so ministers focused their efforts on slave children.

Another dimension of this inhumanity was the sexual violence. The rape of black women was pervasive. Slave girls were often forced to provide sexual acts to the master or face a flogging. Some whites took black women as concubines. As a result, male slaves often chose partners from neighboring plantations so they wouldn't have to watch the abuse and rape of their wives.[10]

After many years of petition, protest, escape, rebellion, and violence, American slavery was finally abolished in 1865 (long after Spain, Holland, Britain, France, and other nations had done the same) and impoverished ex-slaves spread throughout the country. But after a few decades migrants encountered communities called "sundown towns," which outlawed blacks and other minorities from the 1890s to the 1940s, some into the late 1960s.[11] Blacks moved to what they assumed would be friendlier cities and towns than in the South, yet were confronted with violence and intimidation at the hands of whites who disliked the idea of blacks in their communities. This was largely a racist reaction on the part of northern whites after a brief period of post-Civil War idealism. James Loewen writes, "Outside the traditional South—states historically dominated by slavery, where sundown towns are rare—*probably the majority of all incorporated places kept out African Americans.*"[12] Sundown towns and sundown suburbs still exist throughout America. Intentionally all-white, they seek to remain so. Because of this trend, blacks congregated in the big cities, where it was more difficult to expel growing minority populations, though some cities tried. Whites there did everything possible to keep black families out of their neighborhoods and confine black men and women to low-paying, segregated, menial work. Cities refused to invest in black areas of town, as did the white business class, which also overcharged blacks for goods. The police ignored (and committed) crimes against blacks. Institutional racism ensured blacks were excluded from New Deal programs that alleviated poverty, including Social Security. Whites barred blacks from voting and holding political office, denied them home loans, banned black students from colleges, and educated younger students in inferior facilities.

As blacks intruded on white areas and demanded basic human rights, white hate grew to unprecedented levels that persisted for a century. Consider the pamphlet that was distributed in 1956 to 10,000 men and women at a White Citizens Rally Against Integration in Montgomery (which the mayor attended):

> When in the course of human events it becomes necessary to abolish the Negro race, proper methods should be used. Among these are guns, bows and arrows, sling shots and knives.

We hold these truths to be self evident that all whites are created equal with certain rights; among these are life, liberty and the pursuit of dead niggers.

In every stage of the bus boycott we have been oppressed and degraded because of black slimy, juicy, unbearably stinking niggers. The conduct should not be dwelt upon because behind them they have an ancestral background of Pigmies, head hunters and snot suckers.

My friends it is time we wised up to these black devils. I tell you they are a group of two legged agitators who persist in walking up and down our streets protruding their black lips. If we don't stop helping these African flesh eaters, we will soon wake up and find Rev. King in the White House.

LET'S GET ON THE BALL WHITE CITIZENS.[13]

And many whites did just that. The willingness of ordinary people to resort to violence is astounding. It wasn't just in the South; every region was complicit. As the push for equality intensified in the 1950s and 60s, so did the terrorism. Buses and churches were bombed, black and white protesters were beaten with iron bars and clubs, movement leaders were assassinated, white rioters burned black neighborhoods; the police arrested thousands, unleashing attack dogs, tear gas, and water hoses on peaceful marchers. From 1882 to 1968, nearly 1,300 whites and almost three times as many blacks were lynched from the Pacific to the Atlantic Coast; many but not all occurred in the traditional South.[14] Those who executed blacks did so without fear, as their community courts were comprised of all-white juries that routinely exonerated racially motivated murder.

The terrorism of lynching cannot be glossed over. A lynching was public by definition. Thousands of white families would dress in their Sunday best and attend a well-publicized lynching of a black man, woman, or child. The atmosphere was festive and often included refreshments. Spectators took commemorative photographs, sometimes getting them made into postcards to send to relatives.[15] Blacks were not just hanged, but often burned alive, shot, or cut into pieces. Body parts, such as teeth, bones, ears, and genitals, were taken home as souvenirs.[16]

The effects of all this history persist today. A huge wealth gap has existed since slavery. Whites owned thirteen times the wealth of blacks in 2013, up from eight times in 2010.[17] Blacks are three times as likely to be poor, twice as likely to have low-paying work, and twice as likely to be unemployed compared to whites with the same education.[18]

According to the Center for American Progress, minorities comprise 30 percent of the citizenry, but 60 percent of our prisoners, the vast majority in for drug offenses. Blacks are not more likely to use drugs, but are far more likely to be stopped, searched, and arrested. For all crimes, they face harsher prison sentences and are more likely to be executed.[19]

Both armed and unarmed blacks are more likely to be killed by police than armed or unarmed whites. "More likely" does not necessarily mean most victims are black. From January to May of 2015, for example, 135 blacks (29 percent of victims) died in encounters with police, versus 234 armed or unarmed whites (50 percent). But the black population in the U.S. is only 13 percent, versus whites' 63 percent. This means blacks are killed disproportionately: they are killed at a higher rate than whites, when considering demographics. The same can be said of many other problems discussed in this book. There are more poor whites in the U.S., for example, but blacks are more likely to be poor than the average white person. At times, however, blacks are atop the numerical list. Of the 102 unarmed people killed in the aforementioned period, 15 percent were white, 32 percent black. Unarmed citizens killed by police were twice as likely to be black than white.[20] Anger over this and the predictable acquittal of the accused boiled over into protests and riots in 2014 and 2015.

Not only must blacks struggle against intergenerational poverty and police abuse, many live in high-crime neighborhoods. White denial teaches that there is simply something wrong with black culture or black parenting, which leads young black men into crime. But where poverty exists, crime will flourish, regardless of ethnicity or skin color. Attorney General Ramsey Clark put it best:

> Mark the part of your city where crime flourishes. Now look at the map of your city. You have marked areas where there are slums, poor schools, high unemployment, widespread poverty; where sickness and mental illness are common, housing is decrepit and nearly every site is ugly—and you have marked the areas where crime flourishes.... Poverty, illness, injustice, idleness, ignorance, human misery, and crime go together. That is the truth. We have known it all along. We cultivate crime, breed it, nourish it. Little wonder we have so much. What is to be said of the character of people who, having the power to end all this, permit it to continue?[21]

More and more Americans now recognize the historical causes of black poverty and how poverty breeds crime and violence. But we have a long way to go. Tim Wise's *Colorblind: The Rise of Post-Racial Politics and the Retreat from Racial Equity* makes this point. Research indicates about 60 percent of whites will admit to trusting stereotypes of lower intelligence, higher aggression, or laziness in blacks. About 25 percent of whites consider the ideal neighborhood to be completely free of African Americans. At the subconscious level, things are worse. Studies indicate nearly 90 percent of whites hold subconscious anti-black biases, negative associations we don't even realize we have.[22] In experiments, for example, whites describe the actions of blacks as more threatening and aggressive than identical white actions.[23] We hold racist ideas without wanting to.

Whether beyond our awareness or not, this racism perpetuates discrimination, from police killings to hiring practices. Studies show job applications with white-sounding names are 50 percent more likely to earn an interview than identical applications with "black" names, black men without criminal records are less likely to be called back for interviews than white men with criminal records, all other qualifications being equal, and blacks with college degrees are likewise twice as likely to be unemployed compared to whites with college degrees.[24] Because whites have easier access to better jobs, blacks make about 20 percent less than equally qualified whites in all fields of work.[25]

Blacks are discriminated against when seeking housing: borrowers are two and half to three times as likely to be steered into high-cost home loans as whites. Even high-income African Americans are several times more likely to be given a subprime loan than whites with equal or lower incomes.[26] Many white bankers are simply unwilling to offer minorities the favorable terms they offer equally (or less) qualified whites. There are millions of such cases reported each year, and the predatory interest rates are costing Black America billions.

All this while African American children are mired in a national school system that bases school funding on property taxes, ensuring poor neighborhoods have poor schools. Our majority-white schools spend, on average, $733 more on each student per year than majority-nonwhite schools. Some white districts receive twice the funding neighboring black districts receive.[27] Blacks and Hispanics disproportionately suffer with low-quality teachers, crumbling facilities, overcrowded classes, and a lack of books, supplies, and physical and mental health care. Wise writes, "Black students are two to three times more likely to be suspended or expelled than whites, even though they do not, contrary to popular belief, violate school rules disproportionately, relative to white students."[28] Schools with more black kids have more policemen, regardless of actual crime or misconduct rates.[29]

Even African Americans in the upper socioeconomic levels experience higher hypertension, infant mortality rates, and shorter lifespans due directly to stress caused by a discriminatory culture, and blacks are far less likely to receive life-saving drugs and operations than whites of identical diagnoses, insurance, income, and so on.[30] Finally, research shows that people who more strongly oppose social spending to reduce poverty are likely to have the strongest anti-black biases.[31]

That is our history. It is the story of cities across the country, so it is here we turn to Kansas City.

CHAPTER ONE
Slavery and Freedom – 1800-1865

In the early 1700s, French and Spanish colonists became the first to bring black slaves into what would become the state of Missouri. They were seizing Native American land, and enslaving natives as well, as one empire pushed south from Canada and the other pushed north from Mexico. Colonists concentrated their settlements in eastern Missouri near the Mississippi River, along with forts established here and there, including France's Fort de Cavagnial north of the Kansas City area. It is possible the French brought the first black slaves through what would become Kansas City. Spanish holdings were later ceded to the French, who quickly sold all their land west of the Mississippi to the young United States. American settlers were already pushing west from the coastal states. When President Thomas Jefferson began organizing a military expedition to explore his Louisiana Purchase, the land was far from empty.

A black man named York crossed the land that would become Kansas City. He journeyed with a group of thirty-three others, led by U.S. Army captains Meriwether Lewis and William Clark, York's lifelong owner. Traversing Native American land from Pennsylvania to the Pacific Ocean, the expedition mapped the mouth of the Kaw (Kansas) River beginning on June 26, 1804, where Kansas City would one day stand.

From 1804 to 1806, York surely felt a greater degree of freedom than in what is now Kentucky, where he had grown up with Clark. Though mentioned sparingly in the two captains' writings, it is clear York hunted buffalo and worked alongside the white men in their tasks, and prepared meals for Lewis and Clark. He slept and traveled by boat alongside the captains, an image that should replace the traditional one of a Lewis-Clark-Sacagawea trio. The company to a degree embraced democracy and equality; it is recorded that the votes of York and Sacagawea were included in certain key decisions, such as whether to attempt to cross the Columbia River in search of game.[1] York inspired in many Native Americans awe and admiration, a welcome respite from the attitudes toward blacks back east. At an Arikara village, on October 8, 1804, Clark wrote that "many Came to view us all day, much asstonished at my black Servent, who did not lose the oppertunity of [displaying] his powers Strength &c. &c. this nation never Saw a black man before."[2]

York and Clark seemed to have cared for each other. On June 29, 1805, after the captain and others were nearly lost to the Missouri River in a flash flood, Clark writes, "I found my Servent in Serch of us greatly agitated, for our wellfar."[3] When their adventure through the Louisiana Purchase ended, York returned to the typical life of an American slave. He asked Clark for his freedom, but Clark refused for over a decade before finally acquiescing; York spent some sixteen years a free man before his death in 1832. In January 2001, President Bill Clinton posthumously made York an honorary sergeant in the

U.S. Army. York was given the same title in the Missouri State Militia in 2006 by Governor Bob Holden. He was the first African American to travel from coast to coast.

York and his owner came and went through the future Kansas City, although Clark later returned to build Fort Osage east of the area in 1808; both Lewis and Clark served as governor of the territory they explored. Others followed their path to where the Kaw and Missouri meet. François Chouteau and a few French families established a trading post on the south side of the Missouri in 1821, presently northeast Kansas City where Troost Avenue begins (originally a path to the Missouri River used by the Osage Indians, named after Dutch doctor and slave-owner Benoist Troost). The Chouteau family of fur traders can safely be credited with birthing Kansas City, and owning the first slaves in the West Bottoms, one of them a girl named Nancy.[4] John C. McCoy established Westport in 1833 on the Santa Fe Trail (at modern-day Westport Road and Pennsylvania Avenue in Kansas City), which quickly became the new gateway to the Oregon, Santa Fe, and California trails. A group of investors journeyed to the area intending to create an official settlement, building on what Chouteau started in 1821; the "Town of Kansas" was recognized in 1850.

Kansas City proper had 500 residents in 1840, then 2,500 (1853), then more than 4,000 (1860). White settlers brought slaves with them, but both free and enslaved blacks made their mark on the area's development. Primarily, they helped build the towns in Jackson County, such as Westport, Kansas City, and Independence. Sam Shepard, for example, supervised fellow slaves in building the first Jackson County courthouse in 1827 in Independence.[5] Nearby, freewoman Emily Fisher ran a hotel and former slave Hiram Young was a blacksmith and wagon manufacturer, eventually becoming "one of the richest men in Jackson County."[6] He used his wealth to buy his family's freedom, and employed black and white labor, but he also owned three slaves.[7] Free blacks in Kansas City in 1860 included barber James M. Mahoney, father of four; Clarinda Crump, housekeeper, mother of four; Manuel Points, teamster; Thomas Tyler, cook at the Union Hotel; and William Hater, porter at the Clairborne House Hotel.[8]

Today diners enjoy rooftop dining at Kelly's Westport Inn at Westport Road and Pennsylvania Avenue, likely unaware it was once the site of the Boone Trading Post, where blacks were auctioned.[9] By the early 1860s, Kansas City proper had only 166 slaves and twenty-four free blacks[10] and Jackson County nearly 4,000 slaves and 70 free blacks.[11] In 1860, Platte County had more than 3,300 slaves.[12] Clay County (named for southern slave-owner Henry Clay) had 3,455 black slaves in 1861, 26.5 percent of the population.[13] Although Jackson County slave owners involved in large-scale agriculture often had dozens of slaves, most slave owners had but one—a cook or general servant. In 1860, only 4 percent of owners had twenty or more slaves; less than 1 percent had fifty or more.[14] Clay County owners had five slaves on average; the largest farms had twenty to forty.[15]

Southerners migrated to the fertile valley along the Missouri and Kaw rivers, most of them coming from Kentucky, Virginia, Tennessee, and North Carolina. With land going sterile in the old South in the 1840s and 1850s, this move was an economic necessity for farmers. Their migration increased the number of slaves in the area and drove up their value. From the 1830s to the 1850s, a slave in Jackson County consistently cost about $100 more than a slave in Virginia.[16] In the mid-1830s, local slaves were sold for $800-$900; by the late 1850s, buyers were paying approximately $1,000 for black women and $1,300 for black men (sometimes as high as $1,500).[17] Besides cultivating tobacco, corn, and cotton, the area became a leading producer of hemp. Owing to the rapidly growing number of high-value slaves, "Jackson County led the state in aggregate wealth by 1850."[18] Clay County also grew rich—a single day of commerce (January 1, 1859) saw $20,000 worth of slaves sold in Liberty, Missouri.[19] However, the number of slaves in Missouri was limited due to the proximity of free states—owning slaves was riskier when freedom was just a short distance away.

Slaves labored in the fields, or served as masons, bricklayers, smiths, maids, butlers, cooks, gardeners, nurses. Some lived in the homes of their masters, while on the larger farms multiple families were forced to live in a 12 by 14 foot shack. Slaves on larger farms usually specialized in one or two tasks, while those on the smallest farms performed many different duties. Field slaves ate mostly cornbread and potatoes, and were provided with one or two sets of clothing made from cheap material like wool or tow cloth.[20] House slaves fared better, sleeping in attics or bedrooms, sometimes receiving better clothing and nourishment, depending on the income level of the household and the owner's disposition. The closer contact between master and house slave sometimes resulted in a positive relationship, but it also increased the likelihood of sexual abuse. Usually, owners were careful to provide proper medical care for field slaves and house slaves, since there was no value in sick or dead slaves. Accidents, early childhood death, and disease always threatened.

A cholera epidemic in 1849 wiped out many Jackson County families; Jabez Smith lost between 100 and 200 slaves.[21]

Since field slaves usually worked on a small family farm, their owner often worked alongside them. Most often, men left their slave cabins each morning for the fields, women for the owner's house. Trusted slaves were sometimes sent on errands unsupervised. Black John, a slave owned by Colonel John Thornton in the 1820s, would go out hunting in Clay County on his own and was well known for his skill.[22] But an owner usually had an unspoken arrangement with his neighbors and associates—historian Kristen Epps calls it a sort of "neighborhood watch" program. They agreed to keep an eye on each other's slaves. A common practice in the area was to rent out slaves to other whites for short-term work, usually at a rate of around $7 per slave per month.[23] This gave slaves an opportunity to interact with slaves on other farms and in other homes. It also gave them a chance at freedom. Sometimes, in the border counties, when slaves went out to buy goods they'd run into abolitionists and learn how they could best escape to a free state. One abolitionist disguised himself as a peddler, directing slaves to the Underground Railroad when they came up to him seeking to make a purchase.

Slave owners were careful to prevent unsupervised gatherings of blacks. An 1847 Missouri law required the presence of a sheriff or officer during all religious services led by blacks; in 1854, a group of slaves in Platte County were convicted and fined for preaching the gospel to their friends.[24] However, churches gave slaves the opportunity to socialize, worship, and pray together. Besides a church, religious education might take place in the owner's home. The slaves either joined the white family or had a separate service in another part of the house. They were taught to be submissive and obedient to their masters, as unto God. Other social gatherings or celebrations in the slave community usually were held in secret.[25] However, there were times when owners allowed slaves to wed, although it violated state law. A slave named Bill Simms remembered, "If a slave wanted to marry a woman on another plantation he had to ask the master, and if both masters agreed they were married. The man stayed at his owners, and the wife at her owners. He could go to see her on Saturday night and Sunday."[26]

Song was a large part of slave life, whether at rest or work. During the Civil War, a slave named Anisty, working on the Withers' plantation in Clay County, sang:

> *Oh! Hits a long way*
> *To de furwell lane,*
> *Oh! Ma honey, ma honey, ma sweet.*
> *You kin ast brother mink and*
> *You kin ast brother crane,*
> *Oh! Ma honey, ma honey, ma sweet.*
> *Dey'll both look wise and*
> *Dey'll tell you de same,*
> *Oh! Ma honey, ma honey, ma sweet.*
> *Oh! Ma honey, ma honey*
> *Ma heart's delight!*
> *Oh! Ma honey, ma honey, ma sweet*

And George sang:

> *Oh! Jeff Davis, don't you know*
> *I'se got a house in Baltimo?*

Street cyahs runnin' right by de do.
An Oh! Ma little gal Dinah. Oh!
Yass Oh! Ma little gal Dinah, Oh![27]

Receiving one's freedom was a rare occurrence, though not unheard of. The Clay County court freed slaves Tom and Sylvia in 1828. That same year, a free African American named Joseph Collett bought and freed his wife, Hannah, and her children, America and Eliza.[28]

Slaves were passed on to the owner's children. One owner from Platte County wrote in his will: "It is my will and bequest that my daughter Elizabeth McGee have my negro girl AMANDA JANE as her own legal and lawful property forever."[29] Slaves, along with other forms of wealth, were often divided up among family members upon an owner's death. Slaves left out of a will could face the auction block.[30] When blacks were sold, families were often broken up, never to be reunited.

Jabez Smith, who moved from Virginia, owned more human beings than anyone in Jackson County. At that time, slaves received the surnames of their masters. Like many others later on, Malcolm X abandoned his surname, saying it was a vestige of slavery; he replaced "Little" with an "X" for the unknown name of his true ancestors. One of Smith's slaves explained to a companion:

My last name is Smith because I was born into slavery and my master's name was Jabez Smith. You probably never heard of him, sonny, he owned a big farm and about 300 darkies on Lexington road, at Independence, Mo. Yes, sir, Jabez Smith moved from Virginia to Independence in 1844, the same year I was born. I stayed on his place in Virginia until I was 7 or 8 years old, then Jabez Smith moved me to Independence.[31]

Smith brought with him 450 slaves, according to one source.[32] This would have made him one of the largest slave-owners in the United States.[33] The cluster of slave shacks on his main farm in Independence was known as "Nigger Hill."[34] Currently, William Chrisman High School sits on land that once belonged to Smith.

African American oppression was governed by slave codes established first for those living within the entire Louisiana Purchase. Blacks were subject to public whippings for infractions like leaving a plantation without permission or the death penalty for committing a felony. Another code was established in the state of Missouri for black Americans upon their birth: anyone one-quarter black was wholly black, and no free black emigrants were allowed to settle after 1825. After 1837, publishing or circulating abolitionist literature was punishable by a $1,000 fine and two years in prison (first offense), twenty years (second offense), then life (third offense). In 1847, it became illegal to teach blacks, free or slave, to read or write.[35] In Kansas City, no blacks were allowed on the streets after 10 p.m.[36] Jackson County erected a patrol fence guarded by armed men on horses.[37] Clay County had slave patrols as early as 1824. A woman slave named Annice was lynched in Clay County in 1850, followed by Peter in 1855, both for alleged murder.[38] Slave Eph Sanders said that for every kind master in Platte County there were two cruel ones.[39] In 1858, J.C. Iserman of Independence wrote that slave owners were "some of the meanest people who ever trod this earth" and Calvin

Davis of Independence wrote that slave owners "hate a free-state man worse than the Devil"; the next year, after presidential candidate Abraham Lincoln gave a speech in Leavenworth calling for new territories to be free soil, the *Leavenworth Weekly Herald* called him "an imbecile old fogy of one idea; and that is—nigger, nigger, nigger."[40]

Across the country, slaves fought back with acts of resistance, large and small—learning to read or write, working slowly, breaking tools, stealing, running away, and even killing their owners. Kansas City was no different. An 1848 "wanted" ad posted around town claimed that runaway slaves Stephen and John Scott had stolen horses, saddles, guns, and a mule from white folks. A $150 reward was offered for their capture. One of Jabez Smith's escaped slaves was gunned down in the street as he resisted arrest—even then he refused to surrender, so he was beaten to death. It was usually easier for men to escape, since women wouldn't leave behind their children. Slaves who were caught were often auctioned off. Before the sale they were held in a local jail, where they were stripped naked and sometimes assaulted by guards. In an 1848 incident in Liberty, Missouri, a white prisoner beat a slave's head "into a perfect jelly with a stick of wood." Slaves resisted violently at times. Abe Newby, a slave in Platte County, stabbed a foreman to death to avoid a beating. He was sentenced and hanged in 1853 in front of a large crowd. There were other instances of slaves hiding weapons and using them to defend themselves, such as a slave up in St. Joseph who shot his owner in the head in 1859.[41]

Anti-slavery people were not particularly welcome in the Kansas City area. In the early 1830s, when one Joseph Smith declared Missouri to be the Promised Land and Independence to be the site of the Second Coming of Christ, thousands of Mormons (who boasted integrated congregations and black priests) began flooding Jackson and other nearby counties. Their views on slavery, marriage, evangelism, and land owner-ship bred bitter enemies. According to Gordon C. Thomasson, "The immigration of substantial numbers of Mormons, whose land ownership was facilitated through a communal economic system, was seen as a social and electoral threat by older pro-slavery settlers."[42] Five hundred people met in Independence on July 20, 1833, to condemn the Mormon presence, fearful it would draw free blacks to the area and "corrupt our blacks, and instigate them to bloodshed." They declared Mormons were "tampering with our slaves, and endeavoring to rouse dissen-sion and raise seditions among them."[43]

An anti-slavery editorial in a Mormon newspaper prompted a white mob to destroy their printing press and other property. "A Mormon Bishop and elder were tarred and feathered," wrote William H. Young and Nathan B. Young, Jr., in *Your Kansas City and Mine.*[44] The Mormons were quickly forced out of Jackson County through violence. The Missouri Governor declared Mormons enemies of the state in 1838, so they fled to Illinois; it was technically legal to kill Latter-Day Saints in Missouri until 1975, although the law wasn't enforced. The Mormons were not the only religious group with abolitionist sentiments. In 1835, the Presbyterian Synod of Missouri built a statewide abolitionist movement that pushed for a constitu-tional convention that would eradicate slavery.[45]

Missouri was admitted to the Union as a slave state in 1821, after years of bitter conflict in the U.S. Congress—any new state, slave or free, would shift the balance of power in the

Senate and House between pro-slavery and anti-slavery politicians. The Missouri Compromise in 1820 agreed to accept
Missouri, but to also admit Maine as a free state and to deem
all territory west of Missouri and north of the 36th parallel as
free land. Having lost Missouri, abolitionist settlers, black and
white, worked to solidify their control over Kansas. For now at
least, blacks had only to cross the Missouri River into Kansas
territory, or head for present-day Nebraska or Iowa. Slaves
usually escaped on their own initiative or with help from other
blacks, though most escape attempts failed. A secret network of
families, the Underground Railroad, assisted runaway slaves by
hiding them and ferrying them across the river. The Wyandot
Indians were crucial in this effort, at times helping blacks reach
Canada. In the 1840s, many area slaves escaped to Tabor, Iowa.
John Brown helped them, but barely escaped capture in Jackson
County during one of his runs; two of his men were caught and
imprisoned.[46] Now a part of Kansas City, Kansas, the town of
Quindaro became a gateway to freedom for runaways in the
1850s. Quindaro resident Clarina Nichols hid runaways in her
cistern. One winter, a slave named George Washington walked
across the frozen Missouri River and into Quindaro.[47]

The Missouri Compromise collapsed on May 30, 1854,
when Congress voted into law the Kansas-Nebraska Act, introduced by Senator Stephen A. Douglas. It would allow the
residents of the Kansas and Nebraska territories to decide dem-
ocratically whether to permit slavery. Months of fierce debate
over the bill resulted in a crushing defeat for abolitionists, who
rightly held that it violated the Missouri Compromise, which
had drawn a boundary line across the former Louisiana Territory to delineate free and slave regions. Both Kansas and

Nebraska were north of the line. The act was a second major blow to anti-slavery forces in four years. The Fugitive Slave Act of 1850 had declared all citizens and government officials legally bound to help return runaway slaves to their owners.

The Kansas-Nebraska Act and the Fugitive Slave Act all but guaranteed violence between two sides that vehemently hated the ideology of the other. The North was no longer free land, and those who assisted slaves were deemed criminals.

The stage was set for what became known as the era of "Bleeding Kansas." Two opposing forces inhabited Kansas City, and tensions boiled. In 1855, a mob of enraged whites reacted to abolitionist articles in the Parkville *Industrial Luminary* by storming the newspaper building, seizing the printing press, and throwing it into the Missouri River.[48] George S. Park, the paper's editor and the future founder of Park College, was banished from Parkville. In Wyandotte (now Kansas City, Kansas), the anti-slavery Methodist Church North was razed in 1856, and then the pro-slavery Methodist Church South suffered the same fate.[49]

Nationally, the Underground Railroad expanded; tens of thousands of blacks fled north to Canada. Political setbacks sparked the founding of the anti-slavery Republican Party, launched by Alvan Bovay and other socialists in the former utopian, socialist community of Ripon, Wisconsin, in March 1854.[50]

At the 1855 Pro-Slavery Convention in nearby Lexington, Missouri, representatives from slaveholding counties (there were sixteen representatives from Jackson County; only two counties sent more) warned Congress that if it wished to preserve the Union then Kansas should not become free soil.[51]

Pro-slavery and anti-slavery citizens flooded Kansas in an attempt to establish supremacy. The Jackson County Pro-Slavery Pioneer Association was formed in 1856 to help pro-slavery families move into Kansas, and slaves came with them. In the mid-1850s, between 180 and 300 slaves lived in Kansas, a surprising number given the fact it was a free state.[52] On the other side was the New England Emigrant Aid Company, originally formed in Massachusetts, which helped fund abolitionist emigrants to Kansas. These northerners founded Topeka, Manhattan, Lawrence, and other free-soil towns. To counter the threat of "border ruffians" (pro-slavery forces from Missouri), the New England Emigrant Aid Company shipped rifles into Kansas in boxes labeled "Bibles" and helped form local militias. By 1856, free-soil settlers outnumbered pro-slavery forces in Kansas.[53] Abolitionists drove out many slave owners, triggering armed Missourians to push back.[54] They crossed the border, seized polling stations, and cast ballots in support of pro-slavery candidates for the Kansas territorial legislature in 1855. Jeremy Prichard wrote:

> The situation produced arguably some of the most notorious forms of fraudulent voting in 19th-century America. Missouri voters challenged the authority of election judges throughout the territory by threatening them (with death in some instances) for refusing to accept their ballots. The border ruffians...also threatened antislavery voters at election sites, convincing many Free-Soilers to stay home [election] day.[55]

That year Kansas would cast twice as many ballots as there were voters. Leavenworth saw five times as many votes as residents. The result was a powerful pro-slavery government, which established its capital at Lecompton, near the Missouri border, and quickly "passed laws that severely punished anyone who criticized or posed obstacles"[56] to slavery in Kansas. Indeed, anyone who helped a slave escape faced the death penalty or ten years of hard labor.[57] Free-state politicians rejected this government as fraudulent, abandoned their seats, and established their own government in Topeka. U.S. congressmen recognized the government that held true to their private ideologies. President Franklin Pierce rejected the Topeka government and sent cannons and 500 soldiers to their capital and broke it up in 1856.

That same year, the Douglas County sheriff and 800 southerners seized cannons from the pro-slavery bastion of Westport and sacked Lawrence, disarming citizens, damaging houses and businesses, destroying abolitionist printing presses, and blowing up the Free State Hotel. Abolitionist John Brown and his allies hacked to pieces five pro-slavery men at Pottawatomie Creek and fought hundreds at the Battle of Osawatomie. U.S. Senator Charles Sumner was nearly beaten to death with a cane in the U.S. Congress for insulting a pro-slavery senator in a speech called "The Crime Against Kansas." Later, in 1858, a pro-slavery gang executed five unarmed abolitionists in the Marais des Cygnes Massacre. The era of Bleeding Kansas lasted until the start of the Civil War, leaving fifty to seventy people dead. A Union captain described the conflict in Jackson County as "organized assassination."[58] Soon the violence would explode into civil war, and even continue in some parts of the border region after Lee's 1865 surrender, as enraged Confederate guerrillas refused to accept defeat.

In 1860, abolitionists planned to free twenty-six slaves from Morgan Walker's plantation near Blue Springs, but when the infamous pro-slavery guerrilla leader William Quantrill learned of this, he and his allies ambushed the abolitionists and shot them execution-style.[59] Some Kansas City residents wore Bowie knives and pistols openly at the hip. There were occasional shootings in the streets.[60] A pro-slavery mayor was elected and replaced the next election cycle by an abolitionist. According to Rick Montgomery of the *Kansas City Star*, "Mayor John Johnson held office just 35 days before giving in to his wife's urging that they flee the danger in 1855."[61] Of the sixteen city officials in the 1860 city directory, three owned slaves— one rich councilman owned ten, another councilman owned two, and the chief of police owned one.[62] Businesses sought to profit from the conflict; one Kansas City paper lamented that locals "have concluded to go to war to settle their difficulties by bloodshed. (But) we wish to remind them that they can buy powder and lead of (local) merchants at St. Louis prices, and other military supplies much cheaper."[63]

Pouring fuel on the fire was an 1857 Supreme Court decision on a case previously addressed in a St. Louis circuit court and the Missouri Supreme Court. The nation's highest court decided Dred Scott (and all blacks, slave or free) was not a U.S. citizen and could not sue for his freedom. The court declared the Missouri Compromise of 1820 unconstitutional and ruled that Congress had no authority to ban slavery in ter- ritories. In 1858, southern states publicly resumed importing slaves from Africa—a practice that had been conducted ille- gally for fifty years now had the court's blessing. Stephen A. Douglas told the Senate that the year of 1858 saw the import of some 15,000 Africans—more than any other year in American history, and the South was ready with a pent-up demand for slaves to allow further expansion. New fertile land allowed slave owners to continue making high profits off cultivation and allowed increasingly sterile Virginia and Maryland to become "slave-raising" states—profiting from simply breeding slaves and selling them deeper South. More slave states also meant increased pro-slavery representation in Congress.[64] Slavery was growing stronger as time went on, not dying out as some hoped.

Amidst the disappointments, hope prevailed. In the 1858 elections, pro-slavery citizens failed to replicate their earlier, fraudulent success in Kansas, and free-soil politicians won the majority of seats in the territory. An 1859 article in Kansas City's *Western Journal of Commerce* declared, "Kansas is a non-slave-holding country, and all the Dred Scott decisions in the world, or all the congressional enactments that could be piled upon her, would not be able to make her otherwise."[65]

Though Missouri was a slave state, a constitutional convention in early 1861 voted to remain in the Union, fearing her proximity to free states would lead to Missouri's utter destruction should she secede. But when the pro-Confederate governor refused to send troops to aid the Union, northern armies quickly seized Jefferson City and other key towns, such as Kansas City. Federal troops marched in from Leavenworth, Kansas, and established the Camp Union fort at 9th and Broadway. Pro-slavery officials fled to southwest Missouri and established a rogue government, one the Confederacy recognized.

Jackson County as a whole, arguably part of Missouri's "Little Dixie," was largely southern in its loyalties. Only 6 percent of Jackson County voted for Lincoln in 1860.[66] The state itself was more evenly divided, but also leaned toward the Confederacy. Jeremy Neely, professor of American history at Missouri State University, wrote:

> Missouri, befitting its position as a border state, was bitterly divided in its loyalties. Most households...hoped to preserve both the Union and slavery, but a substantial number identified with their native states of the South. The protracted struggle for Kansas had galvanized many Missourians, and in time the ranks of Confederate sympathizers grew, especially after emancipation and the Union army's forceful policies alienated residents throughout the state.[67]

The Civil War began in April 1861, with the Confederacy's foundations laid "upon the great truth that the negro is not equal to the white man; that slavery, subordination to the superior race, is his natural and normal condition," according to Confederate Vice President Alexander Stephens.[68]

On April 20, a pro-Confederate mob attacked and seized the federal arsenal in Liberty, Missouri. In August, the Union declared martial law in Missouri, decreeing that any slave owner who aided the Confederacy would see his or her slaves freed. In September, pro-slavery Kansas Citians sank a major steam ferry to stop slave escapes to Quindaro.[69]

The First Battle of Lexington raged that same month, only fifty miles east of Kansas City. Confederate Major General Sterling Price and his 7,000 troops used hemp bales as shields, which allowed them to advance on 3,500 Union troops defending Lexington. The southern victory is sometimes called "The Battle of Hemp Bales."

During the winter of 1861, Kansas "Jayhawkers" swarmed into Kansas City and Independence and rescued slaves.[70] In 1862, Nancy Pitcher of Jackson County said several of her relatives "have had thare houses burned by [Jayhawkers], thare negros, hoares and everything they had taken from them. They have taken the lives of boys ten years old."[71]

In August 1862, Confederate troops invaded Independence. Colonel John Hughes and William Quantrill launched a surprise attack on Lieutenant Colonel James Buel's forces under the cover of night. Buel had been warned of an attack by local citizens, but was still caught unprepared. More than 300 Union troops were killed and rebel prisoners were freed from the Independence jail. The First Battle of Independence went to the Confederates.

Judge Graves of Kansas City recalled, "When a battle or skirmish was fought near, the wildest excitement would reign and the most extraordinary tales related. After the fight at Independence one woman rushed by frantically exclaiming that the rebels were tearing out the hearts of the men that were killed; that her own son was among them, and she believed the worst."[72]

Kansas City was heavily fortified by Union troops, which drew in frightened people living in the country. Union forces were ordered to nearby Lone Jack, where Major Emory Foster and his 800 troops stumbled upon a rebel camp of 1,600 troops and successfully drove them from the area. A 3,000-man Confederate force arrived and promptly drove the Yankees out of Lone Jack, which was soon abandoned by the rebels as larger Union armies moved in to Jackson County and diminished the enemy's control of the county.

Laura Coates, daughter of Kansas City businessman and abolitionist Kersey Coates, remembered turmoil near her home at 10th and Central, just down the way from Camp Union:

> It is the dead of night, the cannon's rumbling.... I jump from my cot, a startled, wailing child, and run to my mother's side, but she still rocks to and fro.... Her cheek is pale. I press my face against it.... I climb up in her lap, clasp my arms around her waist and hide my face. "Quantrell is advancing!" is the cry of every one.... The cannon was constantly repeating the signals of alarm given by the pickets stationed on the outskirts of the city, the heart of every inhabitant quickened by the sound. Indiscriminate shooting continued among the guards, a bullet whizzing through our bedroom window one morning at the break of day.... I have but to close my eyes to see a motley mob upon a distant hill in the present vicinity of Thirteenth and Wyandotte streets, congregated to witness a most hideous spectacle. A scaffold is outlined in the distance. The figure suspended from its beams is but partially obscured by the curious, morbid spectators. A spy is paying his death penalty![73]

On August 21, 1863, William Quantrill and his guerilla force of more than 400 troops attacked the town of Lawrence and slaughtered more than 150 civilian men and boys in what became known as the Lawrence Massacre. They burned the town to the ground, vengeance for a Union attack on Osceola. Also fueling the anger was a recent tragedy in Kansas City. In April 1863, Union General Thomas Ewing, Jr., issued General Order No. 10, decreeing that anyone who provided aid to enemy guerrillas would be rounded up and imprisoned. Wives and sisters of Quantrill's army throughout the border region were arrested:

> Some of these women and girls were arrested on the public roads and others were taken from the privacy of their home; all were held without bond or bail, awaiting transport and a trial in St. Louis. Some were caught red-handed with percussion caps, lead, and gunpowder, while others were arrested for having bolts of cloth known to be used for sewing guerrilla shirts. Some were suspected spies, some were caught with large stashes of cash thought to be suspicious, and still others were arrested to serve as hostages, only because they were known relatives of men living in the brush.[74]

Makeshift prisons dotted Kansas City. One was a building at 1425 Grand, near where the Sprint Center currently stands. Apparently Union soldiers, using the cellar for storage space, had taken out the support columns. Later, Union commanders' men warned them about the cracking walls, falling plaster, and sinking floors, but to no avail. The commanders used the space as a women's prison. On August 13, 1863, the three-story structure caved in. Four of the 17 female prisoners were crushed to death: Charity McCorkle Kerr, Susan Crawford Vandever, Armenia Crawford Selvey, and Josephine Anderson, sister of one of Quantrill's more renowned men, William "Bloody Bill" Anderson. Another of Bloody Bill's sisters suffered lacerations, a back injury, and broken legs. Other girls were crippled for life. Rumors spread among Confederate sympathizers that the collapse was intentional, especially after drunken Union soldiers took credit for the tragedy, bragging about it one night at a local tavern. There is still controversy today, but little doubt exists that the deaths contributed to the blind rage of Quantrill's men as they butchered innocent people in Lawrence.[75]

After the massacre, General Ewing issued General Order No. 11, ordering what some anti-slavery voices had already called for: removing all citizens from troublesome pro-Confederate counties, an edict approved by President Lincoln. The Union Army marched into the rural areas of Jackson, Cass, Bates, and Vernon counties and evicted everyone, regardless of their sympathies. Residents were forced to migrate out of the counties or into exempted urban areas in the counties like Kansas City, then coerced to take an oath of loyalty to the North. Westport slave-owner John C. McCoy fled to Glasgow, Missouri, writing to a lawyer in Kansas City on November 11, 1863, "I suppose it might not be safe for me to go to Kansas City."[76] Ewing hoped this mass exodus would eliminate aid to Quantrill's forces, but instead it left a massive piece of empty territory for Quantrill to loot. The policy was repealed by Ewing's successor in 1864, but not before it was heavily criticized by northerners and southerners alike, including pro-Union artist George C. Bingham (the owner of the building that collapsed), who painted his famous *Order No. 11* to condemn Ewing and the evacuations.

Frances F. Twyman, a pro-southerner from Independence, said years later:

> If Tom Ewing is in heaven today his inner life must have been greatly changed. Never can I forget the many scenes of misery and distress I saw on the road when people were ordered to leave their homes on a few days' notice. The road from Independence to Lexington was crowded with women and children, women walking with their babies in their arms, packs on their backs, and four or

five children following after them—some crying for bread, some crying to be taken back to their homes. Alas! they knew not that their once happy homes were gone. The torch had been applied—nothing left to tell the tale of carnage but the chimneys. O, how sad![77]

The final battles near Kansas City were engagements with General Sterling Price, whose cavalry swept through Missouri in a last-ditch effort to capture the state for the Confederacy. Unable to take St. Louis and Jefferson City, Price attacked smaller targets, working his way west toward Kansas City, Missouri, and Fort Leavenworth, Kansas. The Second Battle of Lexington occurred on October 19, 1864, in which more than 8,500 rebel soldiers crushed 2,000 Unionists. Price pursued enemy forces to the Little Blue River, a few miles east of Independence, where the Union brigades burned bridges and valiantly held a defensive position on the west side of the river for several hours of battle on October 21. The Confederates overwhelmed them and advanced into Independence. The Second Battle of Independence lasted until the twenty-second. Fighting swept through the town, the bloodiest scenes taking place where the present-day Harry Truman Railroad Depot, U.N. Peace Plaza, and Community of Christ Temple reside. Union cavalry, infantry, and militia of more than 20,000 men counterattacked at various parts of Independence, yet Price's forces drove them out of the town and dislodged defensive positions along the Big Blue River.

Federal armies fell back to Westport, and on October 23, 1864, the largest battle west of the Mississippi took place. Westport had narrowly avoided destruction a year before, when Union General and Senator James Lane had threatened to destroy the pro-slavery stronghold; Lane only backed down when General Ewing sent troops to block his path. General Price had marched south to Little Sante Fe, south of Westport. Major General Samuel Curtis, in charge of the local Union armies, established a new line of defense south of Westport on the north side of the east-west Brush Creek, which currently runs through the Plaza along Volker Boulevard. Armies and artillery lined Brush Creek from Wornall Road to State Line Road. To the south were open fields (present-day Loose Park), from which Price's forces advanced. The battle raged along the creek. Just to the east, Union forces opened a second front by attacking Byram's Ford on the north-south Big Blue River, threatening the Confederate flank. The pincer movement broke the rebel army and forced it to retreat. The Battle of Westport, the "Gettysburg of the West," involved 30,000 men and wrought 3,000 dead, wounded, captured, or missing. The wounded were treated at makeshift hospitals throughout the area, including slave-owner John Wornall's home, now a museum at 6115 Wornall Road.

Two days later, on October 25, 2,500 Union forces defeated Price's 7,000 troops at the Battle of Mine Creek, just over 50 miles south of Kansas City, Kansas, and forced him to flee south into present-day Oklahoma and Arkansas. The northern victory ended the southern threat to Missouri. Though one of the largest cavalry engagements of war, Westport is perhaps an inadequate comparison to Gettysburg, where 165,000 soldiers were involved and 50,000 killed, wounded, captured, or missing. Still, Terry Beckenbaugh of the U.S. Army Command and General Staff College writes that Westport "proved to be more decisive than Gettysburg":

At Gettysburg, Lee's Army of Northern Virginia suffered a sharp defeat, but it retreated in good order and escaped into Virginia as an intact army that continued to fight for almost two years. By contrast, Price's Army of Missouri virtually disintegrated after Westport. Furthermore, most of the large guerrilla bands in Missouri followed Price into Arkansas, so that Price's Raid actually ended bushwhacker and Confederate military activity in the state. Finally, in the 1864 elections, Price's defeat at Westport helped empower the Radical Republicans to electoral victories in both Missouri and Kansas.[78]

By the time the Confederate States of America was conquered in 1865, Missouri had seen more than 1,000 battles, third only to Virginia and Tennessee.[79]

Historian Jeremy Neely wrote that by 1862, "an increasing number of enslaved persons in Missouri seized upon the chaos sown by war to escape to freedom in Kansas."[80] Slaves abandoned white homes and plantations en masse, fleeing to abolitionist areas and Union armies. Though military chaplains helped many reach freedom, hundreds of fugitive slaves could end up following an army across Missouri, prompting the Union to declare in November 1861 they would no longer be welcomed; many generals thus turned them away.[81] There was a great movement of blacks from the countryside to towns. Many passed through Kansas City on their way to Kansas. Judge Graves wrote:

> I had a house girl whose husband had bought his freedom and was saving up money to buy hers. One day she told me she had a sister in town whom she would like to visit. As it was raining I suggested that she take the horse and

buggy, especially as she wished to take her two children. She dressed them nicely and brought them in for me to see; they were very pretty, and she was quite proud of them. I never saw them again. She had gotten their belongings all out of the way without my suspecting anything. The horse and buggy were left on this side of the river, horse taken out and hitched, buggy cushions turned over, and they had crossed over into Kansas and proceeded to Leavenworth.[82]

The *Kansas City Journal of Commerce* reported on April 20, 1863, that "a procession of six wagons, one carriage, five horsemen and ten footmen" came through the city, each wagon holding "from ten to twenty persons—the whole numbering from eighty-five to ninety self-emancipated 'chattels'…. Each family had a heterogeneous collection of household furniture, shotguns, clothing, etc., in their wagons, and all appeared well supplied with the necessaries of life,"[83] likely stolen from their former owners. Watching runaways cross over into Kansas, a Wyandotte resident said, "It was a sight to make one weep, those poor, frightened, half-starved negroes, coming over on the ferry." "Pap" Williams left his family behind when he crossed the river into Leavenworth, but befriended whites who returned to Platte County, Missouri, with him to rescue his family. Runaway Robert Richardson also went back into Platte County to free his family; when a ferryman refused to transport his family into Kansas, Richardson found a canoe.[84]

Missouri had about 115,000 slaves that were soon to join 3,500 free blacks in the state; 8,300 Missouri blacks joined the Union Army.[85] Over 2,000 black Kansans joined. Male slaves from nearby counties headed to Kansas City to enlist. Black soldiers fought in the Little Blue River, Big Blue River, and Westport battles.[86] Some blacks joined General James Lane's originally unauthorized 1st Kansas Colored Volunteer Infantry Regiment, the first black unit to see battle (1862).[87] It should be noted, however, that not all joined voluntarily; General Lane actually forced some blacks he came across to fight, believing it was their sacred duty.[88] But as historian Joe Louis Mattox notes, some lighter-skinned blacks could pass for white, and used this to join Union armies that did not allow black soldiers. (After the war, Cathay Williams, an ex-slave from Independence, disguised herself as a man and became the first black woman in the U.S. Army.) Blacks joined one of the three other Kansas colored regiments or five Missouri colored regiments, which saw fighting across the nation. The 1st Missouri Regiment of Colored Infantry fought in the final battle of the war near Brownsville, Texas, and helped found Lincoln University in Jefferson City the next year. The 3rd Missouri Regiment of Colored Infantry saw action in Louisiana, the 4th Regiment in Mississippi and Alabama. The 18th U.S. Colored Infantry fought in the Battle of Nashville. Still other black Missourians served in Iowa or Illinois armies. In late 1863, the Union declared any Missouri slave owner who allowed his or her slaves to enlist would be paid up to $300 per slave, a program that wasn't particularly popular among the slave-holding class.[89]

Black soldiers were paid less than white soldiers, given inferior equipment, and kept in segregated regiments. When husbands and fathers left to join the army, their wives and children were often violently abused back home. Many white commanders questioned blacks' courage and ability, and refused to promote qualified black soldiers to the rank of officer. However, the close contact between the races changed many minds. A Leavenworth newspaper spoke of Lane's black soldiers after one 1862 battle in Bate's County, Missouri: "It is useless to talk anymore about negro courage—the men fought like tigers." One general said after an 1863 engagement in Oklahoma, "They fought like veterans, with a coolness and valor that is unsurpassed.... Although in the hottest of the fight, they never once faltered. Too much praise cannot be awarded for their gallantry. The question that negroes will fight is settled; besides, they make better soldiers in every respect than any troops I have ever had under my command." Sherman Bodwell, a lieutenant who ran a Sunday school for black children while his unit was in Jackson County, thought blacks "very intelligent." Black soldiers earned the respect and friendship of many whites. Efforts were made to raise wages for black soldiers, and some did become officers. Fort Leavenworth boasted the war's only unit commanded solely by black officers, Douglas' Independent Colored Battery.[90] Nationally, nearly 200,000 African Americans served in the Union Army and 20,000 in the Navy. Perhaps as many as 200,000 black men and women served as army cooks, chaplains, spies, and scouts.[91] About 40,000 black soldiers died in the conflict.

Diane Mutti Burke of the University of Missouri-Kansas City notes that slave owners in Missouri tried desperately and ruthlessly to hold onto their way of life. They threatened slaves to dissuade them from running off, transported them deeper into the South, or sold them to make a profit before none could be made.[92] A slave from Jackson County, Larry Lapsley, remembered his owner quickly took him and all his other slaves down to Texas in 1861.[93] In February 1864, the value of slaves ruined, John W. Rolling of Clay County sold twenty-two slaves for just

$2,080.[94] This was a small fraction of the price ($1,300) that a male slave was fetching in the late 1850s in Jackson County.

If slaves heard their owners aimed to send them to the South, they would often try to escape to a nearby free state. Once sold in the South, they might never be found again by loved ones. ·
Slave patrols and rebel guerrilla groups caught and punished runaways. A $100 reward was offered for returning a fugitive.[95] According to historian Gary Gene Fuenfhausen, some whites in Clay County took out their anger over the Civil War by murdering black slaves. A male slave was murdered in August 1863, and another, on his way back from running errands in Liberty in summer 1864, was killed just "for fun." Sam Marshall, while taking his children to Kansas, was savagely beaten.[96]

Slaves responded by spying on their owners and reporting enemy activity to Union soldiers; some of them were freed when black soldiers organized and raided the homes where their families were held. Overall, slave desertion and the Union occupation crippled slavery in Jackson County. By 1862, hundreds of thousands of dollars in slave property had been lost and most of the remaining slaves were children or the elderly.[97] The same was true elsewhere; Clay County's black slave population fell from 26.5 percent of total residents to 15.6 percent from 1861 to 1864.[98] Their institution in ruins, conservative lawmakers in Jefferson City agreed in 1863 to phase out slavery by 1870, making Missouri the first state to begin the liberation process. A constitutional convention dominated by leftist Republicans sped things along, and Missouri outlawed slavery in January 1865.

Nationally, American slavery was abolished under the Thirteenth Amendment in December 1865.

CHAPTER TWO
Out of the War – 1865-1890

History is not defined by the steady march of progress. There are years of progress and years of regress, depending on how many individuals in a community actively promote equality and justice, and oppose subjugation and violence. Things do not necessarily or automatically get better as time goes on. Slavery grew more ruthless as the human race grew older. Even today, there are more slaves than at any time in human history, some twenty-seven million laborers and sex slaves.[1] Racism is a relatively new phenomenon, like slavery birthed and perpetuated by those who profited from exploitation. And as we will see, racism grew darker in significant ways a few decades *after* the Civil War, in the same way the number of white supremacist groups in the U.S. increased after Barack Obama was elected.

This should come as no surprise, since moral thought, or "human nature," as some call it, is a product of many factors subject to change. Ideology and morality are affected by geography, resources and wealth, political institutions, class structure, religion, education, literacy, individual observation and experience, economics, and so on. And these interact with and affect each other; Will and Ariel Durant wrote in *The Lessons of History,* "Political forms, religious institutions, cultural creations, are all rooted in economic realities."[2]

Racism and slavery were cultural creations, and we can certainly see how economic circumstances affected them. Geography and climate did not make slavery as economically sensible in the North (tobacco and cotton did not grow well), and thus it slowly died out; thoughts on the moral status of slavery changed with it. Slavery itself was an economic revolution that brought with it racism, which was widely adopted by individuals, and collectively within social institutions.

For example, slavery was justified, in part, by the "science" of the mid-nineteenth century, which "proved" people of African descent were more animal than human. Scientists used crude diagrams comparing black and ape facial features (Nott and Gliddon's 1854 *Types of Mankind*), and inaccurate measurements of skull sizes (Samuel G. Morton's 1839 *Crania Americana* and 1844 *Crania Aegyptiaca*) that found whites had the largest brains, followed by Asians, American Indians, and finally Africans.[3]

Yet individual experience is a more immediate factor that changes moral thought. We know hateful ideologies succeed because they are well taught—by parent to child, teacher to student, priest to sinner, government to populace. But observation and experience can change this. One may be born into a society that teaches slavery is a just institution, but countless events, like witnessing the cruelty of a master to his slave, will pull one away from those ideas.

During the Revolutionary War, many people were stirred by the rhetoric and idealism of liberty and freed their slaves.[4] Thomas Jefferson, one of the principal architects of such rhetoric, was not one of them. How can we dismiss Jefferson as a "product of his time" when others were so capable of rejecting oppression based on his very words? Mormons, Quakers, and other abolitionists were products of the same era as slave owners. Jefferson's personal experience, along with many other influences, led him to choose wealth and tradition over mercy and freedom. Other founders did just the same. There is even evidence Britain's steps to abolish slavery in the early 1770s contributed to the push for independence by colonial leaders.[5] And it goes without saying the "product of his time" idea adopts the viewpoint of the oppressor. Black slaves knew slavery was wrong. The idea also encourages us to think of ourselves as simply products of *our* time, dismissing the need for racial progress—in essence, excusing racism or inaction. So as we study a history of race relations, we can acknowledge that people who acted mercilessly or murderously were well taught in the art of racism within a predominantly racist culture. But considering many witnessed or participated in the suffering of fellow human beings—while being well aware of others who supported an end to such suffering—it's difficult to find an excuse for them.

In the same way, there is little excuse for whites today who are made aware of the kinds of racial injustices documented in the Introduction and simply ignore them.

Immediately after the Civil War, there was a surge of idealism regarding race relations. To be sure, there was still violence against antiracists and blacks in the years following the Confederate surrender, but the mood in the North (and even parts of the South) was that a victory for freedom and equality had been won. It was hard won and not just against the Confederacy.

Abolitionist criticism and pressure against President Lincoln and Congress intensified the longer the war went on. Editorials lambasted the president's perceived timidity. Petitions with hundreds of thousands of signatures flooded the U.S. capital. By the end of the war, Lincoln, the Radical Republicans, African Americans, abolitionists, and many common soldiers united in a decision that identified eradication of American slavery as the principal aim of the conflict. Once allowed in, blacks enthusiastically joined the Union Army. Indeed, it was a military necessity for Lincoln and likely saved the Union from collapse. Black courage and friendship dispelled racist myths in the minds of many white soldiers and generals. Some veterans would later help black families build new lives. News reports and political speeches on emancipation changed the thoughts of many common people. Idealism spread. True change was coming.

Under the leftist Republicans, slavery was outlawed, and ex-slaves were granted citizenship, voting rights (for men at least), and equal protection. Historian Howard Zinn writes, "Southern Negroes voted, elected blacks to state legislatures and to Congress, introduced free and racially mixed public education to the South."[6] White and black voters gave Republicans landslide victories across the North in the late 1860s, and even the former slave state of Maryland abandoned the conservative southern Democrats for a spell.[7] The 1870s saw Mississippi elect two African Americans to the U.S. Senate (the first, Hiram Revels, founded the Saint Paul African Methodist Episcopal Church in Independence); there were 20 black congressmen in the House of Representatives, more than half from the South.[8]

Black men exercised their newly granted right to vote, but black political victories often required the support of whites as well. Elections were not enough, however. Despite the plea from black leaders and the actions of General William T. Sherman, blacks were not given land, a key to economic success. But laws granting equality had hopes of enforcement thanks to the Union Army and a political force called the Freedmen's Bureau controlling the South. Overall, the situation of African Americans was improving. Society was growing more tolerant and inclusive. Loewen writes, "In Republican communities, in the period 1865-90, letting in African Americans was seen to be the appropriate, even patriotic thing to do."[9] This did not mean that all white people accepted racial equality. But blacks were welcomed, hired, and voted for in many states, despite the fact that white terrorists continued to torture and execute them.

Much of Kansas City embraced the 1865-1890 idealism. When the war ended, the *Kansas City Daily Journal of Commerce* exulted under the headline "MISSOURI A FREE STATE": "Missouri is free.... We welcome the morning, radiant with golden promise, and grow stronger in the breeze that fans the hills and valleys of a land redeemed."[10] The paper foresaw grander wealth, commerce, and culture for all of Missouri. The city council announced a January 20 celebration, which saw the city

> ablaze with glory over the inauguration of Freedom in Missouri. The city was illuminated at an early hour.... The finest of all was Hammerslough's fine block on the corner of Main and Third streets which was brilliantly lighted from top to bottom and made a magnificent display. Many private residents were illuminated,

and Kansas City from her valleys and heights reflected a thousand brilliant beams in honor of the auspicious occasion.

Meanwhile, cannonballs were booming salutes and bands were discoursing sweet music. At an early hour people commenced assembling at the Court House [for speeches] and a large bonfire was set at the intersection of Main and Fourth streets....

The colored people of the city, rejoicing in their new-found freedom, had organized a large procession with music, and banners and transparencies and mottoes paraded the streets singing the great American hymn of freedom, the John Brown song.... The procession marched down Main street and along the levee until Gen. Curtis, Lane, and company were met and... escorted them to the Court House.[11]

Tens of thousands of former slaves fled the South and headed for Kansas, idealized as a Promised Land. Benjamin "Pap" Singleton (who is buried in Kansas City) traversed the South encouraging this migration, which passed through Kansas City. Some white Kansas Citians formed charities and relief programs to provide black migrants, whom they called exodusters, with food, clothing, and money. The Kansas Freedmen's Relief Association formed to help blacks find housing and work.[12] Some whites reached out in other ways, like Mother Mary Jerome Shubrick, who cared for black inmates at the Jackson County jail in Independence. Upon her death, she was buried amongst blacks. In white-dominated Wyandotte, black veteran Corvine Patterson was elected to the county board of education in 1872, and also served as city marshal and street commissioner. In 1889, he became deputy sheriff. Patterson was instrumental in receiving black migrants into Wyandotte and convincing local civic and community leaders to let them stay.[13] African Methodist Episcopal Church pastor B.B. Watson headed a relief effort for migrants as well.

Suzanna M. Grenz writes, "The citizens of [Kansas City], as well as the mayor, generously aided the exodusters."[14] The *Kansas City Daily Journal* and other papers encouraged citizens to help refugees, who "usually arrived in a wretched condition, most were hungry, many appeared ill and few had the money needed to purchase food and lodging."[15] According to historian Sherry L. Schirmer (*A City Divided: The Racial Landscape of Kansas City, 1900-1960*), "Many of the Exodusters (perhaps a third of the fifteen thousand to twenty thousand who made the journey) found themselves stranded in Kansas City, Missouri, and Kansas City, Kansas, when their travel funds ran out."[16] They established a tent village south of Truman Road between Charlotte and Virginia and were on the brink of starvation when the city allowed them to take up permanent residence.[17] In Wyandotte, nearly 2,000 migrants "camped along the levee, living in tents, rough board shelters, and in tin shacks, in which they huddled together, trying to stay dry and warm. Some begged door to door for food, while others sat mutely awaiting help."[18]

Newly freed people built schools and churches, and found jobs as construction workers, barbers, businessmen, stockyard and meatpacking workers, hotel operators, store clerks, railroad hands, farmers, ministers, principals, and teachers. Even in 1863, runaway slaves found work on the railroad heading west from Kansas City. The *Western Journal of Commerce* reported, "No man is refused work on account of his color, and we yesterday saw a large number of Negroes in one gang industriously at work, and were informed that they have good satisfaction."[19] James Milton Turner, ex-slave from St. Louis, became Kansas City's first black teacher. He began April 16, 1868, making $60 a month.[20] He later became an agent of the Freedmen's Bureau, traveling more than 8,000 miles throughout Missouri, helping to open thirty-two schools and securing $8,000 in annual public funds for black education.[21] Women worked in the homes of wealthy whites or as laundresses, seamstresses, and homemakers, but also created the Women's League of Kansas City to help unemployed black women find homes and schooling.[22]

Jabez Smith once owned a family called the Tuckers; one of those family members, Granville Tucker, became marshal of Jackson County.[23] A black college, Freedman's University (later Western University), was established in 1867 in Quindaro, where slaves had previously escaped to freedom. A black paper, the *Freedman's Record*, appeared in 1876.[24] Black men became mailmen, policemen, and firemen (Fire Station No. 11 was the only black fire company in Missouri at its founding in 1890).[25] Blacks could attend Kansas City University in Kansas City, Kansas, in the 1890s. The Women's Christian Temperance Union opened their doors to African Americans. After the turn of the century, individuals such as the famous J.E. Perry and T.C. Unthank helped open City Hospital No. 2 and Wheatley-Provident Hospital, launching the local black medical profession. Before Wheatley-Provident, only Old City Hospital admitted black doctors and patients; City Hospital No. 2

was the first in the nation run solely by blacks.[26] By 1932, the city had produced more African American medical specialists than any other U.S. city.[27] A fraternal organization called The Knights and Daughters of Tabor, founded in Independence in 1872, offered life and medical insurance to African Americans.[28]

When Kansas City became a center for meat and grain production, the city population exploded. By 1870, there was a total city population of more than 32,000, including 4,000 blacks.[29] Ten years later, there were 8,000 blacks in a city of nearly 56,000. A housing boom along Troost drew many black residents. From 1860 to 1880, the black percentage of the population soared from 4 percent to 14 percent and the city grew eightfold.[30] People abandoned rural areas in the local counties to find work and good schooling in the city. Across Kansas City, whites and blacks lived together in integrated neighborhoods. Though "a few blocks were all-white," wrote author Charles E. Coulter in *Take Up the Black Man's Burden: Kansas City's African American Communities, 1865-1939,* "by 1880, African American families could be found in almost every area of Kansas City, Missouri," and many hotels and boarding houses were integrated.[31] Many parks, drugstores, and restaurants were open to all. For a moment in history the races were largely peaceable, sharing neighborhoods, transportation, and some workplaces and public facilities. But the racial situation was far from ideal.

In Wyandotte, the mayor decided the rising number of blacks had reached an unsupportable level and banned further exodusters in April 1879. The mayor went so far as to pay to transport blacks deeper into Kansas. Officials and vigilantes physically prevented boats from landing. The *Kansas City*

Times called the migrants "human rubbish" and "lazy." City officials protested when the boats—turned away at Wyandotte—dropped off their human cargo in Kansas City and raised money to ship the newcomers off to Manhattan, Kansas. Worse, whites in Leavenworth took advantage of blacks' lack of financial knowledge to con them out of the money they had.[32]

Missouri officially declared slavery abolished in January 1865, but among more than "a hundred counties represented at the convention in St. Louis, only FOUR voted against emancipation. They were Platte, Clay, Calloway and Boone."[33] Platte and Clay are those to the northeast and north of Jackson County, so half the Missouri counties that voted against freedom were in the Greater Kansas City area. Missouri's Radical Republicans made no serious efforts to preserve black males' right to vote,[34] and quickly lost political strength. Conservative and reactionary forces in Jefferson City succeeded in banning interracial marriages (1869) and mixed-raced public education (1880).[35] These edicts were tame compared to the barbaric laws that southern legislatures were passing, but tragic nonetheless.

In the 1860s, the conservative Democrats began to play on fears of interracial mixing for political reasons—they capitalized on the obsessive terror among white men over sexual liaisons between black men and white women to slander the Republicans as the "party of miscegenation."[36] Of course, voluntary sexual relationships between blacks and whites occurred since slaves were first shipped to the American shore. This fear of voluntary racial mixing birthed two myths: first, it was in the black man's aggressive and deviant nature to rape, and second, white women were naturally repulsed by black men. The idea of sexual deviancy in black men still exists today (and many whites see high rates of black single mothers as proof young black men and women are promiscuous, unable to control their sexual appetites).

Black men caught in voluntary relationships with white women were often killed. The women involved in these relationships would deny their role in the liaison, perpetuating the racist sexual myths and allowing the lynchings. White women would take

> cover under the cloak of victimization when discovered. If her parents, husband, or other relatives had been unaware of her illicit liaison with a black man, they could do the work for her, assuming her to be prey and then presenting her as such without dissent. If the family had suspected or known of illicit behaviour, they could bury that knowledge in criminal charges, again with the woman's consent.... As [a] victim, she could in some measure be exalted. Refusal to cooperate could also result in violence at the hands of white patriarchs.[37]

Journalist and sociologist Ida B. Wells, who researched extensively the causes and effects of lynching in the 1890s, wrote:

> With the Southern white man, any mesalliance existing between a white woman and a colored man is a sufficient foundation for the charge of rape. The Southern white man says that it is impossible for a voluntary alliance to exist between a white woman and a colored man, and therefore, the fact of an alliance is a proof of force. In numerous instances where colored men have been lynched on the charge of rape, it was positively known at the time of lynching, and indisputably proven after the victim's death, that the relationship sustained between

the man and woman was voluntary and clandestine, and that in no court of law could even the charge of assault have been successfully maintained.[38]

Wells' words in her *Southern Horrors* pamphlet of 1892 drove white men mad: "Nobody in this section of the country believes the old thread bare lie that Negro men rape white women. If Southern white men are not careful, they will over-reach themselves and public sentiment will have a reaction; a conclusion will then be reached which will be very damaging to the moral reputation of their women." They destroyed her printing press and forced her out of Memphis under penalty of death. Wells then toured the country, speaking in Kansas City in March 1895 to ministers and unionists.[39]

Wells estimated four-fifths of rape charges were in fact adultery.[40]

A charge of rape was usually fatal. Whites in Leaven-worth, Kansas, lynched Richard Wood on January 30, 1887, for alleged rape, and Silas J. Wilson on August 20, 1893, for "disgusting" behavior toward a white woman.[41] In 1866-1867, Daniel Webster, Tom Van Buren, and two other blacks were lynched in Wyandotte for suspected murder. Shawnee saw the lynching of a black man for alleged rape in 1867, then a man named Armstrong in 1871 after he obtained a warrant against white men. In Platte County, 120 people lynched Raphael Williams in 1876 for alleged rape; Charles Reese suffered the same in 1881 for the same crime. In June 1893, the Kansas City Colored Women's League battled to save a black woman from hanging. In December 1896, Leavenworth and Platte County bickered over ownership of an island on the Missouri River where Frank Garrison killed a white man; Leavenworth officials saved him, but then had to avoid a mob of their own constituents. Alfred Brown was nearly lynched in Olathe that same year.[42] The *Examiner* in Independence warned in 1901: "The community at large need not be especially surprised if there is a Negro lynching in Independence. The conditions are favorable at this time. There are a lot of worthless young Negro men who do nothing. They do not [even] pretend to work and stand around on the streets and swear and make remarks about ladies and others who pass by."[43] In Leavenworth, suspicion surrounded the disappearances of three black males. In 1898, the body of Miles Baker, who was in prison for rape allegations, was buried at Mt. Muncie Cemetery—no cause of death was listed on public records. After their 1899 arrests on charges of rape, Ed Fleming and Heck Robinson simply vanished from all public records.[44]

On April 3, 1882, an unknown assailant shot and killed policeman Patrick Jones on St. Louis Avenue in Kansas City. A black man named Levi Harrington, sitting by a boarding house at Ninth and Hickory, heard the shots and found the body. When six police officers arrived on the scene, white citizens pressured them to arrest Harrington. The police, who later reported they believed Harrington innocent, took him into custody and marched him in the direction of headquarters. A white mob followed them. As the police crossed the Fifth Street cable car bridge, a second mob confronted and surrounded them. They seized Harrington, threw a noose around his neck, and hanged him from the bridge. When two officers attempted to free him, a member of the mob shot Harrington in the head.[45]

Although lost to history, there were likely other lynchings in Kansas City proper; a large oak tree in Westport, at Washington and 43rd Street, was known as the "hanging tree."[46] The number of blacks lynched in Missouri and Kansas (sixty-nine and nineteen, respectively) from 1882 to 1968 paled in comparison to the South (Mississippi 539, Texas 352, Louisiana 335, etc.).[47]

Blacks were denied both service and employment at many restaurants, hotels, stores, and theaters. Where they did find work, they were paid less than whites. They were often the last hired and the first fired, therefore facing more frequent unemployment. This set the stage for over a century of intergenerational poverty, the effects of which we still see today. At the same time, revisionist history began. Ex-Confederate John Newman Edwards, editor of the *Kansas City Times*, wrote articles that portrayed the secessionists as victims of northern aggression, encouraged pro-southerners to reenter politics, condemned Reconstruction, and glorified ex-Confederate guerrilla and local outlaw Jesse James. The press would soon portray blacks as the cause of their own poverty.

African American schools were established following the war, as required by the new Missouri Constitution and made a reality by black activists and educators. The first was the Lincoln School, established in 1867, following the creation of the Kansas City Board of Education. It offered high school courses in 1882. But early on, the "Independence Board of Education would only support two grades at [the Douglas School for black children]. They felt that this was all the black children could use or were able to accomplish."[48] In 1870, a room for blacks at the white Benton School downtown opened, though they were kept well isolated from the white students. In the next decade, the state banned integrated schooling. In 1885, 60 percent of eligible black children attended Kansas City schools, compared to less than 50 percent of white children.[49] (If we were to engage in thinking similar to that of modern white denial—"black students' test scores are low and dropout rates high because black families don't emphasize the importance of education"—we might conclude from this that white parents simply didn't care as much about education as black parents, rather than looking for historical causes.) By 1918, there were eight elementary schools and one high school, Lincoln High, for African Americans.[50]

Students benefitted from famous guest speakers like George Washington Carver and from African American teachers who were often qualified to teach at the college level, but were denied employment by universities. Yet conditions at many schools were dismal, speaking volumes of the poverty of black neighborhoods and the obsessive desire of whites to keep non-whites away from their children. In 1889, the student-teacher ratio was 65:1, 25 percent higher than in white schools.[51] In 1921, editor and education advocate Nelson C. Crews of the *Kansas City Sun* believed that it was "an undisputed fact that there never was a time in the history of this city that schools devoted to Negro youth were in a more dilapidated, unkempt and insanitary condition than they are today."[52] The Kansas City Board of Education proved reluctant to equally fund black and white schools. Even while students at black schools suffered in the worst, overcrowded conditions during the 1920s, the board voted to build new schools for white students.

Lincoln High had 750 students in a school designed for 250. Each student shared a locker with one to four other students. There was no library, gym, or science laboratory. The kitchen had old, malfunctioning plumbing, not to mention a gas leak that required every window in the school to remain open. Seventeen teachers worked without desks and six to eight classes took place on the stairs. The district paid black teachers less than white teachers. The Board of Education didn't give in to pressure to build a new black high school for fifteen years, finally opening the new Lincoln High School in 1936. Black elementary schools suffered from decrepit facilities and desks, old books, and a lack of plumbing, which meant students were forced to use outhouses.[53] Nelson Crews maintained that "no city north of the Mason-Dixon line had such deplorable conditions in its black schools."[54]

In the late 1800s, pressure and pleas for equal treatment, opportunity, and political power came from intellectuals like James D. Bowser, newspapers like the *Independent,* the *Gate City Press,* the *Sun,* and the *Dispatch*, and political organizations like the Independent Negro Party and the Negro Protective League.

The Negro Protective League initially formed to investigate and protest police abuse after a killing in the late 1880s. Police brutality enraged black residents, who concentrated at Church Hill (10th and Troost), around Allen Chapel AME, Second Baptist, and other churches. White policemen killed blacks, who were often abandoned by the justice system. Sonny Gibson wrote in *Kansas City: The Mecca of the New Negro* that in July 1888, a white policeman arrested a black woman for "disorderly conduct," striking her in the skull with his nightstick. Then, allegedly, "the woman's brother saw this happening and grabbed the policeman who then shot the woman's brother. Suspicion was cast on the policeman's story because the Negro was shot in the back."[55] This nearly sparked a race riot. Three hundred African Americans protested the violence outside the police station.

The white press at this time was content to ignore the African American community, which soon expanded beyond Church Hill into the Vine Street Corridor, Belvidere and Hicks Hollows, Hell's Half Acre, and between Troost and Woodlawn. When blacks did make the white news, crime was the subject and belittlement the tone. "The Times portrayed African Americans who committed crimes as childish objects of fun and reported their misdemeanors in mocking, playful tones."[56] In *A Rich Heritage: A Black History of Independence, Missouri*, William J. Curtis concurs, writing, "The local newspaper was not sympathetic to the needs and rights of the black community. It offered hostile information at worst or at best condescending paternalism."[57] This tone of paternalism would evolve into something far more sinister after the turn of the century, when racism took a new form.

From 1865 to 1890, poverty was a nightmare. The Hell's Half Acre slum was "one of the worst slums any city has ever seen," writes Tanner Colby.[58] Originally a housing settlement for blacks working on the construction of the Hannibal Bridge in the 1860s, Hell's Half Acre was a collection of shacks along the Missouri River, the only housing some black, German, Italian, and Irish immigrant families could afford.[59] Garbage rotted in the streets, disease and lice spread, and residents fetched water from polluted wells.[60]

The shanty slum offered cheap housing near the rail yards, packing houses, and warehouses where unskilled migrants found their first jobs as laborers and porters.

The high transiency rate in the area indicated that black families left the slum as soon as they could afford better lodgings, for Hell's Half Acre deserved its nickname. A sanctuary for the thugs and grifters who infested the city's nearby train depot and for the barflies and prostitutes who inhabited the area's numerous saloons, its lack of clean water, sanitation, and paving further justified its moniker.[61]

By 1900, 535 blacks occupied 108 shacks, 1,094 whites lived in 136; the horrific conditions bred crime, which only worsened when "virtually ignored by the police."[62] Police indifference was a problem in American ghettos for over a century. Curtis wrote of Independence:

Poverty was so hard after the Civil War that some young men turned to crime as a solution. The county jail on the North Main had a large proportion of black inmates. However, justice then was not too careful to determine if a black person was truly guilty. It is said that many were arrested merely to get workers for the chain gangs to do road work for the county.[63]

As the nineteenth century drew to a close, idealism weakened. The Union Army left the South after the Compromise of 1877, and with it any real chance for the protection of innocent people or enforcement of civil rights legislation. By the end of that decade, the conservative Democrats had regained their former strength in the South. In 1883, the Supreme Court struck down Congress' Civil Rights Act of 1875, which some in Kansas City had labeled meaningless; the *Kansas City Times* said, "The colored people evidently know their place and are possessed of too much common sense to attempt to force themselves on white people."[64] Further, idealism died with the passing of a generation. "By 1890, only one American in three was old enough to have been alive when [the Civil War] ended."[65] Increased immigration from western Europe supplied Democrats with more votes, as the newcomers competed viciously with blacks for work and disliked Republicans for being anti-Catholic. Democratic candidates preyed on these attitudes. American aggression in South America, the Pacific, the Caribbean, and against Native Americans brought a resurgence of racial hate and ideas of ethnic superiority.[66] The increased racism among white voters made black votes less and less appealing to Republican politicians. By 1890, the Grand Old Party retreated from notions of human rights and justice, and the Fourteenth and Fifteenth Amendments, which granted blacks citizenship and voting rights, went unenforced.

Propaganda that stated black officials were too corrupt and too stupid for leadership swept the South. Southern law fell into the hands of the Klan and other white supremacists. Violence restored the rule of white domination. Thousands of blacks and whites across the United States were murdered because of their allegiance to equality or pursuit of opportunity. Fear drove tens of thousands of survivors out of the South. The blacks that remained had little economic independence and became reliant on whites for work and survival. They were quickly stripped of their voting rights, due process, equal protection, and citizenship.

New forms of exploitation and oppression arose. New white fears developed. It was the beginning of the "Nadir," some of the darkest days of American race relations, 1890 to 1950.

CHAPTER THREE
The Nadir in Kansas City – 1890-1950

As the nineteenth century gave way to the twentieth, the fear of blacks grew into an ideology that would dominate white thought for more than a century. It went beyond the fear of racial mixing, and would damage race relations to an extent yet to be undone.

This ideology did not arise spontaneously. As with the birth of racism and the belief in black stupidity and inferiority, there were those who could profit from fear mongering. It began in the 1890s, alongside the wane of racial idealism. White supremacists realized they could rally more support for legislation that withdrew black citizenship and voting rights if the white populace was terrified of the "criminal black man." Politicians realized they could more easily win elections if they stoked and played off white fear. So racism evolved into a fear of the black menace. Colby writes:

> For those keen to present blacks as a threat, the stereotype of blacks as feebleminded children was of little use— children pose no threat. Racism required an overhaul. Blacks needed to be dangerous, disease ridden, violent. These images were pumped into the public consciousness through the work of newspaper propagandists and

political demagogues. Scientists got behind the notion, too, propagating biological and psychological theories to explain the black man's animal nature and his criminal appetites.[1]

These new racist ideas swept over Kansas City. Soon the attitudes of many local newspapers changed from paternalism to fear mongering. Black families were no longer considered victims of poverty and the ghetto; they were the cause. Desperation and hopelessness did not bring criminality; now it was the other way around. As sociologist Kevin F. Gotham writes in *Race, Real Estate, and Uneven Development: The Kansas City Experience, 1900-2000,* "During the first two decades of the twentieth century, local social workers, public officials, and other elites began to associate the presence of Blacks living in a particular area of the city with deteriorating neighborhoods, poor schools, high crime, and other negative characteristics." Local sociologists and the Kansas City Board of Public Welfare released studies that "equated Blacks with moral laxity, instinctively mean character, disorderly conduct and criminality, and property devaluation."[2] This served as white justification for Jim Crow laws.

Poverty indeed grew worse, though mythical black animalism, laziness, immorality, and poor parenting had nothing to do with it. Besides getting shut out of good jobs and good schools, the population of African Americans was growing quickly. By 1910, the city's total population was nearly a quarter-million people, with 23,000 African Americans.[3] The black population jumped 72 percent from 1900 to 1920.[4] World War I drew many blacks to the North to work in war industries. After this, there was another wave of black migration from the

South to the North (and rural areas to cities) as technological advances reduced the need for farm hands. Largely confined to unskilled, low-wage work by white employers, Kansas City blacks averaged $80.61 in wealth per capita; whites averaged $667.96.[5] Another way to assess poverty is to look at property ownership: whites owned more than 99 percent of all property in Kansas City in the early 1910s (although blacks made up 10 percent of the population); only 800 to 1,000 blacks (about 4 percent) owned land on which they lived or worked.[6] Low wages and joblessness meant blacks had to seek low-cost rental options for their families in the slums where health hazards were stunning:

> Hemmed in on all sides, Eighteenth and Vine grew denser. Jerry-built "apartments" were tacked onto tenement homes in back alleys. Families were crowded into crudely subdivided basements. One study conducted in 1912 found that 20 percent of the houses in Eighteenth and Vine lacked any water supply at all, 50 percent had no sink, and bathtubs averaged one per every twenty-two residents. Infection rates ran twice the city average for pneumonia, tuberculosis, and other communicable diseases.[7]

In 1915, one 22-block area contained 4,295 people.[8]

Rows of privies lay just outside the shacks; human waste and flies were everywhere. Obviously, water was not easily accessible. When the Helping Hand Institute set up an ice water station one hot day, it saw a line of 5,000 people.[9] In the Leeds neighborhood (west of the Blue River and south of Raytown Road), homes had only two rooms, some with dirt floors. There was no running water or electricity until the 1930s, so residents used kerosene lamps and iceboxes, and fetched water from hydrants along the unpaved roads. They kept large tubs of smoldering rags near their homes to ward off mosquitoes.[10] A 1913 sociological study noted blacks made up 10 percent of the city's population, but received one-fifteenth of the aid offered by local charities.[11]

In the mid-1920s, the black mortality rate in Kansas City was worse than in New York and Chicago.[12]

The increasing population coincided with increasingly racist policies in housing. Roy Wilkins wrote in the *Kansas City Call*, a prominent black newspaper, that while blacks were concentrated in the business, light manufacturing, and stockyard districts,

> the residential neighborhoods, the nicer sections of Kansas City, were all white. There were ads in the *Kansas City Star* that talked of $5,000-$7,000 houses that could be bought for $750 down—If you were white. A Negro had to cough up $1,000 to buy a smaller house, then run the risk of being "persuaded" out because he dared to wander away from the railroad tracks and the factory sites.[13]

The battle for the east side of the city began. Real estate agents refused to sell homes in "respectable" neighborhoods to blacks, and increasingly worked to steer black families out of white neighborhoods and into black ones.[14] By 1910, Kansas City had a rate of black isolation worse than New York, Chicago, Detroit, St. Louis, Pittsburgh, and other major cities.[15] A more virulent racism infected every corner of the city. Public spaces like the Municipal Auditorium and the Convention Hall established segregated seating. After the 1903 flood, Kansas City's minorities were treated only after white victims received care.[16] Between 1900 and 1910, black teachers could no longer sit with white teachers at Kansas City School District meetings, cemeteries no longer buried the black deceased, and white doctors refused to treat sick African Americans.[17] A. Theodore Brown and Lyle W. Dorsett wrote in *K.C: A History of Kansas City, Missouri*:

> Blacks were being slowly excluded from occupations which many of them had formerly held. White barbers displaced black barbers, the downtown hotels employed fewer and fewer black waiters and bell-boys, and the number of Afro-American nurses for white children declined drastically.[18]

Blacks could enter fewer restaurants and shops downtown. In *A People's History of the United States*, Zinn wrote that a chaplain saw black veterans "unkindly and sneeringly received" here, barred from restaurants where white veterans ate free. Soon public schools would be completely segregated. The Kansas City Board of Education nearly passed a resolution in 1911 that would have fired any black teacher living in a white neighborhood. In 1915, the Kansas City Council passed a law forbidding a black school from being within 2,400 feet of a white school.[19] Even though it was illegal to bar blacks from using public parks, residents erected "Whites Only" signs in Swope Park in the late 1920s.[20] They put up signs on their streets: "Niggers have no business in this neighborhood."[21] The *Star* refused to even print a picture of an African American for many years.[22] The YWCA held minstrel shows, with actresses in blackface, in 1903, 1908, and 1913. The *Star* delighted in their portrayal of "darkey characters."[23]

Violence escalated. As blacks bought or rented houses on the east side, white Kansas Citians bombed their homes using dynamite. Six bombings occurred in 1910 and 1911 on Montgall, just east of Prospect.[24] In a white stronghold along Vine Street, a house was bombed in 1911 to prevent a black family from moving in, and "only one suspect was arrested and sentenced for the crime—a black man charged with trying to scare off whites so blacks could take over [the neighborhood]."[25] Bombs ripped into homes along Troost, Prospect, Kansas, Park, Brooklyn, and Tracy. In August 1925, when Garland Place Apartments (7th and Woodlawn) offered apartments to ten black families, an enraged mob surrounded the place, threatened the families, and forced the owner to rescind the offer.[26] Black homes were set on fire and death threats issued to other neighborhood families. The Kansas City National Association for the Advancement of Colored People (NAACP) legal department did what it could to stop the violence, but white politicians and police offered half-hearted assistance, if any at all. No one was arrested for years, and the white press ignored the events.

In 1919, whites stirred by a local showing of *Birth of a Nation* destroyed two black homes and a church.[27] Members of the Linwood Improvement Association, trying to erect a park as a barrier between black and white neighborhoods, sent a letter to the *Kansas City Call* threatening to bomb sixty-two black homes to clear space.[28] In 1925, Samuel R. Hopkins, president of a realty and loan company, tried to move into an all-white neighborhood and his house was bombed.[29] Explosions rocked the east side well into the 1930s.[30]

The sexual fears of white men over biracial relationships continued to play a large role in the history of Kansas City, Missouri. Kansas City police consistently harassed any black man and white woman seen walking or talking together. They arrested and imprisoned some for this "crime" of fraternizing. They illegally raided homes, too.

In 1900, rumors that black men were assaulting white women swept Leavenworth—one newspaper put the count at thirteen assaults, a number police reports did not support.[31] At a 1910 meeting at St. George's Episcopal Church in Kansas City, white men complained that black rapists lurking on the east side had white women in a state of terror.[32]

Black men were routinely beaten at police stations, whether for alleged rape or mere fraternizing. At the same time, black women could be sexually harassed with impunity. White men who raped black women were well protected by the courts; those who were indicted faced shorter sentences. About the same time that a mentally handicapped black man was given the death penalty for raping a white woman, a white man who attempted to rape a black child was given five years.[33]

On May 3, 1900, twenty-six-year-old Henry Darley was lynched in Liberty, Missouri, for allegedly raping a white hotel waitress with whom he worked. He was hanged in front of the city courthouse by a mob of about seventy-five whites, who broke into the jail and dragged him out for execution.[34]

Some eight months later, on January 15, Fred Alexander, a veteran of the Spanish-American war, was lynched in Leavenworth, Kansas. He was accused of raping and killing Pearl

Forbes—though local doctors who examined her body determined she was not raped. In prison, Alexander confessed to the assault of a woman named Eva Roth, but to the end maintained his innocence in the Forbes case. After his arrest, the press described him as a large black brute—though he stood only five feet, four inches tall. The upcoming lynching was advertised on posters all over town. Kansas City public transportation offered free rides from Leavenworth to the prison in Lansing, Kansas. A mob of 6,000 gathered outside the penitentiary; a leader threatened to dynamite the building if the mob wasn't let in, and people tore up rails from the Santa Fe Railway tracks to use to smash down the gates. They kept the place surrounded for days, preventing the authorities from moving Alexander. At one point, 120 African Americans marched to Lansing to protect Alexander from the mob; deputies disarmed and dispersed them, narrowly avoiding a race war.

Before the mob attacked the prison, Alexander thanked the warden and other guards for trying to keep him alive, and said, "Tell my people and friends good-bye if I should not happen to see them all, that I am not the guilty man." The mob smashed into the prison, possibly aided by guards inside, seized Alexander from his jail cell, cut him apart with a hatchet, and transported him to the site of Forbes' death, at Lawrence and Spruce streets. Five thousand people, including women and children, gathered for the spectacle. The mob doused Alexander with some twenty-two gallons of kerosene, chained him to an iron stake, and lit him on fire.

Alexander's body parts were collected as trophies. Trophy hunters even showed up at the funeral parlor where his body was taken—they cut from the corpse pieces of charred flesh, as Alexander's mother and sister looked on.[35]

In 1904, the citizens of Kansas City, Kansas, nearly witnessed a lynching. Louis Gregory, an eighteen-year-old Kansas City, Kansas High School student, shot a white teenager who was about to beat him with a baseball bat in Kerr's Park.[36] Gregory was arrested, and promptly a white mob made for the Wyandotte County jail. However,

> the Afro-American community had mobilized its own "vigilance committee" composed of about fifteen uniformed veterans of the Spanish-American War. With the Reverend George McNeal at the lead, and the Rev. Thomas Knapper close behind, the contingent marched with Springfield rifles in hand and positioned themselves in front of the jail house door. As the mob approached, Reverend McNeal reportedly made the following pronouncement: "The first man to cross this line is eating breakfast in Hell in the morning." As these words were spoken, his troup [*sic*] readied their rifles. It is difficult to imagine the tension of that moment, but it was apparently an entirely convincing display. The would-be lynch mob rapidly dispersed, and Louis Gregory was saved, although he later received what was considered an extremely harsh prison sentence.[37]

The incident ended the integration of Kansas City, Kansas High School. The state of Kansas violated its own constitution in 1905 with the "Segregation Bill," which allowed segregated schools in Kansas City, Kansas. A separate school for black students, Sumner High School, opened that year, named after abolitionist Senator Charles Sumner.

According to Christopher Lovett ("A Public Burning"), a mob in Olathe, Kansas, lynched Bert Dudley for murder on September 21, 1916.

On August 7, 1925, Walter Mitchell was lynched in Excelsior Springs, Missouri. He was accused of attempted rape of a white girl in the back of a car. According to an Associated Press release in the *New York Times*, a mob of about 1,000 people stormed past the local chief of police and several officers, and into the jail. By the time fifty Kansas City policemen with riot guns arrived, Mitchell was dead.[38]

On November 29, 1933, nineteen-year-old Lloyd Warner was killed in St. Joseph, Missouri. He was arrested for assaulting a twenty-one-year-old white woman. Seven thousand people (men accompanied by women and children) overpowered the National Guardsmen and police, despite being shot at and tear-gassed. They disabled a military tank, smashed down the jail doors with a truck, took Warner from his cell, and beat him to death. They chained his body to a car and dragged him through the black neighborhood, where they hanged him from an elm tree, doused him in gasoline, and set him on fire.[39] Missouri Governor Guy B. Park condemned the violence, saying, "There is no justification for the action of the mob," adding, "Mob violence, whether in the punishment of crime or in attempts to obtain alleged civil rights, is always wrong and is destructive of good government."[40]

In September 1925, a black man in Kansas City, backed by others, staved off a lynching and a bloodbath. A white mob with bloodhounds, hunting for an accused rapist, seized a man named Charles from the Yellow Front nightclub at 18th and Forest.[41] Fellow African American Oliver "Blue" Moore intervened before the lynch mob could haul Charles away, and whites and blacks pulled guns on each other. A crowd of people poured from their homes, cars, and businesses across the city to the scene of the stalemate. Police arrived and took Charles into custody; his protectors remained at the police station until Charles was cleared of all charges and released.

At times the police themselves could be shockingly brutal. In 1926, police officers shot to death unarmed Dorsey Stewart for stealing a ham. The officers went unpunished. In 1931, police arrested Darius Hendricks, a black janitor at the Waldo Theater, for theft. For three hours, they savagely beat him with a bat, garden tools, and wire hangers. Later, the actual criminals were apprehended. The Board of Police Commissioners accused Chester A. Franklin of the *Kansas City Call* of attempting to incite a race riot by reporting on the beating. A grand jury let the police officers go. Hendricks was crippled for life.[42]

A policeman beat a black priest in 1928.[43] Another policeman offered cash to James Price to load oil barrels into a truck at a closed gas station one night. When Price lifted the first barrel, the officer shot him nine times and left him for dead. The next day the officer collected a $25 reward from a local oil company for stopping the "theft." Incredibly, Price lived just long enough to identify the policeman, and when the black press ran the story, "the cop received so many death threats that he had to get out of town."[44]

In 1941, a vice squad stormed Autumn Leaf Club and two officers beat an unarmed Harrison Ware. When Ware seized and struck back with a cue ball, the police officers shot him three times and kicked him as he bled out. One thousand people marched at Ware's funeral in protest.[45] Two years later, a policeman killed an African American male, and only the pleas of voices like the *Call* prevented a full-blown race riot.[46]

Blacks moving into Shawnee, Kansas, encountered burning crosses in October 1949. Whites painted swastikas on doors and shattered windows with rocks wrapped in messages such as, "All niggers that want to be alive in 1950 be out of Shawnee in December 1949."[47]

Despite the obvious risks, some whites were willing to take a stand. White neighbors often stood watch over targeted homes, and a group of white neighbors protected black women from a white mob in 1927.[48] Progressives themselves reacted violently when the Ku Klux Klan, with its 5,000 members in Kansas City during the 1920s, set up a store that sold Klan publications and memorabilia in 1923. They threw bricks into windows. Anti-racists then bombed the Maxwellton Inn, where the Klan had performed an initiation ceremony.[49]

All this is not to say black men committed no crimes. But it is self-evident that stripping people of their Constitutional right to a fair trial, torturing them, and executing them was barbaric toward the guilty and innocent alike.

Kansas City was a dark place. The late Roy Wilkins, former editor of the *Kansas City Call*, remembered:

> White Kansas City was an entirely different place, a Jim Crow town that nearly ate my heart out as the years went by.... One evening on the way home from the *Call*, I jumped up to offer my seat in a streetcar to an elderly white lady. She eyed me frostily, turned her back on the seat, and snapped to a white man standing next to her, "I'm not old enough yet to accept a seat from a nigger."

A few days later I was standing in line in front of a theater ticket window. A white woman immediately in front of me suddenly whirled around.

"I wish you wouldn't stand so close to me," she said.

"But, madam," I answered, "I am not close to you."

"Yes, you are," she hissed. "Entirely too close. I don't want you to touch me."

Hate in her eyes, she looked down to where the hem of my topcoat was grazing her coat. Then she flounced out of line, going all the way to the rear to avoid me.[50]

Wilkins wrote that "schools, hospitals, churches, theaters, and just about everything else were as thoroughly segregated as anything in Memphis. In its feelings about race, Kansas City might as well have been Gulfport, Mississippi.... The longer I lived in Kansas City, the more the racial atmosphere and smug provincialism of the place ground on me."[51]

A real estate tycoon named J.C. Nichols perfected the art of keeping darker people out of white neighborhoods. From the 1910s to the 1940s, Nichols built the most beautiful and expensive areas of Kansas City, such as the Country Club Plaza, Mission Hills, and Prairie Village. He made membership in his neighborhood associations mandatory upon buying a home, and all members were legally required to enforce racial restrictions: homes could not be sold to minorities. He also ensured those restrictions renewed automatically as the decades went on, and that reforming them would be a difficult process requiring the approval of many homeowners.[52] Not that many would be interested in reform. Nichols advertised to scared whites, ensuring them his neighborhoods were safe from undesirables. This was particularly pleasing to whites who felt their "higher status" in society was threatened by middle-class blacks.[53] The terror over economic equality is as prevalent in the history of racist thought as the fear of sexual equality.

As the black population in the city grew, whites fled. Some neighborhoods in Kansas City went from all-white to nearly all-black between summer and fall.[54] Developers across the United States copied Nichols' suburbs and his racial restrictions. Nichols was a giant, one of the most powerful men in the real estate world. He worked with President Franklin Roosevelt to design the Federal Housing Administration (FHA), which ensured government-backed home loans and subsidies were denied to black neighborhoods as a matter of federal policy.[55] A street that runs through the Plaza is named for J.C. Nichols.

Keeping white neighborhoods clean was important, too. In 1926, the city installed a garbage dump in a black area on the east side, at 20th and Woodlawn. Garbage collected all over the city was trucked here for temporary storage.

> Trucks dripping with swill and drawing clouds of flies rumbled daily through blacks' commercial center to reach the new dump. So thick was the miasma rising from the garbage lot that students had to be evacuated from the nearby Western Bible College because they were ill from the stench. Classrooms in Lincoln High and the living rooms of surrounding homes were said to be almost unendurable.[56]

This action violated a recent city ordinance and was a commonly used tactic in cities with ghettos, in no way exclusive to Kansas City nor to the distant past. Educator Jonathan

Kozol wrote in 2000 about the illnesses spreading in the slums of New York City due to this exploitation and negligence in his book *Ordinary Resurrections.*

The politics of the era had an even worse stench. Like conservative Democrats across the United States, Kansas City Democrats used fear mongering to slander Republicans as "nigger lovers" and remove them from power. Beginning in 1904, Missouri Democrats pushed for this, confident the idea of blacks taking over local governments would cause white panic and be a deathblow to the GOP. They also grabbed onto whatever news they could twist to their political advantage. After a black prison guard allegedly beat a white female prisoner with a hose in Kansas City in 1905, the local Democrats seized their chance to vilify the opposition. The story caused an uproar. A second clamor arose over investigations that stated white female prisoners bathed in front of black guards, and that white and black female prisoners shared the same cells. The fact the city government allowed black doctor T.C. Unthank to examine and treat white female inmates enraged white Kansas City.[57] These scandals crippled the Republicans. Plus, the *Kansas City Post* "trumpeted every report of black murder or theft, illuminating its pages with bug-eyed black monkeys riding Republican elephants and truncheon-wielding black gorillas beating white women.... In November, 1908, the Democrats swept every available seat in the county."[58] The state of black Kansas City was already dismal under Republican control, and it now appeared darker days were ahead.

But then Kansas City became "Tom's Town," ruled not by Democrats at City Hall but by the mob boss that put them there. There were mixed results for black Kansas City. Democratic politician Thomas Pendergast, the most powerful man in Kansas City in the 1920s and 30s, moved his businesses of prostitution, strip clubs, sex shows, drag shows, illegal liquor, drugs, and gambling out of white areas and into black ones.[59] Pendergast appointed a thug named Johnny Lazia, who later organized the assassinations of FBI agents at Union Station, as head of the police, and made him responsible for keeping vice in the "right" parts of town. This reinforced whites' ideas of black immorality and deviancy. It was a horrid distortion, as whites owned a "significant proportion" of businesses at 18th and Vine through World War II.[60] The mob itself owned the big clubs, and many used black musicians but banned black customers. The swinging times on the east side under Boss Tom's reign filled white pockets. Only at the end of the war did blacks own 60 percent of the businesses in the district.[61] Many actual black businesses struggled, as banks refused to grant loans, and producers and distributors overcharged blacks for goods.[62]

The speakeasies, brothels, bars, and nightclubs attracted everyone from common citizens to the greatest musicians of the era, like Count Basie, Duke Ellington, and Charlie "Bird" Parker, to gangsters like Pretty Boy Floyd and Face Nelson. Kansas City became known as the beating heart of Depression-era jazz. You could watch plays at the Lincoln Theatre at 18th and Lydia Avenue or the Shubert Theatre at 10th and Baltimore, and movies at the Gem Theatre on 18th. The caliber of dancing, jazz, drama performances, and orchestras in Kansas City was trumpeted nationwide.

But Kansas City also became the country's crime capital, a place where Prohibition didn't exist and vice was king. Heroin and other drugs were a huge problem; young people were especially influenced by idols like Charlie Parker, a heroin addict. In the words of trumpet icon Buddy Anderson, "Kansas City was *screaming*, man."[63]

The Pendergast regime, which launched the political careers of Independence native Harry Truman and other Missouri congressmen, used massive voting fraud, bribes, beatings, and murder to maintain power. The 1934 "Bloody Election" saw three poll workers for Pendergast's rival killed, and others beaten. In 1937 and 1938, investigations showed the Pendergast machine had created some sixty thousand bogus registered voters—and some suspected Truman benefited from this during his political rise.[64] Black leaders like Reverend D.A. Holmes were fierce critics of Pendergast.

But the political machine was popular with the working class due to its welfare system that rescued many from the depths of the Great Depression.[65] Nathan W. Pearson writes, "The base of his support always rested in the poor, the black, the Italian, the immigrant. These groups, disenfranchised by other major political groups, found a benefactor in Tom Pendergast and his ward lieutenants."[66] Pendergast's Jackson Democratic Club had precinct captains give the poor food, fuel, and clothing, and provide holiday meals that fed thousands of homeless, jobless Kansas Citians. Pendergast's regime also provided jobs. Pendergast organized a New Deal-esque public works program that gave $2 million in wages to 22,000 workers, and simultaneously strengthened the machine's popular support and provided workers for his concrete business.[67] Men were hired to build bridges, roads, public buildings like a new City Hall and Jackson County Courthouse. Machines that could have saved on labor costs were abandoned in favor of manual labor.

In 1930, 80 percent of black female workers in Kansas City toiled in domestic and personal service, serving as maids, laundresses, and the like. About 31 percent of black male workers worked in manufacturing industries such as packing houses, with 34 percent in domestic and personal service. Blacks made up 4 percent of the police force, 2.5 percent of firemen, 11 percent of teachers, 5 percent of dentists, and 1 percent of doctors.[68] Many successful professionals lived in nicer apartments and homes at "Negro Quality Hill" on the east side.

During the Depression years, blue-collar jobs on railroads and in packing houses "all but disappeared" as the national economy collapsed.[69] At the same time, unions such as the American Federation of Labor banned black workers, shutting out many from good jobs. Some local unions issued "yellow dog contracts": an employee who signed promised to quit rather than share a workplace with African Americans.[70] However, "In Kansas City, some unions did open their doors to full participation of African American workers. Unions for the building trades, hod carriers, iron workers, rock quarrymen, and truck drivers all admitted black workers. African Americans found employment as bricklayers, carpenters, cement finishers, electricians, painters, plasterers, plumbers, stonemasons, and tile setters."[71] Even so, white employers paid blacks half the weekly wages they paid whites for the same work, and the businesses willing to employ blacks made up only 30 percent of all businesses in the entire city.[72] Whites usually saw to it that blacks were the last hired and the first fired. By 1935, about 25 percent of all black families in Kansas City were on relief. The poverty forced many to open the doors of their decrepit homes to renters. A 1943 study showed that:

Most of the dwellings occupied by African Americans were in need of major repair or had no private bathing facilities.... Higher rents did not necessarily result in better facilities or increased privacy. About one-fifth of all of the dwellings surveyed averaged three people for every two rooms in the building.... Black homeowners, it is apparent, often needed the extra income provided by boarders and lodgers in order to afford the housing they could obtain.[73]

Many homes on Kansas City's east side had leaky roofs, rotten wood, and dead rats in the walls; blacks died from tuberculosis as a result, at a rate four times higher than whites until the 1950s (also, in 1930, the black infant death rate was double that of white infants).[74] The *Call* reported that the Bowery slum in 1925 was the most densely-populated area of the city, with the highest death rate. There was high incidence of "flyblown food, of cellar homes and leaking plumbing, of fire traps and tenement homes."[75] In 1945, 85 percent of all black houses were in need of redevelopment or rehabilitation, and though blacks represented 12 percent of the city population, they occupied half of the city's decrepit homes.[76] The vast majority of these houses were not owned by the residents, but by whites. In 1930, only 16 percent of blacks owned their own homes.[77] Poverty restricted many to low-cost rental options, which meant families could not build wealth for themselves in the value of a home and, hence, had no wealth to pass to descendants. This had lasting effects. Tim Wise wrote that in 2010 white families in the poorest 20 percent of households had, on average, $24,000 in assets from property passed on to them by relatives. Blacks in the poorest 20 percent of households received $57 in assets on average, "for a white-to-black ratio of 421:1."[78]

From the perspective of Pendergast loyalists, Boss Tom was generous, a friend to the poor, a friend to African Americans.[79] One of his friends and allies was Felix Payne, a black Democratic political speaker and owner of the famous Sunset Club and the Kansas City, Kansas Giants baseball team. According to the Special Collections Library at the University of Missouri-Kansas City, Payne was well respected by many African Americans despite his participation in illegal activities; he was allowed to speak at white Democratic rallies and helped generate black support for Pendergast.[80] And that support was genuine. Pendergast himself visited black neighborhoods (usually before election time) with a couple of trucks to give the people free bread and milk.[81] From 1924 to 1938, the number of blacks working for the city increased almost fivefold and social services improved.[82] Though harboring his own racial biases, Harry Truman, judge of the Jackson County Court, formed a friendship with Chester A. Franklin of the *Call* and helped open public homes for disadvantaged black youth. With the mob boss controlling the police department, incidents of police brutality declined significantly. A police officer who shot an African American without sufficient cause was immediately fired.[83] The black electorate was valued for its votes and thus offered better protection by Pendergast than by the former Republican-controlled city government. After Pendergast was overthrown in 1939 for tax evasion, police abuse returned with a vengeance and most black police officers were fired. The end of mob rule also initiated the slow decline of the 18th and Vine jazz scene during the 1940s, as city reformers "cleaned up"

Kansas City and World War II drew many musicians overseas to fight.

In retrospect, Pendergast had little interest in helping blacks rise from the lower class or gain civil rights. His public works plan largely helped white workers. At the beginning of 1933, there were 6,000 men working on projects in the city, but only 120 were African American.[84] Blacks were banned from operating public transportation like buses or trolleys.[85] The Urban League of Kansas City fought to find work for blacks (even creating a janitorial school), but for every success there were still thousands left jobless. Research indicates local relief agencies and charities such as the Provident Association were much more likely to give jobs to whites, while only 25 percent of businesses would even hire blacks.[86]

Nationally, the New Deal was largely intended for whites as well. The dominant types of employment for blacks were excluded from social welfare. Historian Howard Zinn wrote, "Most blacks were ignored by New Deal Programs. As tenant farmers, as farm laborers, as migrants, as domestic workers, they didn't qualify for unemployment insurance, minimum wages, social security, or farm subsidies."[87] Major unions pressured the National Recovery Administration to exclude black workers.[88] Things became so bad in the Kansas City area that federal officials "threatened to cut off funding to projects in Missouri unless racial restrictions on the projects of Jackson County were lifted."[89] Black Kansas City did, however, enjoy free preschool, as well as adult education programs and sewing classes, under the New Deal.[90] There were federal funds for building recreation centers and pools in black areas, and the black death rate dropped by one-third during the Depression thanks to new hospitals.[91] The Leeds neighborhood finally saw paved roads and a new bridge.[92]

In 1950, Nathan B. Young, Jr., asked Carl R. Johnson, president of the local NAACP branch, and Girard T. Bryant, dean of Lincoln Junior College, if the Pendergast regime aided blacks. They replied:

> MR. BRYANT – Very little, if at all. During the Pendergast regime there was a feeling among many Negroes that they could go to their ward or precinct boss and get things done: Little personal things. The lower income bracket had this feeling strongly. But looking at your question broadly, the Pendergast machine was not good for the Negro here. No Negro held any position of prestige under Pendergast. There was the Superintendent of the General Hospital, which was to be expected since it was a separate [black] institution.

> MR. JOHNSON – The only good thing that came from the Pendergast machine and its successors as far as Negroes were concerned could be put this way. The Negroes freshly migrating here from the South were welcomed and told: 1, Now you can vote; 2, And you must be sure to vote; 3, We'll see that you will vote. This was good-sounding news to many who had been denied the ballot in the South. In a way this was a service, and at least the other political forces, the Republicans and anti-machine crowd never approached these newcomers with any such brotherhood of suffrage.

> MR. BRYANT – Yes, these machine politicians would take time to see about Negro families. If a family had to move, the precinct man was on hand to greet them and

help a bit. Those in dire need of food or coal would get a gift. You can't exactly write this kind of politicking off the book even if there is an ulterior motive.[93]

By 1950, blacks were powerful as a voting bloc, but the city government was still totally controlled by whites. Mr. Bryant again:

> We have never had a Negro councilman nor a justice of the peace. Even the few political clerical jobs Negroes have are very minor ones. The only elective officials we have are members of the State Legislature. There are some special appointments in the legal departments in recent years. But we have honestly mighty little to show on the political front for the weight of our votes.[94]

The first African Americans on the Kansas City Council, Bruce R. Watkins and Earl D. Thomas, would not serve until 1963.

From 1890 to 1950, Kansas City blacks did not tolerate all this violence and persecution lightly. A wealth of newspapers, notably the *Kansas City Call*, served as progressive voices and pressured local and national politicians, public and private organizations, the courts, the police department, and common citizens to embrace civil rights. Founded by Chester A. Franklin in 1919, the *Call* grew into the largest black business in the Midwest, one of the six largest black weeklies in the nation.[95] Franklin had to set the type himself in the early days, as the local typesetter's union forbade members from working for a black editor.[96]

The *Call* successfully fought to overturn the ban on black jurors during World War II.[97] *Call* writer Roy Wilkins led boycotts of local segregated theaters. He later became a famous civil rights speaker, a leader of the NAACP, and W.E.B. Du Bois' successor as editor of the *Crisis* journal. Kathryn M. Johnson, "credited by many as the first field worker for the NAACP," began her Kansas City activism in 1910.[98] She helped open NAACP branches across the country. Lucile Bluford, who attended the University of Kansas in 1932 and then worked for Franklin, sued the University of Missouri-Columbia in 1939 when she was refused admission to its journalism school. Bluford and the NAACP won their case before the Missouri Supreme Court in 1941. But rather than accept black students, officials at the university shut down the entire journalism school. Bluford later replaced Franklin as head of the *Call.*

The common people rose up to push for change. There was a huge rally to protest employment exclusion at wartime production plants, for instance. Carl Johnson told Nathan Young, Jr., that

> The largest contribution towards the fight for civil rights was during World War II when the government set up war industries here and plants started out with a policy of wholly excluding Negro workers. Because Negroes were hungry and needed money badly, and at the same time saw so much Government money being spent here, they went on an all-out fight against discrimination of this type. Their wants and the immense war activity had dramatized their second-class status. It shocked their patriotism too! So some 13,000 Negroes gathered at the Municipal Auditorium in March, 1942, and staged an organized protest. This helped to speed up President Roosevelt's [Fair Employment Practices Committee] directive for the entire Nation.[99]

Throughout American history, blacks joined whites in labor organizing, when workers of all colors united for a common cause, like higher wages, safer working conditions, fewer hours, and even equal treatment. There were thousands of strikes across the nation each year. Workers in Industrial America earned starvation wages, and had to risk losing their limbs or lives on the job. Many realized their true conflict was not race but class, the fact that the few became extremely wealthy off the labor of the many. But corporations often stoked racial tensions by hiring unemployed blacks to replace white strikers, since they could pay them even lower wages with less threat of resistance. This often sparked resentment and even violence among whites toward their black replacements.

The Knights of Labor and the Industrial Workers of the World welcomed blacks, women, and immigrants. Many of their founders and members were socialists or communists who called for "equal rights for all without distinction to sex or race" (to quote an 1883 socialist congress in Pittsburgh).[100] Many socialists understood the relationship between race and class: racist doctrines justified economic oppression by capitalists (employers). Just as emancipation would mean the end of free labor for slave owners, human equality would force business owners to pay blacks the same wages as whites. Racism served to prevent this, just as sexism and xenophobia prevented the same for women, undocumented immigrants, and others. Further, racism discouraged diverse workers from uniting. In 1931, James P. Cannon, former editor of *Workers' World*, a Kansas City socialist newspaper, wrote:

> In its struggle against the workers' emancipation movement capitalism plays upon all the dark sentiments

of ignorance, prejudice and superstition. This is seen daily and hourly in its endeavors to divide the workers and oppressed people along national, racial and religious lines.... [White workers are] inflamed against the foreigner, the Jew and the Negro. Communism cannot be other than the mortal enemy of these devastating prejudices.... Communists must be the heralds of a genuine solidarity between the exploited workers of the white race and the doubly exploited Negroes.[101]

This is not to say all socialists or unions accepted blacks. Yet many radicals saw the closing line of *The Communist Manifesto* ("working men of all countries, unite!") as a cry for racial equality in the fight for class equality. It is telling that the Communist Party of the United States ran a black man, James W. Ford, for the vice presidency in 1932.

In Kansas City, people like Herb March of the Young Communist League and socialist Charles Fischer united blacks and whites at places like the Armour packing house, where blacks were fired first and underrepresented in better positions. They formed a union that became the largest racially diverse organization in the city, with leaders from both races. In September 1938, after a pay dispute involving unpaid blacks, 400 black and 600 white workers occupied Armour together for days. "It left a unity of friendship that couldn't have been created in any other way," Fischer recalled.[102] The strikers won their demands.

Black and white members of the Kansas City branch of the Communist Party marched through the city together to protest unemployment in 1931.[103] Black communist Abner Berry gave speeches around the city. Eric Foner wrote in *Give Me Liberty!*

that black and Irish Kansas Citians formed a coalition to elect pro-union mayor Tom Hanna.

The city has a tumultuous history of labor disputes indeed. Striking railroad workers in Argentine and Kansas City, Kansas, shot train cars and ran one train off its track and into the Kansas River, killing three men. Railroad workers in Kansas City participated in a national 1877 strike. At the Ford Motor Company Winchester Avenue plant in 1937, 1,400 workers enraged Henry Ford by stealing power fuses to cripple assembly lines, and welding shut the gates.[104]

Black and white Kansas City hack drivers went on strike together in 1904. Their white employers only rehired the white workers. When workers at meat packing plants left the job in protest that same year, the employers hired black strikebreakers to take their place. The employers armed the strikebreakers in hopes of inciting the strikers to violence. A massive walkout occurred in 1917 when male and female workers of both races, again from the packing houses, demanded decent wages for women and an eight-hour work day. Thousands went on strike. Five packing plants came to a standstill. Freight handlers and soap factory employees abandoned their jobs and joined the ranks. Labor won the dispute, and the workers were rehired with better wages.[105]

Then, on Valentine's Day 1918, hundreds of black and white women abandoned a local commercial laundry to strike for the right to unionize, an eight-hour work day, and better pay, for they suffered working conditions "among the worst in the city."[106] Within five days, 1,000 workers were on strike, as others walked out of their own laundries. Strikers smashed windows, lit bundles of laundry on fire in the streets, and sent a laundry truck flying off Cliff Drive. The police beat women vandals.[107] Attempts at negotiations stalled when white strikers refused to participate unless black workers were also allowed at the table. Quickly the activism grew into a general strike, with 15,000 people walking off the job, "tying up streetcar service, bakeries, restaurants, building sites, breweries, and buildings with elevator service."[108] The city ground to a halt. Schirmer writes, "Even the arrival of the Seventh Regiment of the Missouri National Guard failed to end the strike, which lasted six days before union leaders accepted a wage offer from the laundry owners."[109]

Despite setbacks, the black community found ways to take care of itself. Some, like Minnie Crosthwaite, battled poverty. She was the first black social worker in Kansas City and an invaluable asset to the Wheatley-Provident Hospital. There was also Samuel Eason, who rented a house to found the Niles Home for Negro Children. The Urban League offered job training, employment services, and established nurseries and other facilities. Credit unions opened with the express purpose of offering African Americans the same interest rates on loans as whites. And new job opportunities opened up. Working as a railroad porter became a prestigious job for African American men; others became doctors, lawyers, businessmen.

During the First World War, Vernon C. Coffey of Kansas City, Kansas, was color sergeant of a segregated unit that patched roads and constructed ammunition parks in Europe. His unit was decorated by the famous general John Pershing. He later became associate minister at the First A.M.E. Church in Kansas City. In World War II, Jack Bush, Buck O'Neil, Bruce R. Watkins, and others shipped out to fight in Europe and Asia. Some African Americans trained for the war at Western University in Quindaro, Kansas, and at the Civilian Conservation Corps in Liberty, Missouri. As men left to serve on the front, women gained more opportunities to work in the plants, factories, and packing houses, and found jobs as typists, secretaries, and telephone operators. The black community raised hundreds of thousands of dollars for the war effort, and witnessed military parades through the 18th and Vine District.

Churches and social organizations were the heart of the community, and grew a culture of volunteerism and cooperation. You could join the local chapter of the Negro National Education Congress, the NAACP, or numerous other groups and charities. The Paseo YMCA and YWCA provided educational, spiritual, and athletic opportunities. The Kansas City Monarchs, baseball's longest-running franchise in the history of Negro Leagues, was a powerhouse of black baseball from the 1920s to the 60s. The Monarchs launched the professional career of Jackie Robinson, and their games attracted mixed-race audiences of nearly 20,000. Satchel Paige and Buck O'Neil captivated fans. O'Neil remembered:

> The Kansas City Monarchs. It had the same meaning as the New York Yankees would have had for a boy 40 years ago. Just to tell the fellas back home, very cool-like, mind you, "Yeah, I'm going to be playing for the Kansas City Monarchs," was quite a thrill. Quite a thrill....
>
> We carried ourselves like Monarchs wherever we went, and to people all over, we were Monarchs. We were in the front row, man, the front row. We stayed at the best hotels, ate in the best restaurants; they just happened to be black.[110]

O'Neil later became the first black coach in Major League Baseball, for the 1962 Cubs.

African Americans could attend classes at Western University or other colleges on the Kansas side. Men could join the Ivanhoe Club or other social groups; women joined the Matinee Matrons, Forget-Me-Not Girls, and Merry-We Social. On warm summer days, African Americans could head down to the "colored" pool at 27th and Woodlawn. They could attend picnics, pageants, and parades. In Parade Park, many enjoyed boxing matches, concerts, horse or pet shows, cookouts, games, and contests. There were conferences, political rallies, demonstrations, and speeches. W.E.B. Du Bois spoke at the Ebenezer A.M.E. Church, Marcus Garvey, the leader of the "back to Africa" movement, spoke at St. Stephen Baptist. Paul Robeson sang at the Grand Avenue Temple, and boxing champion Joe Louis stopped by for a party in the 18th and Vine District.[111] The Fourteenth Annual National Convention of the NAACP was held in Kansas City, Kansas, in 1923 to honor John Brown; it was the first NAACP convention held west of the Mississippi. Ten thousand people attended an award ceremony for George Washington Carver at the convention hall in Kansas City, Missouri.[112] There was an annual ball at Paseo Hall. There were bowling alleys and restaurants in the 18th and Vine District. You could feast at Arthur Bryant's Barbeque, Black Hawk Barbeque, or Old Kentucky (later Gates) Barbeque. Starting in 1950, you could listen to KPRS 103.3 (Carter Broadcast Group), the oldest black-owned radio station in the country. It is no wonder Sonny Gibson called his collection of articles and photographs *Kansas City: The Mecca of the New Negro.*

CHAPTER FOUR
Hold the Line at Troost – 1950-1970

Until the 1950s, 27th Street was the informal boundary line
between blacks and whites in east Kansas City, though it
was not a perfect barrier. In 1940, 71 percent of blacks lived
between Troost and Jackson, and Independence Avenue and
31st Street.[1] Nearly 90 percent of all minorities lived in segregated neighborhoods.[2]

So far, the white effort to keep African Americans contained
in the northeast region of Kansas City had succeeded. But as
the black population outgrew their districts in the early 1950s,
they needed somewhere to expand. The whites on the east side
now faced the terrifying reality of blacks moving south and en-
croaching into their neighborhoods and schools. Colby writes:

> Emboldened by the rising consciousness of civil rights,
> black families began to move out. [But] the well-to-do
> whites on the west side were going to make damn sure
> that their side stayed whitest the longest. City officials
> drew a boundary right down the middle of the city along
> its longest north-south thoroughfare, Troost Avenue. Let
> the east side go black, it was decided. We'll hold the line
> here. Still today, nearly every zip code, every census tract,

every voting ward—and, for a long time, every school district—all split right along Troost.[3]

With the boundary drawn, or "redlined," white flight from the east began. But they did not go passively. As African Americans pushed further south into white neighborhoods, the Kansas City School District reorganized school zones *each year* to keep black schools black and white schools white. For example, Central High School went from 100 percent white to 99 percent black between 1954 and 1968.[4] This will be discussed momentarily. In addition, whites launched another series of arson strikes and bombings against new black neighbors from 1940 to 1962. The Paseo area was hit particularly hard. A bomb would have killed an entire family living on Paseo in 1952, were it not for an individual who bravely grabbed the bomb from the house and hurled it onto the driveway. A family moving into Raytown saw their home set on fire and bombed in 1962.[5]

This migration pitted black families, organizations, coalitions, and legal forces against the racist practices of the real estate industry, banks and lending institutions, home builders, developers, and neighborhood associations. But the rapid advance of the black community was to a large degree organized by white profiteers called blockbusters, predatory real estate speculators. Real estate agents refused to sell or rent to blacks, as agreed upon by homeowners in traditionally solidified segregated areas. But others realized there was more profit to be made by orchestrating a perfectly legal scam. First, predatory speculators bought a home in an all-white neighborhood and rented it to a black family. It was then a simple matter to convince the neighbors that more were coming. The terror spread and whites sold like mad. The speculators purchased the homes at discount prices and then sold them to blacks at inflated costs. The only problem was that lenders denied home loans to blacks. A solution was conjured:

> So those brokers would offer to finance the purchase themselves for an outsized down payment and an unreasonable monthly note. Trapped in tenements most of their lives, having never dealt with complex mortgage instruments, black families would take the deal. Falling behind on the note almost immediately, they'd find themselves foreclosed on in a matter of months. The deed would then revert back to the broker, who'd turn around and sell it again.[6]

The redlining of Troost brought wild profits for blockbusters and suffering for the black community. Further, white real estate agents generally ignored the east side as if it did not exist, unless dealing with a black client, who was promptly steered to that side of Troost. Developers and businesses moved to the white side of town. Johnson County employed racial covenants to forbid home sales to blacks and other minorities. Much of this was dramatized in Whitney Terrell's *The King of Kings County*. Blacks wanting newly built homes could rarely get them. Despite the growing black population, "only 106 building permits were issued for new single-family black housing"[7] from 1940 to 1958. The banks denied home loans to black Kansas City for decades ("$642 million in home mortgages were written in 1977, less than 1 percent of which were issued east of Troost"[8]). The stagnation and poverty this created can be seen to this day, and in many ways is still perpetuated in Kansas City and across the United States. Tactics for keeping areas white include "jacking up property taxes, opting out of public transit systems, [and] redistricting their zoning codes to prohibitively expensive homes."[9] In other words, whites have kept minorities out by taking advantage of the poverty created by racist individuals and public policies of the past.

Kansas City underwent "urban renewal" in the 1950s and 1960s to save itself from deterioration and fiscal death, but it proved to be a harmful policy for poor blacks and whites. American urban renewal "destroyed thousands more units than it replaced and dislocated tens of thousands of small businesses and residents."[10]

Under federal housing laws passed in 1949 and 1954, city governments could claim the right of eminent domain to bulldoze slums and clear the land for redevelopment. The laws were well intended—to encourage the building of government-owned, quality homes in former slum areas with federal subsidies. Unionists, social workers, housing activists, and others lent their support to the plan. But they were given little say in crafting federal or local legislation. Instead, downtown business interests and the real estate industry took control. The National Association of Real Estate Boards labeled public housing "socialism" and sought to ensure that slum clearance in the downtown area would pave the way for private development.[11] They also wished to enforce racial separation:

> [The] NAREB did not just see public housing as simply in competition with the private sector. The real estate organization perceived public housing as the opening wedge of a campaign to attack housing discrimination, reduce class and racial residential segregation, and in effect, challenge the institutional foundations of the seg-

regationist private housing market.... The maintenance of housing discrimination and segregation was a source of political and economic power of the NAREB that real estate elites worked to protect and sanction through federal policy.[12]

In this way, private power protected its interests and ensured that urban renewal would meet the needs of the free market instead of the needs of the poor whose homes were taken and destroyed. Due to the influence of the National Association of Real Estate Boards and other organizations and corporations, the housing laws of 1949 and 1954 granted near total local control and left little teeth for the federal government to ensure federal funding was spent on human needs. The projects benefitted big business far more than the common people.

Eighty million dollars, two-thirds provided by the federal government, were spent on eighteen urban renewal projects in Kansas City from 1953 to the end of the 1960s. The downtown neighborhoods of poor blacks and whites were seized and flattened, most of them converted into commercial and industrial districts. This was a national trend. Across the U.S., poor areas were obliterated and replaced with gleaming office towers and luxury apartments.[13]

More than 5,100 acres were redeveloped in Kansas City, displacing 1,783 blacks and 1,960 whites in this period. Nationally, blacks resided in nearly 70 percent of all dwellings that were destroyed for urban renewal; some called it "negro removal."[14] Some 755 Kansas City businesses were leveled and replaced by large corporations. The Northside project (1953-1960) replaced decrepit housing with parking lots. The South Humbolt (1956-1965) and Eastside (1958-1965) projects replaced housing with the freeway loop.[15] Kevin F. Gotham writes, "The purpose of the 54.2 acre Attucks project [1953-1960] was to clear predominantly Black neighborhoods adjacent to downtown."[16] Highway 71 (Bruce R. Watkins Drive), which took 50 years to complete (1951-2001), ran through mostly black neighborhoods: Ivanhoe, Beacon Hill, and Key Coalition. Some 10,000 residents, of all races, were displaced during this period. Many homes and businesses left standing were very close to the roadway, causing disinvestment. Residents complained the highway had divided black neighborhoods, so many pushed for bridges and stoplights to keep the neighborhoods connected. Mamie Hughes—Jackson County legislator, member of the Panel of American Women, and equality advocate who represented the communities and informed residents of their property rights—led this effort.[17]

The city did build some public housing for displaced residents, but it was strictly segregated—in direct violation of new federal civil rights legislation. For example, there was Riverview Homes for whites and Wayne Miner Court for blacks. The Guinotte homes (for whites) replaced a peaceably integrated neighborhood. Nationally, the National Association of Real Estate Boards and other powers worked to keep public housing away from wealthy white neighborhoods and in the inner cities.[18]

In Independence, a black neighborhood called the "Nigger Neck" (at what is now Delaware Street and Bess Truman Parkway) was destroyed to create separation between black and white neighborhoods. McCoy Park replaced the black neighborhood and served as a no man's land; plus, it improved the scenery around the Harry S Truman Presidential Library and

Museum. In her poem "Memories of a Neck Child," resident Alversia B. Pettigrew wrote:

URBAN RENEWAL raised its angry hand,
Moving and splitting black families all over the land.
We all had to move out of the NECK like a flashing spark.
Independence had to make way for the "much-needed" McCoy Park.
Certainly, the prices offered some were quite meager;
But there was no choice, for the City was eager.
Then, the bulldozers rushed in, piling THE NECK in a heap.
Some folks shouted for joy...others would sit and weep.
An "ALL-AMERICAN CITY" was the plot of this story,
Leaving many NECK families deep in debt and full of worry.[19]

In Independence, families were compensated $200 for moving expenses, with a possible $500 in additional financial assistance if certain qualifications were met. Historian and African American Joe Louis Mattox worked with the Land Clearance for Redevelopment Authority of Independence, Missouri, to help uprooted families find and move in to affordable, safe, and sanitary homes. Though proud of this work, he remembers, "People who worked in the program were suspected of being insensitive and uncaring," viewed as assisting in the local government's "negro removal."

"There are some who see me as having 'betrayed the black community' for the work I did. Or, that I was a 'tool for the white man,'" Mattox wrote. There was, after all, intense anger over the program: "There were protests. There were objections and opposition. Condemnation proceedings slowed the process of relocation. Requests for rezoning were proposed, contested and denied."[20]

Gotham concludes in his essay "A City Without Slums" that the promises of revival offered by Kansas City's politicians, businessmen, and real estate elites were empty. Seizing the homes of the poor and redeveloping the land for private industry did not save the inner city from exodus and decay. It only contributed to Kansas City's decentralization. Affordable housing in the central city disappeared, forcing more people to look elsewhere. During suburbanization and white flight, from 1950 to 1970, a half-million residents spread out from the central city into a massive geographic area.

With Troost Avenue selected as the wall between white and black Kansas City, the KCMSD allowed the eastern schools to go black, while protecting the western schools against integration. Paseo High went from all-white to 98 percent black between 1954 and 1969. Southeast High experienced the same between 1954 and 1973. Every public school east of Troost was 90 percent black by the 1970s. But Southwest High, west of Troost, remained less than 1 percent black from 1955 to 1970.[21] Whites protested fiercely when the KCMSD let the Benton school go black—it was set on fire days after opening for the 1953 school year.[22] Black and white students sometimes fought during the transition years. At Central Junior High School in the late 1950s, a favorite weapon was a sharpened beer can opener.[23]

The poverty and segregation on the east side deeply compromised the education of black youths. In the late 1950s, only 11 percent of Kansas City blacks attended college and only 20 percent graduated from high school.[24] After national desegregation was ordered in 1954, Missouri essentially handed the decision to comply with federal law over to municipalities and school districts. These forces then took up the mantle of keeping "niggers" out of white schools, which they achieved by changing neighborhood attendance zones year to year. It is important to note the *Brown v. the Topeka Board of Education* ruling gave no timeline or due date for desegregation, calling only for "all deliberate speed." This resulted in little change throughout much of the country for years. Many states, cities, and districts had no qualms about blatant violations of the Supreme Court decision. Keeping schools white was too important. Missouri districts could integrate if they chose, but were in no way required to do so by state law. The Kansas City, Missouri School District chose not to integrate.[25]

Until 1968, there were no blacks on the school board to represent black families.[26] This begs the question of whether to blame the victims for their condition in society or those who held economic and political power. It was white school board members who perpetuated separate and unequal facilities. This era was marked by "overcrowding in the Black schools east of Troost and underutilization of White schools west of Troost."[27] This helped "reinforce in the minds of White residents that Black schools were inferior and substandard, a claim consonant with the negative stereotypes and prejudices of today."[28] The 1960s saw a busing program attempt to alleviate the crowded conditions of black schools, but blacks shipped to white schools were kept in isolated classrooms, as they had been in the Benton School nearly a century before.[29]

But throughout the 1940s, 1950s, and 1960s, progressives and antiracists pushed back. Integration advocates, neighborhood coalitions, and some city politicians and educators condemned the school board's tactics. Blacks and whites rallied at a June 1963 KCMSD board meeting to protest. In July, the Kansas City chapter of the Congress of Racial Equality organized sit-ins and pickets of the board meetings. A lawsuit from the federal government brought the segregation policy to an end when the Department of Health, Education, and Welfare sued the KCMSD in 1973.[30]

People like Esther Brown were an early force to bring about change. Brown, a Russian-Jewish radical from Kansas City, took up residence with her family in Johnson County after World War II. Already a member of labor organizations and various leftist groups, Brown began a journey as a civil rights activist when her maid, Helen Swan, described to her the horrendous conditions of the black Walker School in nearby South Park Township. White students had enjoyed a better school building for some time, but in 1947 a new $90,000 elementary school was built for the 222 white students. The 44 black students in the community had to remain where they were (eight grades with only two teachers), even though the tax dollars of black families were also used to construct the new school. The Walker School was a "dilapidated two-room shack with an outhouse, poor heating, and a flooded basement."[31] According to the Kansas Historical Society, the school had dirt floors and limited classroom materials.[32] This being 1947, there was no national legal mandate for integration, only for equal facilities. Kansas statutes, however, did require integration in smaller cities.

Brown worked with Helen Swan, community leader Alfonso Webb, and other black parents, educators, and activists to form an NAACP chapter for South Park in 1948. The resistance from the school board and the white community was vicious. Brown was invited to an open meeting in the new elementary school's gymnasium, where she faced hundreds of enraged parents. The chairman of the school board crowed, "All of a sudden we seem to have a racial problem in South Park. Well, let me tell you that no nigger will get into South Park as long as I live."[33] The crowd screamed things like "Go back where you came from, nigger lover," and cursed at Brown; one woman attacked her with an umbrella.[34] Brown later received threatening calls and a cross was burned in her front yard.

With petitions and protests gaining only vague promises or patronizing offers, Webb (the new chapter president) and the NAACP sued the school district in May 1948. Brown worked to get Elisha Scott on the case, an attorney who pushed to allow black children into the new grade school.

The black community boycotted the Walker School and held classes in living rooms instead. Brown traveled across Kansas to raise money to pay the teachers' salaries and keep the lawsuit alive. "She spoke to community groups, churches, fraternal orders, social clubs, veteran organizations, NAACP branches—anyone who would listen."[35] When her massive letter-writing campaign didn't bring in enough cash, she used her own savings. She raised more than $3,000 and spent $1,000 of her own funds. Due to her efforts, newspapers and publications from the *Kansas City Call* to the national NAACP's *Crisis* magazine devoted space to the struggle in Johnson County. Brown split her time between fundraising and substitute teaching in black homes if one of the teachers grew ill. She was labeled a communist by her father-in-law and slandered by the FBI. But on June 11, 1949, the Kansas Supreme Court ruled in *Webb v. School District No. 90* that the school district was in violation of state law, and required the new grade school to be opened to African Americans.

The school board scrambled to prevent integration, promising to retrofit Walker School or build a brand new school for blacks. Yet in the fall of 1949, black children showed up at South Park Elementary to attend class. They were allowed in by the new principal, Charles H. Rutherford (who was also labeled a "nigger lover" and a "communist"). Brown bought new clothes for all the new pupils of the school. The *Webb* case ended segregation in Johnson County. Later, Shawnee Mission High School opened to the former Walker School students; they would no longer be bused to Sumner High.

Esther Brown headed to Wichita and then Topeka to fight for integration. She became an integral part of the historic *Brown v. Board of Education of Topeka* case, advising the Brown family, raising money, and determining strategy with Roy Wilkins, Walter White, and Thurgood Marshall (later the first African American on the U.S. Supreme Court). She later advocated for fair employment policy in Kansas City, pressured the KCMSD to integrate, pushed for the establishment of a new junior college downtown rather than in the white suburbs, served on the Jackson County, Missouri Civil Rights Commission, and founded the Panel of American Women.[36] Importantly, Brown understood the grand American hypocrisy of the era, saying in a 1948 speech to the Kansas NAACP, "Until Jim Crow is abolished, the words 'democracy,' 'freedom,' and 'justice' used so freely to support our foreign policy will ring hollow throughout the world."[37]

While residents pushing for positive change consistently ran into roadblocks—for example, 150 black students attempting to enroll in a white public school with better facilities were blocked by a court edict[38]—progress was made in higher education as African Americans gained greater access to Kansas City's colleges. Rockhurst College, a Catholic institution east of Troost, admitted blacks to summer programs in the mid-1940s, and to all semesters in 1949. The University of Kansas City, a private college (now UMKC, public), admitted Harold Holliday in 1948. Holliday later became a Democratic politician and served in the Missouri House of Representatives starting in 1964. According to William H. Young and Nathan B. Young, Jr., the University of Kansas City was "believed to be the first private college in the middle southwest to admit Negro students to all the phases of its program—to the college of liberal arts as well as to the graduate school."[39] By 1950, the University of Kansas City had 150 black students.[40] In the late 1960s, more junior colleges, such as Penn Valley, were established. Headway in public education administration came in 1964, when Dr. John Ramos, Jr., became the first African American to sit on the Kansas City Board of Education.

Still, the cycle of segregation, poor schools, joblessness, and poverty was unbroken. With so much at stake, housing rights became a national priority for blacks, especially after *de jure* victories regarding segregation and discrimination in education (1954), employment and public facilities (1964), and voting (1965). But U.S. government policies that could have helped black Kansas Citians in the 1960s only improved white lives. The Federal Housing Administration offered government-backed housing loans to help low-income people enter the mortgage market, but the program was designed for and benefited whites. Nearly all the loans went to them.

Federal Housing Administration loans and the G.I. Bill in the 1930s and 1940s essentially built the white middle class, pumping $220 billion into housing and education for white Americans.[41] Not even black veterans received such aid. The Federal Housing Administration under the Roosevelt administration redlined minority areas of municipalities and withheld government aid from those sections of the country. It was a similar story in the 1960s. FHA subsidies for new home construction (under Section 235 of the 1968 Fair Housing Act) were distributed in a decentralized manner, overseen by real estate businesses and banks.[42]

These were the same powers that historically condemned any ban on racial discrimination in housing as an assault on the Constitution, private property rights, freedom of choice, and Christian values.[43] They not only oversaw the enactment of the 1968 law, they wrote it.[44] So blacks were marginalized. Some look at government programs and believe their failures to simply be part of the nature of government programs. But this denies historical contexts. The program was successful for whites. Failure is sometimes due to prejudice, or the destructive influence of private powers on public policy. In this case, the National Association of Real Estate Boards and other corporate organizations made the majority of decisions in housing policy that affected the common people.[45] Perhaps if the fair housing laws were written and enacted by social workers, housing advocates, community leaders, sociologists, neighborhood coalition leaders, and the very people they were designed to help, things would have been different. Predictably, the private sector built 72.4 percent of new homes where least needed, in the white suburbs of Kansas City.[46]

Segregation hardened. Poor whites were directed into the suburbs and blacks into the inner city.

The blockbusters of Kansas City and elsewhere took advantage of the FHA program. Exploitation and fear mongering became even more profitable. Because of the Housing Act, lending standards were lower, credit more available, and the risks of lending covered by the government. Blockbusters continued to buy bad houses for next to nothing and sell mortgages to African Americans at high prices; when the family defaulted and lost the home, the FHA fully reimbursed the blockbuster the price of the mortgage.[47] When a home was foreclosed,

> [Department of Housing and Urban Development] guidelines mandated that the property remain vacant until the government decided what to do with it, a process that could take months or years. Abandoned homes began cropping up all over formerly vibrant communities. They quickly went to seed, attracting vagrancy and crime.[48]

In this manner, east Kansas City deteriorated. Abandoned homes and buildings multiplied, businesses and services disappeared, houses decayed, property values fell, poverty worsened, and crime rose. Discriminatory practices were fought viciously by the local NAACP, the Community Committee for Social Action, Freedom, Inc. (formed by Bruce R. Watkins and Leon Jordan), the Congress of Racial Equality, and neighborhood coalitions like the 49/63 Neighborhood Coalition, led by the president of Rockhurst College. Their protests were backed by the findings of the National Commission on Urban Problems, the President's Committee on Urban Housing, the U.S. Commission on Civil Rights, and other groups, which "agreed that the nation's housing woes were either directly or indirectly linked to the practices of the FHA."[49]

Plunging property values, crime waves, dwindling populations, and shrinking tax revenues worried city councils across the country.[50] From the mid-1960s to the mid-1970s, total employment in the inner city plunged about 20 percent. "Urban Renewal had not halted decentralization trends but reinforced the exodus of people and industry, creating more urban blight and exacerbating the urban housing problem."[51] As whites continued to isolate themselves, city services declined in black areas and white businesses relocated.

Again, progressive activists fought back. In 1955, Earl T. Sturgess, pastor at the Southeast Presbyterian Church, led an effort to prevent white flight from Benton Boulevard, selling "Not for Sale" signs to residents for their lawns.[52] Civic and religious organizations persuaded the city council to ban blockbusting in 1964. The Kansas City, Missouri Human Relations Commission launched a public awareness campaign to prevent panic selling. Politicians condemned the tactics of the real estate industry. Neighborhood coalitions formed to maintain integration. There were petitions and protests at City Hall against blatant violations of the anti-blockbusting law. Though the good fight was fought, the division of city neighborhoods continued through the 1960s and 70s.[53]

Yet success was found elsewhere. The half-million dollar, 3,000-capacity swimming pool in Swope Park had banned blacks since opening in 1941. Blacks were confined to a section in the park called "Watermelon Hill."[54] The local NAACP sued the city in August 1951 when Esther Williams, Lena Rivers, and Joseph Moore were turned away from the pool (*City of Kansas City v. Esther Williams*). Carl R. Johnson of the Kansas City NAACP and Robert L. Carter from New York City represented Williams, Rivers, and Moore,[55] and Thurgood Marshall came to Kansas City to serve as the lead attorney.[56]

The NAACP argued the local black pool was inferior, while city lawyers justified segregation by citing "the natural aversion to physical intimacy inherent in the use of swimming pools by races that do not mingle socially."[57] The city government feared a race riot, as thousands clashed violently in St. Louis in 1949 when the public pools were integrated. When the U.S. District Court ruled in favor of the NAACP, the city shut down Swope Park. The city appealed, but the U.S. Supreme Court ruled that unless equal facilities were built for blacks, the city was in violation of federal law. Swope Pool opened for both races on June 12, 1954. The riot police placed outside the pool proved unnecessary. Rather than revolt, many whites simply stayed away. Attendance dropped by more than 60 percent.[58]

Progress was also seen in the world of sports. The Kansas City Chiefs hired the first full-time black scout in professional football history, Lloyd Wells, in 1963. Wells found and recruited many talented black players, and in 1969 the Chiefs became the first team to play a majority-black starting line.[59] Hal McRae also broke barriers as the first African American to lead a Missouri professional sports team when he became manager of his former team, the Kansas City Royals.[60]

Activists were inspired by bus boycotts in Montgomery, Alabama, and rallied into action after Martin Luther King, Jr., spoke at St. Stephen Baptist Church in Kansas City on April 11, 1957. Some 2,500 flocked to hear him.[61] He gave the same speech he gave in St. Louis the night before, called "A Realistic Look at the Question of Progress in the Area of Race Relations." He cried out for a

> new world in which men will be able to live together as brothers. This new world in which all men will respect the dignity and worth of all human personality. This new world, in which men will beat their swords into plowshares, and their spears into pruning hooks. Yes, this new world in which men will no longer take necessities from the masses to give luxuries to the classes. This new world in which men will learn the old principle of the fatherhood of God and the brotherhood of man. They will hear once more the voice of Jesus crying out through the generations saying, "Love everybody." This is that world. Then right here in America we will be able to sing with new meaning:
>
> *My country 'tis of thee,*
> *Sweet land of liberty,*
> *Of thee I sing.*
> *Land where my fathers died,*
> *Land of the Pilgrims' pride,*
> *From every mountainside,*
> *Let freedom ring.*[62]

Stirred by his call, Kansas Citians pushed harder for equality. In 1958, elementary school teacher Gladys Twine and a society of black women called the Twin Cities formed the Community Committee for Social Action. They demanded that the five largest downtown department stores—Macy's, Jones Store, Kline's, Peck's, and Emery, Bird, Thayer & Company—end segregation at their dining counters. After a massive public awareness campaign, the Community Committee for Social Action announced a boycott in December 1958. The Reverend Arthur Marshall declared, "If they walked in Montgomery, surely we can stop buying in Kansas City."[63] The committee found allies in Lucile Bluford of the *Call*, the local NAACP, and many community and religious leaders, both black and white. The picketing and boycotts slashed holiday sales, and after the committee threatened a march downtown, the stores capitulated. Lunch counters desegregated in February 1959. These actions influenced lunch counter sit-ins across the country in the following years (including a quite famous one at a Woolworth's store in Greensboro, North Carolina, in 1960).[64]

In 1963, sixteen activists (four white) marched into Fairyland Park in Kansas City (75th and Prospect) and refused to leave. The park was whites only except for one day a year. The activists were arrested and jailed. Then a black barber named Richard Robinson, his brother Charles, and nine friends sat down one morning at the Peerless Cafe (3115 Prospect) and refused to leave unless they were served. The Peerless Cafe closed that day and never reopened.[65] Alvin Brooks, head of the Kansas City Congress of Racial Equality, investigated restaurants and bars that lied about fire marshal limits to keep out blacks, or charged them double to enter.[66] The passionate Reverend Wallace Hartsfield of the Metropolitan Missionary Baptist Church led mass protests against downtown stores like

Kline's, Macy's, and Peck's in 1964.[67] And Kansas Citians jour-neyed to join the marches in the South. People like Sister Barbra Moore, a nurse supervisor at the old St. Joseph Hospital, and Father Al O'Laughlin of St. Peter's Catholic Church marched with Dr. King from Selma to Montgomery, Alabama, in March 1965 to push for voting rights, which were key to voting racist politicians out of office. Hostile southerners attempted to run over two of O'Laughlin's fellow priests.[68]

The work of groups like Freedom, Inc. (the oldest black political organization in the country[69]) and an emboldened black electorate launched Bruce R. Watkins to the Kansas City Council in 1963. Watkins worked for a clean-up campaign of the inner city and to get more blacks on the police force. At that time, white police officers still followed and harassed African Americans in the company of white women or in pre-dominantly white areas. Two white policemen viciously beat a black man on the Plaza in September 1965, outraging the black community. In 1966, the Interdenominational Ministe-rial Alliance led a march to police headquarters to protest mis-treatment.[70] That same year, Watkins became the first African American in the Jackson County administration; he returned to the city council in 1975, and had an unsuccessful run for mayor in 1979.

Freedom, Inc. produced many more successful candidates and campaigns. Leon Jordan, who would become Missouri's most powerful black politician, was elected to the Missouri General Assembly in 1964. Jordan's grandfather fought in the Battle of Westport, his father was a civil rights activist, and his wife, Orchid Jordan, later became a Missouri state legislator.

Watkins helped push forward legislation to end segregation. In April 1964, the people of Kansas City voted on a ban on racial discrimination in public facilities. Freedom, Inc., Watkins, Jordan, and others rallied 18,000 black voters. It was one of the largest voting drives in city history.[71] Supporters parked a hearse and coffin outside their headquarters with a banner that read, "LAST RIDE FOR JIM CROW...VOTE 'YES' APR. 7TH."[72] The law passed with a mere 50.9 percent majority after a fierce battle between civil rights activists and the white business class.[73] Segregation, while not overthrown, was now illegal in Kansas City.

In 1966, a new voice for social, political, and economic equality sounded from Oakland, California, in the form of a black socialist organization that spread quickly across the United States. The Black Panther Party, founded by Huey Newton and Bobby Seale, was largely inspired by the ideology of Islamic minister Malcolm X. The Black Panthers, founded the year after Malcolm X's assassination, aimed to promote self-defense and use of Second Amendment rights, to unify workers against capitalist exploitation, to embrace black pride, to make African Americans politically powerful and economically self-sufficient, to end illiteracy, hunger, and poverty in black communities, and to fight and die at any time for freedom. Marxist ideas of giving power to the common people attracted many. So did the idea of revolution. In 1967, with violence increasing against non-violent protesters and little being done to alleviate discrimination and poverty, hundreds of riots raged across the nation. Eighty-three people perished during the worst rioting in U.S. history.[74] Many had been killed in urban race riots in 1966, 1965, 1964, and long before then as well. The Black Panther

Party and its message of self-protection appealed to those who saw King's pacifism as inadequate. There was simply too much rage over white oppression. The Panthers wanted change, as outlined in their *Ten Point Program and Platform*:

1. *We want freedom. We want power to determine the destiny of our Black Community.*

We believe that black people will not be free until we are able to determine our destiny.

2. *We want full employment for our people.*

We believe that the federal government is responsible and obligated to give every man employment or a guaranteed income. We believe that if the white American businessmen will not give full employment, then the means of production should be taken from the businessmen and placed in the community so that the people of the community can organize and employ all of its people and give a high standard of living.

3. *We want an end to the robbery by the capitalists of our Black Community.*

We believe that this racist government has robbed us and now we are demanding the overdue debt of forty acres and two mules. Forty acres and two mules was promised 100 years ago as restitution for slave labor and mass murder of black people. We will accept the payment as currency which will be distributed to our many communities. The Germans are now aiding the Jews in Israel for the genocide of the Jewish people. The Germans murdered six million Jews. The American racist has taken part in the slaughter of over twenty million black people; therefore, we feel that this is a modest demand that we make.

4. *We want decent housing, fit for shelter of human beings.*

We believe that if the white landlords will not give decent housing to our black community, then the housing and the land should be made into cooperatives so that our community, with government aid, can build and make decent housing for its people.

5. *We want education for our people that exposes the true nature of this decadent American society. We want education that teaches us our true history and our role in the present-day society.*

We believe in an educational system that will give to our people a knowledge of self. If a man does not have knowledge of himself and his position in society and the world, then he has little chance to relate to anything else.

6. *We want all black men to be exempt from military service.*

We believe that Black people should not be forced to fight in the military service to defend a racist government that does not protect us. We will not fight and kill other people of color in the world who, like black people, are being victimized by the white racist government of America. We will protect ourselves from the force and violence of the racist police and the racist military, by whatever means necessary.

7. *We want an immediate end to police brutality and murder of black people.*

We believe we can end police brutality in our black community by organizing black self-defense groups that are dedicated to defending our black community from racist police oppression and brutality. The Second Amendment to the Constitution of the United States gives a right to bear arms. We therefore believe that all black people should arm themselves for self defense.

8. *We want freedom for all black men held in federal, state, county and city prisons and jails.*

We believe that all black people should be released from the many jails and prisons because they have not received a fair and impartial trial.

9. *We want all black people when brought to trial to be tried in court by a jury of their peer group or people from their black communities, as defined by the Constitution of the United States.*

We believe that the courts should follow the United States Constitution so that black people will receive fair trials. The 14th Amendment of the U.S. Constitution gives a man a right to be tried by his peer group. A peer is a person from a similar economic, social, religious, geographical, environmental, historical and racial background. To do this the court will be forced to select a jury from the black community from which the black defendant came. We have been, and are being tried by all-white juries that have no understanding of the "average reasoning man" of the black community.

10. *We want land, bread, housing, education, clothing, justice and peace. And as our major political objective, a United Nations-supervised plebiscite to be held throughout the black colony in which only black colonial subjects will be allowed to participate for the purpose of determining the will of black people as to their national destiny.*

When in the course of human events, it becomes necessary for one people to dissolve the political bands which have connected them with another, and to assume, among the powers of the earth, the separate and equal station to which the laws of nature and nature's God entitle them, a decent respect to the opinions of mankind requires that they should declare the causes which impel them to the separation.

We hold these truths to be self evident, that all men are created equal; that they are endowed by their Creator with certain unalienable rights; that among these are life, liberty, and the pursuit of happiness. That, to secure these rights, governments are instituted among men, deriving their just powers from the consent of the governed; that, whenever any form of government becomes destructive of these ends, it is the right of the people to alter or to abolish it, and to institute a new government, laying its foundation on such principles, and organizing its powers in such form, as to them shall seem most likely to effect their safety and happiness.

Prudence, indeed, will dictate that governments long established should not be changed for light and transient causes; and accordingly, all experience hath shown, that mankind are more disposed to suffer, while evils are sufferable, than to right themselves by abolishing the forms to which they are accustomed. But, when a long train of abuses and usurpations, pursuing invariable the same object, evinces a design to reduce them under absolute despotism, it is their right, it is their duty, to throw off such government, and to provide new guards for their future security.[75]

Such an ideology was a declaration of war against the powerful. The FBI, which has a long history of working to destroy leftist and civil rights organizations (the NAACP, the Southern Christian Leadership Conference, the Student Nonviolent Coordinating Committee, etc.), installed spies, helped assassinate Black Panther Party leader Fred Hampton in Chicago, forged letters to create disunity, illegally imprisoned activists, and attempted to discredit the Party through propaganda.[76] The FBI authorized municipal police to terrorize members at home, at meetings, and at protests. This crackdown again revealed Constitutional rights as meaningless when racism permeates the police, the local and federal governments, the military, and the courts. When Bobby Seale was arrested for protesting at the Democratic National Convention in 1968, he was not allowed to choose his own lawyer—he was gagged and bound in the courtroom.[77] He was sentenced to four years in prison. Many leaders were forced to flee the United States to avoid death or imprisonment.

A Kansas City chapter of the Black Panther Party launched in 1969 (there was also a Nation of Islam mosque built here). The chapter was chaired by Pete O'Neal, a man inspired by *The Autobiography of Malcolm X* and influenced by experiences similar to those of the slain leader. Raised in the slums of Kansas City, he spent much time as a child in the bars on 12th Street, running errands for hustlers and pimps. He later joined the Navy, but was discharged and imprisoned for stabbing a man in the chest, nearly killing him, for insulting a woman. After his release he returned to Kansas City, where he "lived by his hustle: stealing, running cons, and pimping."[78]

After he joined the freedom struggle, he helped found the Black Vigilantes in 1968, which grew into a Black Panther Party chapter after O'Neal visited Oakland and got to know Party leaders.[79] "To O'Neal…[his chapter] represented a lifeline out of an abyss of drugs and aimlessness. He blazed with purpose: End racism and class inequality, fast."[80] He boldly announced the launch of his chapter in the hallway of police headquarters!

O'Neal was a magnetic young man possessed of bottomless anger. He was an ex-con who'd found a kind of religion in late-'60s black nationalism, a vain, violent street hustler reborn in a Black Panther uniform of dark

sunglasses, beret and leather jacket. With pitiless, knife-
sharp diction, he spoke of sending police to their graves.[81]

The chapter created social programs to lift Kansas City blacks
out of poverty. Its "three major survival programs included a
free breakfast program, black history classes, and free health
screening for sickle cell and hypertension."[82] Food donations
from local businesses fed 700 children each day.[83] Big food
chains like McDonald's donated food, while pharmaceutical
firms contributed vitamins. This generosity came in the wake
of threats by O'Neal, who said: "We went to white businesses in
our community, businesses that were exploiting our communities…[and said] if you were going to be in our community you
were going to support the uplifting of our community or bad
things could very well happen to you."[84]

Still, the Party's work and rhetoric appealed to many, black
and white, interested in equality and in black history. The Party
offered educational opportunities. "Hang the Honkie" parties
were community meetings that introduced whites to the horrors
of slavery and oppression; this glimpse of true history left many
whites terrified, tearful, and angry enough to join the fight for
human rights.[85] Nationally, the Party was renowned for organizing dozens of community programs such as free clothing,
shoes, food, education, legal representation, and health clinics
for communities of color. The Panthers have largely been erased
from American history textbooks, and when they do appear
the focus is usually on their dark sunglasses, black berets, and
menacing guns. The Party did see the need for the violent over-
throw of an oppressive government if their demands for equal
rights went unmet. O'Neal called it "a goal worth struggling

for"[86] and once said, "I would very much like to shoot my way into the House of Representatives.... I mean that literally."[87] But that is not the singular legacy of the organization.

Reynaldo Anderson (*On the Ground: The Black Panther Party in Communities Across America*) points out other Kansas City organizations, like the NAACP and the Social Action Committee of 20, cooperated well with the Black Panther Party at first, despite their differing views on militancy. Black Panther Party members were well represented on community committees and at speeches and rallies.[88] And of course they held their own mass rallies, promising revolution. The Party led a march against City Hall to protest an ordinance that banned the burning of garbage in residential zones, a surefire way to worsen the conditions of a ghetto if the government refused to offer garbage removal services.[89] "Also, Kansas City Panthers made close alliances with organizations of welfare mothers, church community outreach workers, religious missionaries, and others."[90] The Panthers received support from the white community, too. The Methodist Inner City Parish, for instance, offered Party members work, office space, transportation for food deliveries, and bail money in case of arrest.[91]

Women were deeply involved in the Black Panther Party. Charlotte Hill, an eighteen-year-old student at Wyandotte High School, joined in 1969. She organized meetings at school to teach African history and attended Party rallies and classes, before graduating and going to live with Party members in Kansas City, Missouri. She went through the same military drills and firearm training as men, helped build the health care and food programs, and was made deputy minister of culture and deputy minister of finance. Hill told author Gaidi Faraj in 2005 that although Panther women faced frequent sexual pressure and advances from the men, and sexism in general, the Party aimed to liberate women and promote equality—it was "empowering," a "source of pride" and "strength."[92]

The U.S. government worked to destroy the Kansas City Panthers along with all the other chapters. Faraj notes that "Kansas City was probably one of the more difficult cities to resist police aggression because of the power and influence of Police Chief Clarence Kelly," who spent over 20 years as an FBI agent (and would later become director after J. Edgar Hoover died).[93] The FBI worked with the Kansas City Police Department to install spies in the Party, to arrest members on trumped up charges, to destroy property such as food meant for distribution, and to generally slander the Panthers to discourage support and membership. Hostilities between members and the police were venomous. Members referred to police officers as "pigs," and accused them of illegally funneling weapons to white supremacists called the Minutemen. Pete O'Neal tried to draw the police into a war that would show the true nature of police brutality.[94] He also tried to expose Kelley for allegedly falsifying a report when a police officer committed suicide; the doctored report allowed the officer's widow to receive insurance money. The Panthers invaded Kelly's church during a service. At a press conference to address the matter at the police station (December 5, 1969), Kelley was perturbed to see O'Neal and other Panthers arrive, and ordered them removed. The Panthers refused and brawled with the police. O'Neal and others were handcuffed and arrested.[95]

Several factors made the Black Panther presence in Kansas City a brief one, only about a year. O'Neal admits he lost a lot of support in the black community by denouncing the Methodist Church for not giving enough to the Party.[96] Then, when white police officer John E. Dacy was shot and killed during an armed robbery involving hostages, the Party exalted in the victory. Its response triggered the NAACP and other moderate civil rights groups to withdraw their support. Working-class blacks, who made up the base of the Black Panther Party, supported the killing more readily than blacks of the middle and upper class, who were less radical.

During the same period that the black revolution was being crushed locally and nationally, "overtures were made to the black business class, which included local Kansas City citizens,"[97] wrote historian Reynaldo Anderson. Upper-class white support for black banks and businesses was meant to prevent their radicalization and support for the Party, and to draw higher-income African Americans into a more conservative and controllable fold that emphasized racial advancement through higher education and other methods. Newspapers like the *Kansas City Star* praised black capitalism and the success that came by playing by the rules.

Beyond diminishing support, the Panthers faced increasingly heavy persecution: police raids, beatings, and arrests. After the assassination of Fred Hampton in Chicago, a group of black ministers saved the Kansas City chapter from a potentially fatal police raid. They stood protectively before the Party headquarters and refused to move. By January 1970, the Black Panther Party was all but finished in Kansas City.[98] It broke into smaller revolutionary groups, like the Sons of Malcolm, to try to survive. Pete O'Neal, facing a harsh prison sentence for moving weapons from Kansas into Missouri, escaped police surveillance and fled to Sweden in 1970 with his wife, Charlotte Hill O'Neal. They made their way to Tanzania two years later. Nevertheless, the Kansas City movement left behind programs to feed children. In 1982, the national Party ceased operations due, in part, to decades of intense government repression. One could argue that the Panthers left a legacy of increased interest in black studies and opposition to state power, support for socialist ideas like worker ownership of businesses and government, and the acceptance of force by many as a proper response to tyranny and violence.

After riots ravaged the U.S. in 1967, violence exploded again in 1968 after the assassination of Martin Luther King, Jr. Though King held to his belief in nonviolence, he believed, like the Black Panthers, W.E.B. Du Bois, A. Phillip Randolph, and other black leaders, that socialism could end poverty for blacks and whites alike—not state or totalitarian socialism, but a democratic socialism. At the 1967 Southern Christian Leadership Conference convention in Atlanta, King said:

> The movement must address itself to the question of restructuring the whole of American society. There are forty million poor people here. And one day we must ask the question, Why are there forty million poor people in America? And when you begin to ask that question, you are raising questions about the economic system, about a broader distribution of wealth. When you ask that question, you begin to question the capitalistic economy. And I'm simply saying that more and more, we've got to begin to ask questions about the whole society. We are called upon to help the discouraged beggars in life's marketplace. But one day we must come to see that an edifice which produces beggars needs restructuring. It

means that questions must be raised. You see, my friends, when you deal with this, you begin to ask the question, Who owns the oil? You begin to ask the question, Who owns the iron ore?....

A guaranteed annual income could be done for about twenty billion dollars a year.... If our nation can spend thirty-five billion dollars a year to fight an unjust, evil war in Vietnam, and twenty billion dollars to put a man on the moon, it can spend billions of dollars to put God's children on their own two feet right here on earth.[99]

King noted in a letter he penned while in a Selma, Alabama, jail cell in 1965, "If we are to achieve a real equality, the U.S. will have to adopt a modified form of socialism."[100] He told his staff in 1966:

You can't talk about solving the economic problem of the Negro without talking about billions of dollars. You can't talk about ending the slums without first saying profit must be taken out of slums. You're really tampering and getting on dangerous ground because you are messing with folk then. You are messing with captains of industry. Now this means that we are treading in difficult water, because it really means that we are saying that something is wrong with capitalism. There must be a better distribution of wealth, and maybe America must move toward a democratic socialism.[101]

King knew that under capitalism the few (the "captains of industry," the business owners) were growing wealthy off the labor of the many, the workers, who were paid little, especially blacks. He believed a guaranteed income could correct this.

A sniper's bullet tore through King's face as he stood on the balcony of his motel room in Memphis on April 4, 1968. He was on his way to support the strike of local sanitation workers. An escaped convict, James Earl Ray of Illinois, was hunted down, arrested, and pled guilty, avoiding a jury trial and possible execution. He almost immediately recanted his plea, and spent the rest of his life fighting for a new trial, with support from the King family, who believed the U.S. government orchestrated the slaying. Though Ray died in prison in April 1998, a civil court in Memphis ruled on December 8, 1999, in *King v. Jowers*, that government agencies were complicit in the murder of King. Coretta, on whose behalf the lawsuit was filed, declared, "The Mafia, local, state and federal government agencies were deeply involved in the assassination of my husband."[102] The Department of Justice issued a report attempting to discredit the trial and insisted no further investigation of the assassination was necessary.[103] Some point out government complicity would not necessarily be out of character during the civil rights era. For instance, the FBI worked with the Chicago police to assassinate Fred Hampton. The FBI "tapped [King's] private phone conversations, sent him fake letters, threatened him, blackmailed him, and even suggested once in an anonymous letter that he commit suicide. FBI internal memos discussed finding a black leader to replace King. As a Senate report on the FBI said in 1976, the FBI tried 'to destroy Dr. Martin Luther King.'"[104]

When King died, riots erupted in 125 cities. Washington, D.C., and Chicago were hit hardest. Across the states, rallies and protests turned into shootouts as black Americans and police exchanged fire. Whites were assaulted. Looting and arson destroyed white-owned businesses. The police were overwhelmed, and only widespread military occupation could restore order. Forty-six people died, 2,600 were injured, and 21,000 arrested.[105] Thousands of structures were damaged and incinerated, and tens of millions of dollars' worth of property destroyed.

Kansas Citians watched the nation burn for several days. In Kansas City, Kansas, African Americans held a memorial march for King on Friday, April 5. The city's police force assisted and the district superintendent even participated in the demonstration.[106] Then, on April 7, Palm Sunday, around 15,000 people joined in another march. Episcopal priest David Fly wrote, "On more than one occasion, people in the streets and speakers from the platform congratulated themselves on the nonviolent nature of the march.... While other cities experienced riots in the streets, we proudly said, 'Kansas City is different.'"[107]

Students in the Kansas City, Missouri School District planned their own demonstration on the day of King's burial, which fell on Tuesday, April 9. The closure of schools as part of the national observance of President Kennedy's funeral five years ago was still fresh in students' minds, and many school districts across the country likewise closed to honor King. The Kansas City, Kansas, schools closed when parents and civil rights leaders swore they would boycott otherwise.[108]

The Kansas City school district in Missouri took a different tack and kept school doors open. The board of education and police leaders thought there would be less trouble if students were busy at school.[109] Disgusted at what they viewed as the district's disrespect, students decided to march for King, and staged a walkout. Hundreds of black youths poured out of Lincoln High and Manual High early Tuesday morning and

joined demonstrators at Central High School. The demonstration began peacefully, but then marchers entered Central
Junior High School, screamed that school was out, and threw
textbooks out the window.[110] Word began spreading among
students that the entire Kansas City Police Department had
mobilized and white policemen were surrounding Central. The
situation grew tense; during the 1960s the police force was 94.5
percent white. Their preparation and training to crack down on
a rebellion often translated into the abuse of black citizens.[111]

Two policemen maced students when they attempted to
continue the march from the school grounds.[112] According to
some sources, agitated students shattered the windows of cars
in the Central parking lot and completely overturned others,
though Harry Ross, who led the Manual students, said, "…the
kids at Central was just making a lot of noise, really, I didn't see
them tearing up nothing…. I didn't see no car they had turned
over."[113] Regardless, Central administrators cancelled classes
and ordered the restless students to head home, but the situation escalated. Police threw tear gas; students threw bricks and
rocks.[114] The growing crowd surged past police and marched for
Paseo High, and "vandalism erupted sporadically up and down
Indiana where rioters stomped on cars and threatened residents
with baseball bats."[115] At Paseo High, things also spiraled out of
control. One student remembered, "We [ransacked] the cafe-
teria and broke out a couple windows on the first floor—no—a
whole lot of windows on the first floor and then after that…
everybody went out in front and they jumped on this white
girl."[116]

Police, with dogs and in riot gear, formed a defensive line
on 31st near Troost and blasted the approaching crowd from

Central with mace; the same was done from a passing police cruiser. Screaming students broke and ran, then regrouped, joined the students at Paseo, and angrily decided to seek an apology for police conduct from Mayor Ilus Davis, who had supported anti-discrimination policies throughout the 1960s and had a positive relationship with much of the black community. But not all. One student said after the riot, "The mayor ain't gonna listen to us until some shit happen[s]—other than that, he's going to stay locked up in his office." The student continued, saying: "When you're down at City Hall and he gets on the elevator…if [there are] any niggers on that elevator he's gonna tell you to go on down, let them off and then make a special trip back up to get him…. He don't want nobody on there with him."[117]

The mayor soon met the students at Parade Park. Determined to proceed, the young Lee Bohannon and other leaders convinced the mayor to walk with them downtown and discuss their grievances there.[118] When Davis tried to move with them, two policemen grabbed him, said, "Mayor, you're not going anywhere," and escorted him to a police cruiser. Then, according to David Fly, "all hell broke loose," as students surged forward and ran out of the park.[119]

Some youths pelted the police with rocks as they headed for City Hall. Traffic on I-70 froze as the demonstrators flooded the lanes "like a screaming black river."[120] The news was all over the radio and spread by word of mouth, prompting black residents to leave their homes and businesses, swelling the size of the march. Some whites shut down their businesses and watched anxiously from their windows. Other whites joined the walk. As the city government and the governor of Missouri called up the

Missouri National Guard mid-morning, the crowd had reached around 1,000 people. Joel Rhodes ("It Finally Happened Here: The 1968 Riot in Kansas City, Missouri") writes that "leadership shifted periodically between ministers, established civil rights leaders, and young militants"[121] like Bohannon. No one could control the angriest youths. They ran and shouted and cursed, smashed police car windows, hurled rocks and bottles, and raided delivery trucks. About forty were arrested.

By the time the mob confronted the squad of riot police surrounding City Hall, a podium had been set up from which Mayor Davis and some demonstration leaders pleaded for calm. "A young black woman in her thirties, with tears streaming down her face, told the students they would gain nothing by burning and looting as others were doing in cities across the nation."[122] But the more militant speakers taunted the police and called for violence. Marchers swore at and spat on officers, who formed a perimeter around the crowd. When a bold youth climbed atop a cruiser at about 1 p.m., police pulled him down and struck him. One officer maced a student. The shouting crowd hurled bottles, cherry bombs, and rocks, and one man screamed, "The niggers don't have no country, but before we're through this is going to be nigger town!"[123] Then the police fired tear gas into the mob. Enraged demonstrators split and ran from police pursuers, looting and vandalizing white businesses and parked vehicles downtown. Policemen caught and beat marchers, and unleashed their dogs. White priest David Fly and black priest Edward L. Warner were clubbed.[124] Youths knocked out a policeman and stole his gun.[125] The city plunged into violence.

Blacks armed themselves with rifles and handguns, and shot at police officers from street corners, cars, windows, and rooftops. The mayor declared a curfew. Bruce R. Watkins, Louneer Pemberton, and others were "driving around trying to cool things."[126] Rioters beat or stoned white residents. Some lit Molotov cocktails and firebombed buildings. Flames swept the streets. Businesses were not burned at random, but out of vengeance from years of pent-up anger. Black businesses were not targeted. One rioter said:

> It's like that tire store. Most of their trade is with Negroes. He overcharges $5 a tire so we got him. That ------- drug store. We burned them out because they don't have enough Negro employees. They follow you around like thieves—not all Negroes are thieves—so we got them.... That auto parts place. A lot of us have old cars and have to buy parts there. They charge twice as much as they should. We burned them.[127]

A student said:

> It's some store owners you really hate, but you can't do nothing until something like this break out...[128]

And his friend added:

> You go to the store and if you stay there too long, [they say] Hurry up, boy, Hurry up, git and [they] grab on you and [say] What you got in your pocket, what you got in your pocket.... You go in stores and they say, watch him, watch him, as soon as you come through the door...[129]

The heart of the battle was eight blocks on either side of Prospect Avenue, between 27th and 39th. Between 7 p.m. and midnight alone on April 9, firefighters battled seventy-five fires. Dozens more were neglected and flared out of control. A fire alarm went off at the fire department "at a rate of one every two minutes."[130] In the two days of crisis, 312 buildings burned to the ground.[131] Black youths emptied clips and threw rocks at firefighters to prevent them from reaching the infernos; several firemen were shot and wounded. A fire truck was set on fire. Rioters got their hands on tear gas and opened fire.

Seven hundred policemen and 450 national guardsmen fought in the battle. One unit fired tear gas through the windows of Holy Name Catholic Church (23rd and Benton), where a dance had been organized to distract African American youths from joining the rioters. Police authorities claimed they did not know it was a dance, but assumed the gathering was part of the disturbances. According to David Fly, the police "blocked the wooden basement doorways so that no one could get out of the building," and described a "horrible scene" of screaming youths.[132] When news reports informed the public that Fly, an Episcopal priest, had been part of the march, anonymous callers told his cathedral they would kill him and his family.[133] Father Timothy Gibbons said that inside Holy Name "it was impossible to see. Everyone was blind, choking. Kids crowded up under the bandstand. Some hid in the closet. It was a terrible job getting them out."[134] Dozens were injured.

Overall, police and white business owners shot eleven blacks the first night, slaying one, Leonard Whitmore. There were forty-four Kansas Citians wounded and 175 arrested.[135]

The violence ended as night deepened, and hundreds, possibly thousands, of rioters retreated to their homes on the east side. Of course, the rioters made up only a tiny fraction of the black community: "a small portion of one percent," wrote the *Call*.[136] The *Kansas City Times* ran an article, "Citizens Join in Plea for End to Violence," that captured the sentiment of much of the black population. KPRS news director John L. Frasier said:

> Brothers, yesterday what happened, well, it was wrong. There were teen-agers who were gassed. It is also wrong for you to go out and burn, loot and kill and so forth.... So therefore, you're moving too fast. A little bit too fast.... You won't go that way, you won't get it that way. Let me say this to you—two wrongs will not make a right.

John Palmer, a sophomore at Lincoln High, said:

> I wish to express myself to all young Negroes and black youths of the Greater Kansas City area. I feel that violence will get us as a group no progress. I also feel that violence is not the answer to our situation. I wish that all of you would evaluate the situation within yourselves and then re-evaluate the situation and come to some conclusion that violence is not the answer.

Ex-Kansas City Chiefs cornerback Fred Williamson spoke out as well. An "Uncle Tom" is a black person who seeks white approval, even to the point of betraying blacks:

> I am appealing as a fellow Negro, a brother. Not as an Uncle Tom, because those of you who know me know that I am not an Uncle Tom. But the fighting, shooting and looting that is going on in the Negro community is not necessary and it pains me and hurts me deeply when I read about or hear about one of my fellow brothers being shot or killed in the street.... We have to fight on an eco-

nomical and social level. We cannot fight in the streets with guns and weapons. We cannot win this way.[137]

Yet there was a keen understanding of why it was happening. A student said:

[P]eople are going to get to the point where they don't care anymore and then they are gonna start burning up everything.... When a person is treated so bad for so long and they just can't stand it no more...[that's] where it's gonna end up.[138]

On the morning of April 10, the police tear-gassed angry student gatherings at Lincoln and Central high schools. Officers threw a gas grenade into a girls' restroom; six girls were burned and hospitalized.[139] Things quieted down for the rest of the day, but "that evening everything exploded at once. A fast-moving caravan of cars swept through inner-city streets with an angry load of passengers throwing firebombs in all directions."[140] Arsonists and looters returned with a vengeance to lay siege to white businesses. Black snipers battled with the police and the military "at nearly every intersection along Prospect between Twenty-seventh and Thirty-ninth."[141] "One officer compared the scene to wartime conditions—flames and smoke filled the night air, emergency messages, constant dialogue on the two-way radios, sirens screaming throughout the city, all accompanied by alternating sporadic and sustained weapons volley."[142]

Near the Byron Hotel at 2941 Prospect, a guard helped disperse a mob of looters. He was suddenly shot in the arm and collapsed on the street. Policemen dragged the guardsman to safety behind police vehicles and, believing black snipers to be in the hotel, returned fire. "We put a thousand rounds into that hotel," a sergeant said. Tear gas missiles rocketed into the hotel. In the chaos, three unarmed blacks, who were later determined to be innocent of looting, were killed.[143] Their names were Charles Martin, George McKinney, and George McKinney, Jr. Martin had been drinking heavily and was shot when he failed to follow police orders to move; McKinney and his son were likely mowed down when they burst out of the hotel doors to escape the fumes.[144] The police stormed the hotel and smashed down thirty-three doors, blasting tear gas into the rooms, but found no snipers.[145] State Representative Harold Holliday said, "What happened at the Byron Hotel would not have happened on the Plaza. The police just opened fire on anyone who happened to be in the way."[146]

Unarmed Julius P. Hamilton, visiting an apartment on 30th Street, was ordered out of the residence as the authorities swept the area near the hotel for snipers. A shot rang out nearby, and the tense policemen blew Hamilton away.[147] Lucile Bluford of the *Call* wrote later in her article "Answers Sought By Citizens" how relations between the police and the black community were at "the brink of breakage" because the police lied about Hamilton being in the hotel when he was shot.[148]

Armored personnel carriers crawled steadily through the streets. Police headquarters were located at the World War II Memorial at Linwood and Paseo, and it quickly became a target of black snipers. Police snipers were positioned on the rooftops of St. Joseph Hospital and other buildings. Law enforcement used the cover of darkness for protection: officers caught under fire in the streets shot out streetlights, and police and military vehicles patrolled with lights off. Rioters sped through the city firing from car windows. Albert Miller, flooring his vehicle toward a police barricade, opened fire and was shot to death. The battle damaged elementary schools and gas stations on the east side. Rioters caught and beat a reporter from the *Kansas City Star*, Harihar Krishan, in a back alley. Other *Star* employees were deputized and armed. Police stopped cars on the Plaza and searched them for weapons. Unrest spread as far as Olathe: carloads of black youths threw bottles and stones at windows. The Kansas National Guard mobilized. Johnson County went on lockdown, with police stationed at every access point to the county to "turn occupants back to Missouri if they had no business in Kansas."[149]

When there were no more jail cells, downtown churches served as holding centers for curfew violators. Arrested citizens reported to priests, attorneys, and social workers that the police forced some black women to strip for frisking. "One man reported being made to lie on the street while police kicked him and shot in the dirt beside him."[150] Citizens also said some officers removed their badges to protect themselves from abuse allegations. Officer Richard Goering allegedly pulled an innocent African American named Lester Blue out of a car and beat his face and back with the butt of his riot gun.[151] Other youths said the police handcuffed them, stacked them like sardines in a van, and lobbed in a tear gas grenade.[152] In an interesting parallel to what some whites said about the young black rioters and looters, Harry Ross said the police were throwing tear gas "for the fun of it.... The riot was fun for them, it was something exciting, because it was mostly nothing but young cops." He said the first day of the riot, before curfew, he was driving with friends when the police pulled "up beside us just looking at us and laughing, and they threw some tear gas in the car.... We wasn't doing nothing."[153]

Of course, in the same way that not all African Americans accepted violence, not all white police officers were abusive or heartless. For instance, during the riot that night one policeman mistook a black man on his front porch with a broom as an armed sniper. He shot and killed the innocent man. According to Chief of Police Clarence Kelley, the officer was "horror-struck" and turned himself in. Kelley and the policeman later met with the slain man's widow. "We expressed to her our most heartfelt regret over the tragic mistake," Kelley said. "Indeed, we were sorry beyond words."[154]

By the time the violence ended in the dark hours of the morning, seven Kansas Citians were dead, all black. Hundreds of civilians and officers were wounded. More than 1,000 people were under arrest (788 blacks, some held on $50,000 bail). It required 4,000 policemen, national guardsmen, highway patrolmen, and sheriff's deputies to restore order. Four million dollars' worth of property was destroyed.[155] In the United States, centuries of oppression had repeatedly led to uprisings. Now Kansas City, so long avoiding chaos while revolts engulfed other cities, was in shock. Many had thought the city immune. Harry Ross said, "This riot really surprised everybody in Kansas City because they thought the Negroes here in Kansas City didn't have that much sense, because Missouri used to be a slave state and they thought these Negroes were scared..."[156] As Paul Brink wrote in the *Call*, all the hopelessly naive "talk about racial understanding in Kansas City, a city which prided itself on it, was drowned out."[157] Today's misguided ideas of racial transcendence, of racism no longer being a problem, are nothing new. In 1968, the riot shattered the self-delusions of many Kansas City whites.

There were interesting effects. The Metropolitan Inter-Church Agency charged the Kansas City Police Department with "dehumanizing" actions, and the NAACP, the Congress of Racial Equality, and other groups condemned Chief Kelley and requested a U.S. Department of Justice investigation.[158] Kelley maintained that tear gas was used appropriately and that, in spite of the behavior of "disrespectful and irresponsible hoodlums," officers "showed tremendous restraint."[159] White citizens sent Kelley letters of support, one saying it was "time we quit blaming ourselves and put the blame where it belongs .... After all, we didn't make them black, and that is what they are really frustrated about."[160] Three-quarters of the mail sent to the mayor's office supported the actions of the police.[161]

However, Mayor Davis apologized for the use of gas and his government named Alvin Brooks Kansas City's human relations director. Brooks focused his attention on the roots of black hopelessness and anger; he set aside resources to boost employment and improve housing on the east side. He also created the Commission on Civil Disorder to draft proposals on how to prevent riots. The commission recommended a war on minority poverty and segregation, better job and education opportunities, and reforms in the police department. By 1978, only sixteen of forty-three proposals were fully implemented. The Kansas City Police Department enacted only three of the seventeen reforms directed its way.[162]

In 1967, the city council had finally given in to intense pressure from civil rights groups and passed a fair housing law banning discrimination in sales and rental agreements. But opponents gathered 14,000 signatures in protest, automatically sending the ordinance to a vote by the people. Progressive and reactionary forces both campaigned frantically for support; the latter warned that the measure was communistic, forced integration, and would lead to increased sexual mingling of the races, lower property values, urban blight, and immorality. The vote was scheduled for April 30, but after the riot the city council took matters into its own hands to avoid more violence. It voted to adopt the housing provisions of the federal 1968 Civil Rights Act, making the need for a city ordinance moot.[163] Whites who opposed the fair housing ordinance argued at a City Hall hearing that the move had stolen decision-making power from the people. Nine of the last twelve fair housing laws that went to referendum across the U.S. had been struck down; it was suspected Kansas City would have suffered the same fate. In the opinion of one journalist, "two-thirds of the white people in Kansas City hate Negroes."[164] At one gathering of about 100 citizens in a school gymnasium north of the river, speakers condemned their city councilwoman for not representing the true interests of the people. One woman complained, "The more you give 'em, the more they want."[165]

According to *USA TODAY*, this legislation and the riots prompted middle-income blacks to push out from the east side, leaving only the poorest behind. The third district has lost 60 percent of its population since 1960.[166] Many businesses relocated as well.

The events changed the way some blacks viewed the struggle against racism. Keith Hinch, who worked in a post office, was set to go to trial in April 1968 for refusing the Vietnam draft. He expressed what many black Americans felt: "I didn't feel very beholden towards the United States government towards putting on a uniform—in the first place, I didn't see how the Government was doing anything for me—or for the Black people, I didn't see how Black people were prospering in this country at all." He was questioned by the FBI and later arrested at work; his trial was delayed due to the riots. Hinch was interviewed by Kenneth King about whether he was involved in any organizations before the riot.

> HINCH: I wasn't involved with any. I was sympathetic towards several.... The Black Panther Party, and at that time, SNICK [Student Nonviolent Coordinating Committee], and...CORE [Congress of Racial Equality], but as far as any actual participation—no.

> KING: So you said that your trial was supposed to be held during the riots but...they gave you a continuance.... Would you say the riots affected your political thinking in any way?

> HINCH: I really didn't get "Hip" to what was going on as far as Black people were concerned until Feb. [or] March 1968.... You might say that I became black—maybe a month before the riot. I was aware of what was going on [but] my first development towards understanding the evils that were going on in the country was only on an anti-war level, not on a racial level.... As far as Blacks are concerned...there are many more fundamental causes of social pressure and economic exploitation...but the riots, more or less, gave me a firmer foundation to base my thinking on. I knew I was right in thinking the way I did and the riots just gave me more evidence—proving that I was right.

KING: Excuse me, in which way did the riots give you more evidence?

HINCH: Well, it's kind of hard to explain but I guess what I'm talking about is the fact that Martin Luther King, who was the [epitome] of non-violence, the apostle of non-violence, and…I think my development toward radicalizing myself was not merely just being non-violent radical, but going toward what [Malcolm X] talks about when he talks about…anything [that's] necessary. I really didn't [consider] myself to be really advocating "any means necessary" until after the riot…. I think that the fact that Martin Luther King was killed showed that non-violence as an effective force to justify—to rectify the grievances that Black people have in this country— is totally out of date…. I see the time when it was relevant—where it was a necessary step, in the struggle— but in April 1968…it had just outlived [its usefulness] and Martin Luther King was unfortunately caught. After this—after I saw what was going on in Kansas City and the incident at 30th and Prospect, at the Byron Hotel, I knew then that Black people would have to mount "one hell of a struggle"—by any means necessary to get what they want.[167]

By the time of the interview (1969), Hinch had already joined the Black Panther Party.[168]

Many whites quickly pushed the memory aside and returned to a comfortable place of apathy. A protester predicted right after the riot, "Yeah, it's gonna be forgotten right quick."[169] Bruce R. Watkins told the *Star* in 1973 that there was little awakening among whites and "when the emotions died down, the problems were forgotten because nobody gives a damn about the problems of blacks." Alvin Brooks, Lee Bohannon, and others agreed with his assessment that after five years, "conditions have not changed hardly one bit." Dr. William B. Silverman stressed apathy could cause more violence. Despite some attention given to the east side by the city government and community coalitions, Bohannon said, "The situation is now worse than it was before the disturbances.... Housing is deplorable and there is no adequate housing code. We have absentee landlords who care less than a damn about making repairs on the homes they rent to blacks."[170]

Calvin Trillin, in his May 1968 *New Yorker* article "Kansas City—I Got Nothing Against the Colored," wrote that most whites attributed any police overreaction to simple human error, not racism, and that the violence was seen as "exploitation of the situation by a small criminal element, rather than a spontaneous outburst against white authority."[171] He wrote, "Most of the talk I heard on the subject was critical of those who would try to make the police the scapegoats after they had risked their lives to restore peace."[172]

The white media encouraged apathy. The *Kansas City Town Squire* ("A Distinctive Monthly Newspaper Serving Every Home in the Country Club District and the City of Mission Hills") ran "A special report on how things stand after April's riots" in November 1968. The quotes of black and white citizens selected for this report pushed several themes: deemphasizing racism as an issue, stressing jobs were available for any black person willing to work, and highlighting the drug use and criminality of black youths. Ignored was the fact that black unemployment rates remained double that of whites, and the connection between poverty, hopelessness, and crime, all worsened by racism. The white media preached a message of racial transcendence that highlighted black laziness, poor parenting, and immorality. Excerpts read:

> It doesn't seem to me that race is the issue now.

> Some of the rioting was racial I guess. But a lot of it was done by people who just like to be destructive.

> Race isn't the big problem. I think lots of it is that dope they're usin'.

> It don't matter what color you are.... They'll attack anybody who has a dime!

> It seems to me that a lot of parents ain't usin' enough razor strap.... We've just got to be stricter at home.

> Anybody can find a job.... Things are all right these days.

> There's lots of people walkin' around the streets who are qualified...but [through government employment programs] they can take advantage of it. There's no need for a person down here not to find a job.

> They know they can get ahead, and if we'd just stop our welfare system things would get better. We're the ones who are holding them back—we're the ones who are paying them not to work.... That kind of thing can probably be attributed mainly to environment. She's done that all her life—she doesn't know anything else.[173]

Today, four decades later, some of the area destroyed by the riots has yet to be rebuilt.

CHAPTER FIVE
Progress and Regress – 1970 to the Present

In the era after the 1960s civil rights movement, racism slowly grew socially unacceptable. Yet both conscious and subconscious beliefs in negative black stereotypes persisted alongside the increasing rhetoric of racial transcendence. Progress in civil rights led many Americans to convince themselves that racism and discrimination were dark memories left behind in the 1960s, that society had advanced to a point where equal opportunity and prosperity were available to all, if only one had the fortitude to succeed.

This belief is perhaps even more dangerous than blatant racism. White denial, whether the denial of history's lingering effects or the denial of present-day racism, encourages one to look at the condition of Black America without any historical context. This is our great regression, a line of thinking that parallels ideas from slavery days, when the "problem" with African Americans was their "nature," their "childish stupidity." They were slaves because they were good for nothing else; their innate condition led inevitably to their societal condition. Likewise, if racism is a thing of the past (and surely a few decades is enough to undo centuries of institutionalized oppression), what else can explain the condition of blacks today but their "nature" and "culture"? Laziness, irresponsible parenting, shortsightedness, lack of individualism, and innate immorality, anger, and aggression *must* be the causes of black poverty and crime. Not everyone believes this, but those who do keep racism alive. Progress can construct illusions. So can the ticking of a clock.

There was real progress, of course, since the 1960s, owing to the legal attacks on injustice, the grassroots campaigns, civil disobedience, and, arguably, the riots. Many minds changed and so did laws. Society changed tremendously for the better. But the movement still had a mountain to climb.

The fight to improve housing in recent decades showed progress was still difficult to come by after the 1960s. In Kansas City, city council members, neighborhood groups, and activists battled for an end to Section 235 of the 1968 Fair Housing Act, which gave subsidies to private firms for low-income home construction, only to see these firms ignore the intended minority areas. The 49/63 Neighborhood Coalition, the Blue Hills Community Association, and the Marlborough Heights Neighbors sued the federal Department of Housing and Urban Development, one action among many around the United States to protest the abuses of Section 235. In 1973, President Nixon responded by suspending federally subsidized housing programs rather than reforming them—a move that failed the downtrodden residents. The real estate industry, neighborhood developers, mortgage lenders, and others

> refused to invest in city neighborhoods without the backing of government support or subsidies. In Kansas City, after the federal government halted the Section 235 program, many real estate companies and lending institutions closed their offices in the central city rather than

attempt to market loans to low-income people without the government's backing. By 1978, no prominent real estate company had offices in the central city, east of Troost.[1]

Disproportionate poverty led to disproportionate suffering. The poor housing on the east side proved deadly in July 1980, when the city suffered through seventeen consecutive days of 100-degree heat. Without air conditioning, 115 Kansas Citians died. Three times as many of these fatalities were black than white.[2]

In the era of conservatism and deregulation, the ghettos were left to rot. The Reagan and Bush administrations slashed funding for subsidized housing by 80 percent and handed over many public housing projects and other government programs to private powers.[3] Well-paid manufacturing jobs for low-skill workers went overseas. At the same time, the war on drugs, the mass imprisonment of nonviolent ghetto residents, began.

In 1980, Kansas City ranked tenth on the Census Bureau's list of most segregated cities.[4] Many realtors and landlords continued to discriminate against blacks looking for a place to live. Research from the late 1980s indicates blacks were still more likely to be steered east of Troost by real estate agents, and more likely to be charged higher rent by landlords or turned away from apartment complexes altogether. Getting a loan in black areas was still difficult. There were no black-owned banks or insurance companies in the 1970s. In 1988, a tiny fraction—only 2.3 percent—of the nearly $100 million loaned by the city's eight largest banks went to minority-majority areas. A 1991 study showed blacks were 2.8 times more likely to be denied a housing loan. Income wasn't the reason. Higher-income blacks were slightly more likely to be rejected by lenders than lower-income whites.[5]

A more recent study reported that residents of the Kansas City metropolitan area filed nearly 600 housing discrimination complaints in the five-year period of 2005-2010.[6] And modern lenders still engage in predatory and racist practices that mirror the blockbusters. Wise notes an estimated two to four million cases of racial discrimination in housing occur annually in the U.S.[7] He writes:

> Although sometimes this discrimination manifests as outright denial of rental property or denial of mortgage loans to people of color, far more often it takes the shape of racial "steering" (whereby people are relegated to same-race neighborhoods, no matter their own desires for integrated spaces), or the offering of housing to people of color on terms far less desirable than the terms offered to whites.[8]

It is still more profitable to prey on African Americans than to deny them loans. Minorities are far more likely to be offered subprime (high interest, low protection) loans by banks and other lenders regardless of qualifications like income, credit score, and debt. Even wealthier blacks are more likely to be offered higher interest rates than poorer whites. In New York City, as just one example, "black households with annual incomes of $68,000 or more are five times more likely to have a subprime mortgage than white households with similar or even less income."[9] The lighter your skin, the easier it is to get a loan with favorable terms. Such practices mean black individuals pay tens of thousands, even hundreds of thousands of dollars

more over the life of a mortgage (billions collectively), putting
them at higher risk of default and foreclosure.

In October 2014, the National Fair Housing Alliance
added Kansas City neighborhoods to its discrimination complaint against Bank of America, accusing the bank of properly
maintaining its foreclosed homes in white suburban areas, but
allowing its foreclosed homes in poor black and Latino areas to
fall apart.[10] Too few care about the plight of the poor.

Poverty is difficult to escape no matter how hard one works,
contrary to conservative rhetoric. Poor children attend inferior
schools, which hurts academic performance, as does the psychological damage of growing up in poverty, to be discussed
later. Low test scores deny students entry into universities
(black students in Kansas City average 14.5 on the ACT, as
we will see). Many won't apply to community colleges, feeling
incapable, hopeless, or utterly burned out. Low wages, particularly in a time of exploding tuition costs, further restrict access
to higher education. Low-wage work is the future for most
poor children. The cycle continues from there, generation after
generation. Only 34 percent of Americans manage to reach a
higher income quintile before they die, the lowest quintile is
the most difficult to escape, and people in the middle are just
as likely to fall on the social ladder than climb it.[11] Add to this
racial discrimination past and present and it grows obvious
why blacks are disproportionately poor. Jim Crow was not
that many generations ago, nor was slavery itself, when blacks
started with nothing. Yet some whites view black poverty as
evidence of blacks being lazier than whites, just as black crime
is evidence blacks are more deviant and low test scores a sign

of lower intelligence or inferior parenting somehow unique to black people.

With the combination of poor schools, government and private sector disinvestment, and discriminatory practices, slums became a permanent scar on the American landscape decades ago. Little has changed; urban space today is sharply divided between wealthier, white suburbs and poorer central cities dominated by minorities.

Despite this, there were substantial personal victories in the last several decades in the quest for equality. In the 1970s, several black women moved into positions of power. Gertrude H. Keith was elected the first African American woman on the Kansas City, Missouri, school board in 1970, and Leona P. Thurman, who received her law degree in 1949, served as the city's first black female attorney.[12] Dr. Julia Hill became the first female president of the local NAACP in 1971, and Orchid Jordan served in the Missouri House of Representatives from 1970 to 1986.

Former Kansas City NAACP President Lee Vertis Swinton became Kansas City's first black state senator in 1980. Other men rose to positions of national power. Bill Clay of St. Louis became the first black politician to represent Missouri (First District) in the U.S. Congress; he served in the House from 1969 to 2001. His son, William L. Clay, Jr., succeeded him. Kansas City saw its first black U.S. congressman with the election of Alan Wheat, who represented Missouri's Fifth District (which includes Kansas City) from 1983 to 1995. He was succeeded by Emanuel Cleaver, who served as Kansas City's first black mayor starting in 1991. These four gentlemen make up the only African Americans to ever represent Missouri at the national level, all in the House of Representatives. Yet oppression and poverty caused blacks to be underrepresented in Congress throughout U.S. history: 131 blacks have served in the House and only nine in the Senate.

For Kansas City, the 1970s opened and closed with assassinations of prominent African Americans. On July 15, 1970, Missouri State Representative Leon Jordan was blown away by shotgun blasts while leaving his Green Duck Tavern at 26th and Prospect. Jordan was a legend: he graduated from Lincoln High School, attended Wilberforce College, served in the Army and for the Kansas City police force, trained and led the national police force of Liberia in Africa, founded Freedom, Inc. with Bruce Watkins, and fought for civil rights as a community organizer and state politician. At 1 a.m., three black men pulled up in a brown 1960s Pontiac as Jordan was walking to his car. The first gunshot shattered Jordan's leg, and he collapsed. Before Jordan could get to the .38 caliber pistol he kept in his pocket, one of the assailants got out of the car and fired rounds into his groin and chest. The murder launched one of the largest investigations in Kansas City history, led by Sergeant Lloyd DeGraffenreid, a black detective and Jordan's friend.

At the time, the FBI was still operating under Hoover and the counterintelligence program that spied on civil rights leaders. It focused its covert attention on Lee Bohannon, Jordan's political rival for the upcoming Missouri General Assembly election, a Kansas City black activist, and member of the Social Action Committee of 20, which the FBI deemed a "militant" organization. Bohannon told the *Kansas City Star* in 2010 that he suspected the FBI had wanted to ruin him, perhaps by pinning the murder on him. Some speculate that the FBI may have wanted to ruin Jordan, too. Orchid Jordan (his wife) and others believed at the time that white political opponents in Jackson County had recruited the black men to make the hit.[13]

But there was evidence the Black Mafia, a crime organization that controlled the east side from 1969 to 1970, might have played a role. According to a federal report, the Black Mafia was making $190,000 a day through the sale of heroin, cocaine, other narcotics, prostitution, gambling, and other vice. Authorities believed the gang was responsible for seventeen murders. Further, it was recruiting black youth, primarily drug users, to commit bank robberies and muggings. A source told the *Star*, "They got kids who would kill their mamas to get a reputation."[14] Leon Jordan was a staunch opponent of the drug trade, which led to a falling out between him and James Dearborn, a Black Mafia leader. Jordan had taken steps to destroy drug trafficking, prompting the authorities to investigate the mob. But after hundreds of interviews, more than a dozen polygraph tests, several court trials, and more than 100 suspects fingerprinted, the case remains unsolved to this day.[15]

Due to the efforts of people like civil rights activist Alvin Sykes, the Cold Case Squad at the Kansas City Police Department reopened the Jordan murder case in late 2010. New evidence suggests the Italian mob had the murder weapon in its possession and recruited three African Americans to make the hit. If true, it would not be the first time, nor the last, that blacks were paid to kill for the white mob; they killed prosecution witness Sol Landie in Kansas City, for example, in October 1970.[16] This is the mafia that began in Kansas City in the 1910s when "Joe Church" and "Sugarhouse Pete" Di-Giovanni arrived from Sicily and remained well connected to the mob in other American cities. Pendergast took over during the Prohibition Era. Investigators suspect that "Shotgun Joe" Centimano, who ran Joe's Liquors at 19th and Vine, provided the murder weapon. The mob was still a dangerous piece of Kansas City's landscape at this time. For instance, "the River Quay entertainment district west of the City Market became a mob battleground with bombings, murders and attempted murders through the 1970s," as civil war broke out in the family over control of certain territories.[17] Jordan battled white politicians who, supported by the mob, sought to control black voters and limit the influence of Freedom, Inc. Between this and his efforts to fight narcotics, Jordan would have been a prime target. However, Centimano had connections to both the Black Mafia and the Italian mob, and one source claims the two cooperated in Jordan's assassination.[18]

The murder at the other end of the decade took out another powerful leader. Bernard Powell was killed in April 1979. He attended Central High School in Kansas City, joined the NAACP at the age of thirteen, marched with King in Alabama, became the director of the local Congress of Racial Equality, and worked for much of his life with the Urban League of Kansas City. In 1968, he helped found the Social Action Committee of 20. He pushed for increased activism, investment, and employment in the Kansas City ghetto—the latter taking a big hit during the recession of the 1970s, when blacks lost their jobs at almost double the rate experienced by whites. A jobless black Kansas Citian told the *New York Times*, "The truth is that black people ain't no closer to catching up with whites than they were before. A black man can work hard, if he can find work, but there's no catching up with what whites got already."[19]

Powell always wore a black beret in support of black power. Jackie Robinson, a former public relations worker for the Social Action Committee of 20, shot Powell in the head at Papa Doc's East Side Social Club. Although not a racially motivated murder, the black community lost another of its most influential leaders. Powell was a great Kansas City civil rights leader, one who dreamed of becoming the first black governor of Missouri.[20] The state is still waiting for this "first" to occur.

A year after Powell's murder, a young black saxophone player named Steve Harvey was beaten to death with a baseball bat in Penn Valley Park on November 5, 1980, by nineteen-year-old Raymond Bledsoe, a white man with a history of harassing African Americans and an intense hatred of homosexuals. Bledsoe and two friends left a party that night and headed for Penn Valley Park, a meeting place for homosexual men. Once there, Bledsoe and his accomplices assaulted a gay white man in a park bathroom. The victim was allowed to go free, but Bledsoe soon found Harvey, chased him into the center of a sports field, and beat his skull in with a bat. The murderer later bragged about it. The assailants were soon arrested, and Bledsoe's friends testified against him. Still, an all-white Jackson County jury found him not guilty in August 1981.[21] Blacks and whites alike were outraged.

Harvey's friend, Alvin Sykes, launched the Steve Harvey Justice Campaign. At a speech to the Crimes of the Civil Rights Era Conference in Boston (April 2007), Sykes reflected, "I knew you couldn't do anything on the state level, so I called the Civil Rights Division of the Justice Department. When I first talked to them, they said there was nothing they could do."[22] Sykes gathered thousands of signatures and sent a petition to the

Justice Department. He reminded the Department of a federal statute making it illegal to injure or threaten to injure someone at a public facility due to race, color, religion, or national origin. Bledsoe's former girlfriend testified to the FBI, which found the first man that Bledsoe beat. Bledsoe was tried in federal court. His lawyers attempted to convince the jury that it was a hate crime not against race, but against sexual orientation, since Bledsoe was on the hunt for gay men in the park. The distinction was important as sexual orientation was not mentioned in the statute. The prosecution countered by emphasizing that Bledsoe let his white gay victim live but executed a black man. The all-white jury found Bledsoe guilty, and he has been in prison since 1983, the longest-serving convict in a civil rights violation sentence in U.S. history. Sykes, however, has had to argue recently to keep Bledsoe in prison, as the murderer is now eligible for parole. As Sykes told the *Star* in 2013, he is concerned Bledsoe is capable of further racial violence, including violence against him.[23]

Sykes later started the Emmett Till Justice Campaign. Steve Harvey's widow was a relative of Emmett Till, a boy murdered in 1955 in Mississippi for reportedly flirting with a white woman. His killers were also acquitted. Sykes pressured U.S. Senator Jim Talent of Missouri in 2006 to introduce to Congress the Emmett Till Unsolved Civil Rights Crime Act, which would establish a cold case unit at the Department of Justice. Sykes testified to Congress in support in 2007, and the act passed in late 2008. In a 2013 interview with KCUR Kansas City Public Media, Sykes explained what inspired the legislation:

> While I was pursuing Steve Harvey's case and going back and forth to Mississippi and Tennessee and all these

places down south, I kept hearing about these stories of not famous people who disappeared in the middle of the night, and nobody ever found. People would say, "Well, you know so-and-so we never seen or heard nothing from him again." And that was kind of a catalyst for me. I [started] thinking about these other cases, because a lot of them were never reported.

So, [there are] all these unsolved civil rights murders that don't have notoriety, that nobody is looking for, and I can't make a blank-blank justice campaign for each case. There needs to be some systematic means of going and looking at each of these cases.[24]

Other problems plagued Kansas City. After all, the Reverend James L. Betts, head of the Ku Klux Klan in Missouri, said that Kansas City was the best area in the state to recruit new members.[25] A study of convictions in 1993 found blacks received sentences about fifteen months longer for drug crimes (and over six months longer for property crimes) than whites.[26] Most convicts were unemployed. In 1985, the regional NAACP called for a boycott of Dillard's department stores for discrimination in hiring practices, mistreating minority employees, and insisting on using white models in their catalogs. People rose up in protest. They organized pickets twice a week against stores in Kansas City and St. Louis. NAACP signs in Kansas City read: "Dillard's Discriminates Against Blacks - Minorities in Jobs" and "NAACP Calls for a 'Fair Share' of Jobs from Dillard's." Dr. Zelma E. Davis, local NAACP president and president of Penn Valley Community College, led the charge.[27] William Dillard, the store founder, signed an agreement in 1986 promising to broaden opportunity for blacks in his workplaces. And yet an article from the *Phoenix New Times* in 1993 explained Dillard's was still facing "a slew of racially charged complaints" and lawsuits, and that "in the areas in which it pledged to improve, Dillard's has done little, if anything."[28] In 2008, the NAACP reported in its Economic Reciprocity Initiative Report that Dillard's still refused to participate in their survey that helps track diversity efforts, a survey embraced by many of the nation's largest companies.[29]

Several years after the protests of Dillard's ended, Kansas City celebrated a huge victory with the election of Emanuel Cleaver II, its first black mayor, a testament to reformed racial attitudes in a city about 26 percent black. However, it came somewhat late in the game: black mayors had already been elected to cities such as Detroit, Los Angeles, and Washington, D.C., in the 1970s, and Chicago, Philadelphia, and New York in the 1980s. Cleaver, a former Methodist minister and city councilman, was also a distant cousin of Kansas City Black Panther leader Pete O'Neal. At times, Cleaver pressured U.S. presidents, albeit unsuccessfully, to pardon his cousin so he could return to the United States. Cleaver was a product of the radical era, like O'Neal. An article from 1991, the year he took office, noted:

> In 1972, a young Emanuel Cleaver described himself as "a militant, a revolutionary, and a radical" in his fight against racism. But in his 12 years on the City Council he has emerged as a voice of moderation, and he acknowledges that his militancy has modified. He now considers himself a negotiator. "I learned you can't agitate and legislate at the same time," says Cleaver.[30]

Cleaver served until 1999. In 2005, he was elected by the Fifth District to represent Missouri in the U.S. House, where he is still serving. Midway through his time as mayor, Cleaver saw the end of the infamous *Missouri v. Jenkins* case, which had broad ramifications for the Kansas City, Missouri School District.

The case began in the 1970s, at a time when the state of Kansas City schools was a significant issue. Black and white teachers went on strike for forty-two days in 1974 and again, three years later, for fifty-four days. The strikes, organized by the American Federation of Teachers, pushed for better wages, smaller class sizes, sick leave, better working conditions, and other demands. The district sought court edicts to end the strikes or weaken them through restraining orders. Violations of court orders earned strikers fines or jail time. Union leader Norman B. Hudson was put behind bars for violating court injunctions during the 1974 strike. The strike beginning March 1977 shut down ninety-two schools and left 51,000 students out of class.[31] On April 7, 1977, the *Star* ran the headline "127 Teachers Arrested in School Disturbances." The strikes were "divisive" and "undermined parental confidence in the school system."[32]

This turmoil, however, was not the worst of it. The KCMSD was bleeding students. White flight to the suburbs meant the loss of thousands of students and the beginning of a severe funding crisis. Upper- and middle-class blacks had also abandoned poorer minority areas. In the late 1960s, the district had more than 70,000 students; by the mid-1980s, 35,000; by 2014, around 17,000.[33] In the past, schools were segregated but the district as a whole was more racially balanced. By the late 1970s, 60 percent of the district's students were black, most very poor.[34] So prospects were bleak: school funding was based on the district's property values, and white voters consistently rejected funding initiatives.[35]

With only low-income families remaining, the district was desperate to bring students back. As a district of the poor, test scores were dismal and facilities crumbled. Conditions grew increasingly horrific. Broken toilets and plumbing systems, leaky ceilings, lack of air conditioning and heat, and enormous rats plagued most city schools.[36] As noted earlier, the district technically went along with the *Brown* decision, but divided attendance zones along Troost to maintain racial separation, until it was commanded to stop the practice by the Department of Health, Education, and Welfare (HEW) in 1973. After this, HEW and the district tussled over appropriate means of desegregation, and in 1977 the conflict culminated in a move by the district that can only be described as desperate. The largely white KCMSD administration sued the "HEW, the Department of Housing and Urban Development (HUD), the Department of Transportation (DOT), the state of Missouri, and eleven suburban school districts, arguing that the combined policies of these various entities all contributed to racial isolation in the Kansas City schools and that, alone, the district would be unable to resolve the problems."[37]

The district was not actually concerned about "racial isolation," but rather the worsening funding crisis. This was not a push from civil rights progressives. In the bizarre series of events that followed, District Court Judge Russell Clark in 1983 threw out the KCMSD lawsuit, believing that the district and Missouri were both culpable of illegal segregation. The district suddenly found itself as the defendant. Clark sought out the NAACP and the American Civil Liberties Union to join the case, but they declined. Liberal attorney Arthur Benson was found to take the case, and in 1984 Clark ruled that racial imbalances were due to unconstitutional segregation perpetuated by district policies. Unfortunately, the judge could not specifically address equal school funding, as the Supreme Court ruled earlier in 1973 (*San Antonio v. Rodriguez*) that districts have no right to equitable funds, ensuring to this day an education system that offers vastly unequal educational opportunities for children. Those unlucky enough to be born in poor, minority-dominated districts attend crumbling, underfunded schools, while students in wealthy white areas attend schools outfitted with all the amenities, thanks to high property values.

Clark's judicial solution was to mandate heavy investments in the KCMSD to entice whites back to Kansas City schools. From the mid-1980s to 2003, more than $2 billion was poured into district schools, funded partly by doubled property taxes and increased income taxes in the city, but mostly by state funds.[38] The district spent around $11,700 per student, higher than any district in the United States, adjusted for the cost of living.[39]

The billions invested under the *Missouri v. Jenkins* case raised teacher salaries, built fifteen new schools, renovated fifty-four, and shrank class sizes. Neighborhood schools were all but eliminated, converted instead to specialized magnet schools in which families could choose to enroll their children (or join a waiting list). Joshua M. Dunn, in *Complex Justice: The Case of Missouri v. Jenkins*, wrote:

Every high school and middle school and half the district's elementary schools became magnet schools with special themes such as classical Greek, Slavic studies, and agribusiness. Special themes required special facilities, such as petting zoos, robotics labs, and a model United Nations facility with simultaneous translation capability. One high school was so extravagant it was dubbed the "Taj Mahal"....

Arthur Benson, and his expert witnesses[,] assured Judge Clark that if he ordered the requested improvements, the school district would draw tens of thousands of white students from the suburbs back into the district. Much like the *Field of Dreams*, the premise was "If you build it they will come." But the students never came.[40]

The number of white students bused in from the suburbs never exceeded 1,500 a year.[41] The same families that participated in white flight only years before were not so easily bribed into returning and joining integrated schools. Some view Clark's experiment as a classic example of the futility of "throwing money at a problem," but the truth is more complex. More money is sometimes an effective solution. The United States is characterized by well-funded, well-performing white schools and poorly-funded, low-performing minority schools. But simply "throwing money" at schools while ignoring the impact of intergenerational poverty will not remedy the root cause of racial performance gaps in education. An impoverished environment can devastate a child's physical and psychological well-being. Children who grow up in poverty (regardless of their parents' race) are far more likely to experience high-stress homes, absent parents, homelessness, hunger, abuse, exposure to alcoholism, drug use, crime, and poor health. Kansas City youth speak of these things in *I'm Not No One* ("All of a sudden I hear a gunshot, jus one, and it's not that unusual, but it sounded really close. I really thought nothin' of it at first until one of my friends looked out the front window to see my brother laying there wit a pretty decent sized blood stain on his shirt." Another: "I was sleeping in a chair until I was 8 years old"). These experiences lead to depression, low motivation, developmental delays, decreased memory capabilities; unsurprisingly, test scores correlate closely with income.[42] A 2015 study, "Association of Child Poverty, Brain Development, and Academic Achievement" (*JAMA Pediatrics*), found that parts of the brain tied to academic performance are 8-10 percent smaller in our poorest children. In the late 1970s, non-white unemployment was a colossal 17.4 percent; in the 1980s, black businesses were worse off than in the 1960s, the number of known drug houses in Kansas City increased tenfold, and the number of homicides peaked to 140 in 1989; by 1990, three in four black babies were born to unwed mothers.[43] Perhaps if billions had been invested in alleviating minority poverty in Kansas City, the outcome of this experiment would have been different.

Money also can't change racial attitudes, and the heart of the matter was race. What caused white flight to the suburbs? What prevented whites from returning? And in *Missouri v. Jenkins,* whose interests were being protected? Who represented the predominantly black students and parents in the district? Consider that

[Judge Clark] repeatedly ignored the preferences and complaints of black parents whose children were the subject of his experiment. Many black parents objected not only to their children being bused long distances, but also to the fact that most of the new schools emphasized exotic themes rather than the basic skills so many students lacked. When the black school superintendent, the black members of the school board, several dozen black pastors, and the local chapter of the NAACP asked the court to institute a more modest magnet plan, they were rebuffed. The longer the case went on, the deeper grew the schism between black leaders and parents and the white judges, lawyers, and experts claiming to represent black interests.[44]

Black interests were sacrificed in the attempt to draw higher-income whites back to the central city. Clark decreed that magnet schools must remain 60 percent white and 40 percent black, a well-intended effort to create true integration, but one that proved disastrous for the black community. It meant schools went underused by whites and blacks alike. If enough white students could not be drawn in, black students were kept out. Thousands of black students could not attend the magnet schools of their choice, schools with empty seats. The KCMSD experiment was created by whites and, whether intentional or not, for whites. In her review of Dunn's *Complex Justice*, Emilye Crosby of the State University of New York wrote:

It is easy to understand the black community's anger when the judicial focus on integration translated into greater resources for white students. Given persistent white reluctance to attend the Kansas City public schools, Judge Clark's initially rigid 6-4 black-white ratio for magnet schools meant far greater access for the white students than black, many of whom were blocked from schools even when they were under-enrolled. Similarly, white suburban students received door-to-door taxi rides to city magnet schools, while black students negotiated a complicated city-wide transportation system. Perhaps most important, there is little to suggest that Clark's approach improved the educational quality for most African American students. (The district also grew more segregated.) Moreover, following a pattern that is repeated throughout the history of desegregation, African Americans were largely excluded from any meaningful role in decision-making—from the first desegregation plan in 1955 through the evolving remedial plans that emerged from *Missouri v. Jenkins*....

[Dunn] appears to repeatedly downplay the impact of race and racism, both in terms of the problems facing the Kansas City schools and in terms of the broader national challenge of providing quality education, regardless of race....[45]

Better schools and teachers were a noble and much-needed goal, but not "magnets that spend more time and money trying to recruit white students than trying to teach black students,"[46] as black parents protested. Even the conservative Cato Institute noted in 1997 that the plan neglected "the needs of inner-city blacks for health care, counseling, and basic instruction in reading, writing, and arithmetic," and that the district had discovered that it was easier to meet the court's 60/40 integration ratio by letting black students drop out than by convincing white students to move in. As a result, nothing was done in the early days of the desegregation plan about the district's appalling high school dropout rate, which averaged about 56% in the early 1990s (when desegregation pressures were most intense) and went as high as 71% at some schools (for black males it was higher still).[47]

So the experiment was indeed a failure. It left whites disinterested (they already had superb schools) and blacks further marginalized. Massive investment could not undo the trend of racial isolation, nor did it change white attitudes toward blacks and their schools. The black student population continued to decline, and test scores remained low.

Black Kansas City at the time certainly didn't ignore the role of racism in this failure. In 1989, black parents sued the state and the KCMSD in federal district court because their children were barred entry into magnet schools. The parents argued for vouchers that would allow them to attend private schools. They said the integration plan was "victimizing them and their children rather than removing the barriers of illegal discrimination."[48] Black families formed a political organization that worked to take over the school board and end magnet schooling. There were other issues to address as well: civil rights leader Nelson "Fuzzy" Thompson, who worked with Dr. King in the South, helped protest the lack of minority contractors and crews during the construction of the new Central High School, and was arrested for it in 1990.[49]

Things unraveled in June 1995, when the U.S. Supreme Court threw out Clark's integration plan. By a five to four ruling, the Court decided *de facto* segregation could not be solved using such methods as court-ordered property taxes. States, cities, and districts were not violating the Constitution if racial isolation existed after the end of legal segregation. Clarence Thomas wrote, "...*de facto* segregation (unaccompanied by discriminatory inequalities in educational resources) does not constitute a continuing harm after the end of *de jure* segregation. 'Racial isolation' itself is not a harm; only state enforced segregation is."[50] After this, state funding was reduced in Kansas City and property taxes lowered. The district court handed control back to the KCMSD. The district was left to deal with some lavishly expensive schools, some only half-full, on a budget reduced by hundreds of millions of dollars.[51]

The turmoil continued. Superintendents came and went rapidly (twenty-seven from 1969 to 2011). Over the course of the experiment, the percentage of whites in the KCMSD *dropped* to 24.1 percent. White flight continued on as usual, and today the KCMSD is only 9 percent white.[52] Underutilized schools were shut down. Abandoned schools now dot the city, slowly taken over by weeds. The Paul Robeson Middle School for Classical Studies on Holmes Road is a lonely sight to behold. Southwest High School closed in 1998. Westport High, Southeast High, Horace Mann Elementary, the Douglas School, all empty.

The Missouri Board of Education stripped the district of accreditation in 2000 due to poor test scores. The KCMSD was able to show enough improvement to gain provisional accreditation later that year. But between 2000 and 2010, 18,000 more students fled for suburban, private, and public charter schools. With only 17,000 students—most all impoverished and black—and a budget deficit of $50 million, the district shut down 28 schools in 2010, about half its facilities. Seven hundred jobs were eliminated. The next year, the KCMSD again lost accreditation. Fewer than 25 percent of grade school students were reading at grade level in most schools. The district failed eleven of Missouri's fourteen performance benchmarks. Worse, unaccredited districts had to pay to bus students to neighboring districts if families wished to leave.[53]

In 2007, the district handed over the seven schools east of I-435 to Independence. Gwendolyn Grant, president of the Urban League of Greater Kansas City, praised the transfer of schools because it reorganized the sub-districts to allow more African American representation on the school board. Grant wrote:

Free at last, free at last. Thank God almighty, we finally have an opportunity to wrest educational control of our children from the benighted....

If these changes take effect, African Americans in Kansas City will be able to elect a majority of the school board and thereafter, control the educational destiny of our youth. Although blacks in leadership positions on the school board is not a panacea for black children, it is time for African Americans to govern this dysfunctional school district.

The KCMSD has had a majority black student population for nearly 40 years. During that period, majority white and often racially divided school boards have presided over a system with high drop out rates and low achievement levels. These miseducated students beget miseducated children who become pathological adults perpetuating cycles of poverty and ignorance. The community suffers.[54]

Integration proponents faced an uphill battle, as "virtually every attempt in the last three decades to seek a metropolitan-wide solution to the problem of school segregation had met with fierce opposition from suburban residents, property owners, and political elites."[55] The Independence city government, for example, complained in the late 1970s that busing would damage the education process and incite whites to violence.[56] After *Jenkins*, integration was put on the back burner, given the KCMSD's other challenges.

Although Kansas City's second black mayor, Sylvester "Sly" James, elected in 2011, proposed a mayoral takeover of the KCMSD, the effort was unsuccessful. In late 2014, the state gained the power to seize control of the district and potentially dismantle it permanently, but soon after the district earned provisional accreditation and began inching up toward full accreditation. At about the same time, controversy arose over a proposed partnership between the KCMSD and Academie Lafayette, a successful K-8 public charter school with a black principal and many black administrators and teachers. Academie Lafayette sought to launch an International Baccalaureate high school, and proposed using the historic and recently reopened Southwest High in the KCMSD, which was underutilized. It served only 400 students, mostly black and poor. Under the plan, Academie Lafayette would run the school, integrating their charter school students with an equal number of KCMSD students. The International Baccalaureate program could also draw economically advantaged white families living nearby out of private schools and back to the district.

Though the plan won support from African Americans like Mayor James and KCMSD Superintendent R. Stephen Green, it came under fire from groups like the NAACP, the Urban League, Urban Summit, Freedom, Inc., Southern Christian Leadership Conference, Metro Organization for Racial and Economic Equity, and the Black United Front. They argued that the 400 students already at Southwest would be displaced. Academie Lafayette's K-8 student body was mostly non-poor and 67 percent white. If the new high school attracted white students previously attending private schools, this could create a relatively wealthier, white-majority high school in a district that otherwise had very few white or non-poor students. Further, Academie Lafayette junior high students would be admitted automatically to the high school, whereas district students would need to score high enough on a test to get in. If the district eighth-graders were tested on the Academie Lafayette pre-International Baccalaureate curriculum, this would likely mean even fewer blacks could get into the new high school. Finally, the school could have drawn financial resources and white students away from Lincoln College Preparatory Academy, the district's successful, selective, majority-black International Baccalaureate school, which would hurt its effectiveness, possibly lead to its closure, and worsen segregation. Lincoln itself was underutilized, leading some to question why the district needed a second International Baccalaureate school.[57] Others believed funds and gifts, like the Stowers Foundation's proposed $2 million to renovate Southwest, would never have been given to a majority-black school like Lincoln.

The plan fell apart in March 2015. *Tony's Kansas City*, a popular news blog where one can get a taste of vile modern racism by skimming the reader comments on stories related to African Americans, saw these anonymous posts:

> Every single one of those groups have the same agenda... lower standards for African American youth. Keep them dumbed down, reinforce their permanent victim-hood ideology, and insure that there will be generations of welfare slaves on the plantation. One need only look at the graduation rates of KCPS, the low, and I mean bottom of the barrel low, reading comprehension and math skills. Compare the black students to students of any race north of the river, south of Grandview, etc. The most egregious crime of all, is that inner city black adults are so willing and eager to guarantee that their children will have the same shit sandwich life that they have. With the caveat that they live long enough to reach adulthood. natch[58]

> Regular people would be astounded at the interplay between wealthy NIGGERS and the various "schools" and "academies" set up in Kansas City. These coons have constructed a wonderful mechanism for screwing whitey and boy, they do it with zeal, everyday...[59]

> One thing worth noting is The Black Power Establishment does not want Black people who are educated and think for themselves or they would throw these corrupt individuals from power. Gone would be the corrupt clergymen, activists, community organizers and politicians

and other assorted grifters, mountebanks and hustlers who make up the Black Power Establishment. Black ignorance is the source of power for the race pimps. The fact is that in two generations, Southwest High School has gone from being a top quality high school, one of the best in the country that prepared its grads for the Ivy League and other top universities to being a cesspool of crime and ignorance.... This does show a cultural shift in the demographics of the area and of Kansas City in general. One cannot blame the current state of Southwest High School or the Kansas City Public Schools (KCPS) on racism, white privilege or white flight or any other Leftist buzz word. The fact is that sixty years of a welfare state has created a pathological society in the inner cities of America. Lyndon Johnson and the welfare state did not create a Great Society but sick society and these scholars we have seen at Southwest High School are products of this sick society and are Lyndon Johnson's grandchildren.[60]

The story of Kansas City's nearly segregated schooling is far from unique. Rather than peaceably integrating into a diverse and inclusive education system, American schools are more segregated than half a century ago. Education activist Jonathan Kozol wrote in *The Shame of the Nation: The Restoration of Apartheid Schooling in America*:

Many Americans I meet who live far from our major cities and who have no first-hand knowledge of realities in urban public schools seem to have a rather vague and general impression that the great extremes of racial isolation they recall as matters of grave national significance some 35 or 40 years ago have gradually, but steadily, diminished in more recent years. The truth, unhappily, is that the trend, for well over a decade now, has been precisely the reverse.

Schools that were already deeply segregated 25 or 30 years ago, like most of the schools I visit in the Bronx, are no less segregated now, while thousands of other schools that had been integrated either voluntarily or by the force of law have since been rapidly resegregating both in northern districts and in the broad expanse of the South.[61]

The concentrated minority poverty caused by long years of oppression has not disappeared. Economics, legal precedents, and racial avoidance today work in tandem to keep black and brown students in inner-city schools, which are often abysmal. The Civil Rights Project in 2012 found that three-quarters of black students and 80 percent of Hispanic students attend minority-majority schools.[62] And, sadly, only 9.3 percent of U.S. teachers are black.[63] "Legal precedents" include the steps that the executive office and the Supreme Court took in recent decades to undermine integration efforts. The Reagan administration slashed financial aid provided to school districts that were enacting integration. *Oklahoma City v. Dowell* (1991) decided that desegregation orders were temporary, that federal orders would be relaxed and then lifted. Other cases in the 1990s, like *Jenkins*, followed this pattern, and cities across the nation set about dismantling integration initiatives. Indeed,

U.S. Supreme Court decisions over the last two decades have forgotten or refuse to acknowledge the historical basis of racial segregation or consider how vestiges of the past continue to affect the present.... Supreme Court decisions on school desegregation in the 1990s reflected an entrenched ideology that has come to accept racial segregation as natural or accidental, inevitable, and un-solvable.[64]

Integration is not hoped for because it will "save" black children, keep them from crime or raise their test scores. That idea perpetuates the myth of black inferiority, implying that if only black kids were sitting next to white kids, how they would shine. The abolition of poverty, the abandonment of racist thought, and the establishment of equal school districts would together accomplish those things. Integration is needed because separation and isolation are breeding grounds for misunder-standing, fear, and hostility. Interaction helps diminish racism. White soldiers of the Civil War forsook racial prejudice and helped their black comrades build new lives because they served with and unexpectedly befriended men of color. Some religious fundamentalists come to accept homosexuals when they find themselves working together and conversing. Young students' fear of special needs children fades away the longer they share a classroom; integration serves a moral and social purpose.

While divisions between white and black schools in Kansas City are deep, there are schools with better racial compositions outside the KCMSD. Unfortunately, most of these schools are diverse only in skin color, not income levels. For example, Silver City Elementary in Kansas City, Kansas, is 41 percent black, 13 percent white, and 33 percent Hispanic, but 94 percent of the students are on the Free and Reduced Lunch Program[65] and childhood poverty in the neighborhood is worse than 95 percent of all U.S. neighborhoods.[66] Raytown Central

Middle School is 40 percent black, 47 percent white, and 9 percent Hispanic, but nearly half the students qualify for Free and Reduced Lunch, and some are homeless—displaced and living with relatives or other caretakers. "We're in one of the wealthier areas," a counselor there once said, "meaning we don't have trailer parks." In one elementary school in Grandview with similar demographics, many students have experienced hunger, neglect, abandonment, roach-infested homes, crowded beds, homelessness, violence, sexual abuse, imprisoned fathers, and mentally unstable mothers. Some of the most emotionally traumatized children come to school each day in unwashed clothes smelling of secondhand smoke and cat urine. Teachers in these schools have the immense task of teaching and attending to serious emotional and physical needs.

The only schools left in Kansas City proper with high white populations are private schools. Visitation Catholic School, for example, is 91 percent white and 1 percent black. It's the chosen favorite among wealthy white families who live along Ward Parkway and in nearby neighborhoods. Between tuition costs ($6,300 a year per student), fundraising, and investments from the parish across the street, the total annual operating sum is over $2.7 million.[67] A black man and Hispanic man clean the building after school.

In some of the neighborhoods off Ward Parkway, the median household income is more than $250,000 and the median home value nearly $1 million, making it one of the richest areas in Kansas City. The population is virtually all white.[68] (Ironically, at the end of the nineteenth century, "Millionaire's Row" was actually on Troost, between 26th and 32nd.) The students enjoy membership at the Carriage Club and regularly shop and dine on the Plaza. Some interrupt school for vacations to California, Chicago, or Colorado. They live privileged, mono-cultural lifestyles. They don't know how other children live.

Jonathon Kozol writes:

> What saddens me the most...is simply that [poor] children have no knowledge of the other world in which I've lived most of my life and that [rich] children in that other world have not the slightest notion as to who these children are and will not likely ever know them later on, not at least on anything like equal terms, unless a couple of these kids get into college. Even if they meet each other then, it may not be the same, because the sweetness of too many of these inner-city children will have been replaced by hardness, some by caution, some by calculation rooted in unspoken fear. I have believed for 40 years, and still believe today, that we would be an infinitely better nation if they knew each other now.[69]

This entrenched social and economic separation is now an accepted part of life in Kansas City. In 2011, researchers from Brown University and Florida State University ranked Kansas City twenty-third among America's most segregated cities. Integration here is better than in Detroit, New York, Chicago, Los Angeles, and St. Louis, but worse than Nashville, Richmond, Minneapolis-St. Paul, Phoenix, Las Vegas, and Atlanta.[70] The ranking is an improvement from previous studies, owing in part to an increasing black population (13.4 percent of the greater metropolitan area in 2011) and middle-class blacks joining whites in the suburbs. But segregation is not the deadliest issue.

There's been a sharp increase in the number of extremist hate groups in the U.S. since Barack Obama's election.[71] Regression always threatens to undo the gains for which so many fought. A twenty-one-year-old white man who read hate group literature allegedly massacred nine African Americans at Emanuel African Methodist Episcopal Church in Charleston, South Carolina, on June 17, 2015. The tragedy revealed how far white denial and ideas of racial transcendence could go. The suspect posted photos of himself online in a jacket with historic flags of apartheid regimes in Africa.[72] In other photos, he held the Confederate flag. The attack coincided with the anniversary of Denmark Vesey's planned slave revolt of 1822; Vesey helped found the church where this attack occurred, and possibly planned the revolt there.[73] The suspect reportedly told the congregation before firing that he was there "to shoot black people" because "You rape our women and you're taking over our country."[74] The Department of Justice announced it would investigate the killing as a hate crime. Yet *Fox News* anchor Steve Doocy said, in a segment labeled "Attack on Faith," that it was "extraordinary" people were calling this a hate crime based on the fact that it was a "white guy and a black church." The segment even included a carefully selected conservative black pastor who said the attack was really about hostility toward Christians, and urged pastors to arm themselves.[75] Casting this as an attack on faith reflects the conservative worldview of the network, which appears more comfortable reporting on hostilities against Christians than African Americans. By June 20, the suspect's anti-black manifesto had been found online; he had sought to spark a race war.[76]

Leftist publications pointed out the shooting and its aftermath fit into many disturbing patterns in American history: violent whites targeting black churches, the mainstream media reflexively labeling white shooters as "mentally ill" versus "thug" or "terrorist" for nonwhites, and the tendency of news reports to imply the victims of white terrorism were complicit in their own deaths.[77] We hear the same of police victims.

As noted in the Introduction, racist thought (both conscious and subconscious) affects police conduct. FairImpartial-Policing.com/bias provides links to many important studies. "Seeing Black: Race, Crime, and Visual Processing" (*Journal of Personality and Social Psychology*) showed how police officers associate innocent blacks with criminality and aggression. "The Police Officer's Dilemma: Using Ethnicity to Disambiguate Potentially Threatening Individuals" from the same journal showed ordinary civilians in simulations are far quicker to shoot armed blacks than armed whites, and decide faster to spare an unarmed white than an unarmed black. "The Correlates of Law Enforcement Officers' Automatic and Controlled Race-Based Responses to Criminal Suspects" (*Basic and Applied Psychology*) found that during simulations police officers with anti-black biases shoot unarmed black suspects more often. "The Consequences of Race for Police Officers' Responses to Criminal Suspects" (*Psychological Science*) showed police officers are more likely to mistakenly shoot unarmed blacks than unarmed whites. Fortunately, the bias diminished with extensive time in the simulation. In fact, "Across the Thin Blue Line: Police Officers and Racial Bias in the Decision to Shoot" (*Journal of Personality and Social Psychology*) credited time in simulations when police officers (who had implicit biases) did *not* use lethal force in a biased way during tests. In 2012, blacks who were not attacking an officer when killed made up 39 percent of police victims, way out of proportion to a small black population of

13 percent (compared to 46 percent of victims being white, when whites are nearly 70 percent of Americans).[78]

Kansas Citians consistently gathered for vigils and protests after senseless police killings of black males in other cities, like Eric Garner in Staten Island, twelve-year-old Tamir Rice in Cleveland, and Walter Scott in North Charleston, all of whom were captured on video. In November 2014, police arrested four people protesting the verdict of the Michael Brown case for civil disobedience at a gathering by the J.C. Nichols Fountain. Participants chanted, "No justice, no peace, no racist police."[79] The next month, a Black Lives Matter protest, organized by One Struggle KC, held up traffic on I-70, and seven people were arrested for civil disobedience. One large sign read: "Sorry for the disruption. We are trying to change the world."[80]

On August 9, 2015, the anniversary of Michael Brown's death, protests against police brutality popped up across the country. One hundred Kansas Citians protested outside the Ward Parkway Center; four were arested for civil disobedience. Others held a prayer rally in Swope Park, which included a mock funeral with hearses and a motorcade for the nearly 700 Americans killed by police in 2015 up to that point.

The aftermath of these shootings are revealing. Some conservative whites interpret each decision of the courts as a "yay" or "nay" on racism. For example, they viewed the "not guilty" verdict in the Michael Brown case as proof the killing wasn't racially motivated, even at a subconscious level. But this is problematic because racial prejudice, whether conscious or subconscious, has infected the courts themselves. As earlier noted, blacks receive longer sentences and are more frequently executed on death row than whites who commit the same crimes. If we were to use the logic that a "not guilty" verdict meant racism wasn't a factor, we could extend that reasoning to say it wasn't a factor in lynchings in the United States. After all, whites who murdered blacks in the nineteenth and twentieth centuries were consistently declared not guilty because the judge and jury held the same prejudices as the accused. The events of today have similarities: officers who use excessive force against blacks are nearly always exonerated, including Rodney King's attackers in Los Angeles in 1991 and those who in 2014 killed Tamir Rice, a boy with a pellet gun (in an open-carry state) who was given no chance to surrender and no first aid after being gunned down. Nearly 1,000 Kansas Citians gathered in protest after the court acquitted the policemen who brutally beat Rodney King. The verdict sparked the 1992 Los Angeles race riot; Mayor Emanuel Cleaver asked that the Kansas City police stay out of sight to avoid a confrontation with protesters.[81]

Activists confronted other challenges, too. When Neo-Nazis rallied outside the Jackson County Courthouse downtown in November 2013, an anti-Nazi protest of 300 people organized across the street, and civil rights groups held their own meetings and rallies to counter the hate group's message and decry its presence.[82] That same year, Kansas Citians denounced the candidacy of Edward Stephens, who ran for a position on the Park Hill school board. Stephens was backed by the extremist right-wing American Freedom Party, which promised white voters that Stephens would "represent the interests and concerns of White American school students." Stephens advocated keeping poor and minority students out the district and "removing materials that promote racial diversity" in the district curriculum.[83] In the much more tolerant American society of 2013, he lost miserably.

On November 14, 2009, black religious leaders gathered across the street from the Power and Light entertainment district downtown with signs that read, "End Corporate Racism," "No Jim Crow," and "Never Again." They were protesting discriminatory dress codes at Power and Light that banned baggy clothing and athletic wear usually worn by African American males. The city filed a discrimination complaint against Cordish Co., the corporate owner. A black family sued Power and Light in federal court when the Mosaic Lounge turned them away but allowed in similarly dressed whites. The city council quickly banned discrimination of this nature. Power and Light yielded to pressure and relaxed its dress code in 2010.[84] Other cases around the nation dealt with similar policies.

In March 2014, Glen Cusimano, club manager and security chief for Cordish, sued the corporation for racial discrimination. Cusimano claims he was told to hire a "rabbit," a person given a cash payment to agitate black patrons, help create a disturbance, and give clubs an excuse to eject the "troublesome" African Americans. The "rabbit" corroborated this accusation in a sworn affidavit.[85] Less than two weeks later, two black men sued Cordish in federal court for denying them entrance to clubs and ejecting them using the same "rabbit" technique.[86] In June of 2015, a federal judge threw out this case, citing a legal technicality and lack of evidence, despite the testimony of ex-employees who said they were ordered to keep out blacks.[87]

Racial tensions have been exacerbated by events at the Country Club Plaza, a focal point of controversy in Kansas City. Some black teenagers—a tiny percentage of black teens that enjoy evenings on the Plaza—have caused serious distur-bances. On one chaotic night in April 2010, police called in ad-ditional officers and used pepper spray to break up fights among black youths. One person was arrested for robbery, another for assault. Someone was rushed to a hospital after being discov-ered lying in a parking lot with a broken jaw and head injuries. The police said they handled thirty-five calls. Their report also documented:

- Crowds gathering in front of businesses and blocking entrances.
- Traffic being brought to a standstill by crowds of youths flooding into streets.
- Crowds harassing customers and blocking the foyer of P.F. Chang's restaurant.
- Numerous reports to police and Plaza security of being harassed and intimidated.
- A 16-year-old girl being run over by a stampede of youths.
- A girl on a prom date pushed into the Cheesecake Factory fountain by a group of youths.
- A couple being assaulted and robbed in the parking garage at Nichols Road and Pennsylvania Avenue by at least 15 juveniles.[88]

In September 2013, police used pepper spray to break up a fight by the J.C. Nichols Memorial Fountain.[89] In February 2014, several fights broke out at a crowded movie theater; officers arrested three black youths.[90] In April 2015, two black males were arrested for vandalizing cars by leaping onto hoods.[91]

Reports of these incidents, and many similar ones, often included the sizes of black crowds on the Plaza at the time—300, 500, 700, 900 black youths—implying, whether intentionally or not, virtual armies of troublemakers. Some residents and conservative bloggers even used the word "riots"—despite the very low number of actual arrests. Still, businesses and restaurants feared these episodes would scare away customers. African American community leaders like Mayor James, Chief of Police Darryl Forté, and activist Alvin Brooks urged black youths to refrain from illegal behavior and black parents not to leave their teenagers unsupervised. The city government established a curfew for minors, increased the police presence on the Plaza, and devoted resources to expanding activities for black youths on the weekends. These incidents strained race relations, likely making many whites suspicious of the black youths they passed on the Plaza streets.

One resident told KMBC-TV:

> Well I work by the plaza and I can tell you I have never seen a group of white kids running around causing problems. Have not seen a group of Hispanic kids running around causing problems. That goes for Chinese, Korean, or every other race out there. You want to make it a race thing so I am going to call it like I see it.[92]

Another added:

> The problems on the Plaza are with BLACK teenagers. Call it what you will—since there are no white teens causing the problems. This is a problem for anyone who enjoys the Plaza—so we all get to suffer because of the lack of parenting of these black delinquents.[93]

In comments on online reports, readers, whether local or from across the country, were not so tactful:

Part of the problem is that slavery was abolished.[94]

Not only should abortion be a legal choice, it should be mandatory for certain people. This country needs nigger control[95]

Time for blacks to go back to Africa[96]

Whites build and maintain livable civilizations....Blacks completely destroy civilization until it is nothing more than grass and sticks. We all know the partial solution for Kansas City. Curfew on all blacks after 5 PM city wide AND restricted area where they can not go. Of course this will not be done, thus Kansas City is doomed and everybody there know it.[97]

I remember the riots and the curfews...I was born and raised here. I know from first hand accounts the destruction that Negro's do to any place they gain a foot hold. And ive yet to have a person tell me of a town or city populated and ran by Negros that prospers. Here is a hint, THERE ISNT ONE.[98]

I would like to be down on the plaza when these riots take place. I can never time this right. Damn. I would relish the opportunity to hand out some justice Kansas city style to these sub-humans....Trust me the good folks of KC will not let the Plaza go down....The Niggers will not win this one....I think I will go to the Plaza this weekend to see if I can find an opportunity to live my American Dream.[99]

The bullet size really doesn't make that much difference if you remember to put 3, 4 rounds into the Negro....You NEVER, EVER want the Simian to live. Then he will get a squid lawyer and sue you for "hate" crimes. Every police officer I have ever spoken with about this situation has said to finish the person off so as to avoid real problems. A dead negro can not testify. A live wounded Negro is "god" and his word will never be doubted. Remember, you are White and thus you are guilty.[100]

You enjoy what this area of your city means to you. The Niger enjoys destroying it. To him, it represents WHITE MEN. He loves the feeling of destroying all that which is White. Why do you thinks Nigers target White women for rape? Revenge. Hate. Getting even. It isn't just that White Women are so damn better than African sows. Everybody knows that. It is the wonderful feeling of DE-STROYING anything White. The more your city politicians attempt to keep the Nigers out, the more then will want in. They will win. They will form flash mobs, they will still show up and jump, jive, prattle and annoy White people. THEY LOVE THAT. The more problems they cause, the happier they are. If they can't be White and enjoy the White World then they will destroy it for you.[101]

If the disturbances on the Plaza reinforced white suspicion and fear, race riots in places like Ferguson (2014) and Baltimore (2015)—erupting after deadly incidents involving unarmed blacks and police officers—did the same but to a much greater degree. These riots, like those in the past, were initiated by a very small percentage of the black population within each city, but reflect the anger of oppressed, marginalized, and impoverished people. Similarly treated groups around the world also explode into violence and destruction, and poor U.S. whites have a long history of rioting, too (the 1863 New York Draft Riots, for example). Riots can have positive effects—those of the 1960s certainly impelled civil rights legislation forward, and the riots in Ferguson sparked a national dialogue on race relations and pushed federal and local governments to put body-mounted cameras on police officers. Yet the riots also damaged race relations because they reinforced in white minds stereotypes of the "aggressive," "violent," "criminal" black man, even though the majority of black residents protested peacefully and black leaders repeatedly urged nonviolence. Many whites saw the main cause as blacks who simply "like to be destructive."

Police abuse has also severely strained race relations. In 2005, a black family in Kansas City, Kansas, sued after five white police officers entered their home without a warrant during a birthday party. In the ensuing confrontation, they beat adults and children with fists and flashlights, spouted racial slurs, and fired pepper spray. In 2007, Sofia Salva was pulled over (for fake tags) on her way to the hospital. She was pregnant and bleeding, as video shows she calmly told two Kansas City officers. "How is that my problem?" one of them replied. The police jailed her for outstanding warrants. She miscarried the next day. That same year, even the police chief wanted an officer fired for driving his nightstick into the mouth of a cuffed black man. In 2010, Carlos McCain, while complying peacefully with police orders, was slammed to the pavement. In August 2014, graphic designer Jasmine Taylor filed a complaint against the Kansas City Police Department after an officer purportedly struck her in the face and knee during a traffic stop, sending her to the emergency room. A black boy in second grade, hysterical after being teased in class, was cuffed like a criminal that year.[102]

In other incidents, Kansas Citians died in confrontations with the police. In July 2013, unarmed African American Ryan Stokes allegedly refused to obey police orders and was shot in the back and killed by a black officer, who thought he had a gun. A gun was found in a nearby car, where police claim Stokes hid it before he was shot. Stokes' mother says the police told her he was shot in the chest.[103] The officer got a commendation. Four months later, a white man named Nick Simonitch, possibly mentally ill, attacked an officer with a bat and was killed. In separate incidents in 2014 and 2015, African Americans Carlos Davenport and Javon Hawkins threatened officers with swords, and were shot and killed.

Some Kansas Citians believe that because they refused to follow police orders or, in other cases, committed crimes, the victims "had it coming." This is a standard never applied to their own children, siblings, parents, or spouse. If one of their family members disobeyed the police or broke the law, no matter how unlikely that may be, they would want the police to find a non-violent solution, at the worst use nonlethal bullets. They would want officers who used unnecessary deadly force to lose their jobs and be imprisoned; that is, they would want justice. The fact many whites can say the killing of Ryan Stokes or Tamir Rice was justified but cannot say the same if it were their sons exhibiting the exact same behaviors speaks to the white devaluation of black lives.

On July 10, 2015, a policeman pulled Sandra Bland over in Waller County, Texas, for failing to signal. Their interaction grew heated. The officer arrested her. Three days later, Bland was found hanging by a garbage bag in her cell. It was ruled a suicide. Many were suspicious, as Bland was about to be released on bail and the sheriff in charge of the jail was once fired for racism and police brutality. In Kansas City, there was an ugly reverberation. On July 27, KCTV5 reported that a white supervisor at Adam's Mark Hotel hung a "slave doll" in a hotel office doorway with a plastic bag. An antiracist protest outside the hotel followed. The supervisor was reportedly fired.

Hate crimes occur too frequently in Kansas City. In May 2008, two white men were found guilty of murdering an African American named William McCay. The court held that it was "a violation of his civil right to walk down a Kansas City street unmolested because of his race."[104] A man and woman from Independence drew a swastika and "white power" on a black family's driveway, then threw a gasoline bomb against their house.[105] Journeys, a store in Overland Park, made national news when Keith Slater, a black student at Missouri State, discovered the customer name on his return receipt read, "DUMB NIGGER."[106] Racist graffiti was left at a church in Leavenworth in 2003, on Kansas City residences in 2007. In 2004, "white power" and "KKK" were painted on a black family's fence in Kansas City, Kansas. Klan fliers appeared in Olathe in 2005, Overland Park in 2008; 2012 saw racist leaflets from the extremist Council of Conservative Citizens distributed to homes in Blue Springs. Then three people pled guilty to breaking into a biracial man's Independence home, writing racial slurs on his walls, and later setting the place on fire to convince him to move out. In 2009, a drunk man yelled racist remarks at his noisy neighbor and shot up his house; he didn't want his street to become "the hood."[107] A parolee celebrating his release from prison used a racial slur against a black guest at a party in Platte County in 2013. In the argument that followed, he assaulted the guest with a log, threatening to slit his throat and murder his family.[108] In February 2014, black firefighter Eric Sanders sued the Kansas City Fire Department for tolerating a "racially hostile" work environment, where the word "nigger" is dropped right and left and African Americans are ostracized.[109]

During the 2014 Martin Luther King, Jr., holiday weekend, the *Star* ran a front-page article highlighting the obsessive terror over interracial couples that still grips some of white America. Robert and Carrie Cleveland, after moving into their new home in Kansas City, were terrorized repeatedly: they found their tires slashed and a "for sale" sign placed in their yard; their lawn was vandalized; their sons' bikes were stolen; their eldest son was threatened on a YouTube video; and a neighbor swore at them and told them their sons could not use the community pool. It all sounds familiar. The idea that racism is over is an old white delusion. In 1963, polls showed 60 percent of U.S. whites thought blacks were treated equally![110] If whites could be so blind then, could we not be blind today, when racism is more subtle? There is much more tolerance, to be sure, but we cannot overlook modern racial injustices like they did.

Nationally, blacks and whites commit hate crimes against each other. In 2014, about 63 percent of hate crime victims were targeted due to their blackness, 23 percent targeted due to their whiteness. The Department of Justice estimates over a quarter-million hate crimes occur annually, over race, religion, sexual orientation, etc.[111]

But perhaps most common in Kansas City and elsewhere are simply unwelcoming looks. One white Overland Park, Kansas, resident described on *CNN iReport* how he and his black female coworker felt at a restaurant one night in 2009: "The entire time we had people watching us and whispering and gawking…. I pointed this out to her and she was indifferent with 'you seem surprised'…. She said 'have you ever taken a black girl out before?' I said no. She explained that this is a taboo."[112]

Overall, the conditions of black Kansas City today are not so different than in decades past. Black-on-black crime remains a huge problem. Drive-by shootings and other forms of gang violence cut short young lives. This characterizes any American ghetto. However, rather than some innate moral depravity special to African Americans, it's the product of a history of white hate, isolation, and poverty. Any serious study of human history shows poverty spreads crime like theft and murder. Research indicates violent crime falls dramatically just when people have jobs.[113] Crime is a creation of socioeconomic conditions, not race. And it is only worsened when businesses refuse to hire ex-felons (most of whom are just nonviolent drug users) and the government bans them from receiving food stamps, subsidized housing, and other forms of aid.

Further, a society that offered few legal protections encouraged vigilante justice within an oppressed community. From the beginning, the Kansas City police did not do enough to protect the rights or physical well-being of blacks; instead, many officers victimized them. Few white politicians or policemen made any serious attempt to eradicate vice from black areas; on the contrary, illegal (often white-owned) businesses on the east side were protected as long as they remained there.

On top of all this, the authorities generally showed indifference toward the ghetto; when one African American murdered another, there was little investigation. Many policemen cared little for black victims, and when murder or theft is ignored, what better incentive could there be for the perpetuation of such acts? Roy Wilkins lamented, "Getting Kansas City's police to enforce the law in black neighborhoods was almost impossible.... The official attitude seemed to be, 'Well, there's one more Negro killed—the more of 'em dead, the less to bother us. Don't spend too much money running down the killer—he may kill another'"; Representative Harold Holliday said, "People tend to spend time and energy on things they think are important. And the police don't think that crime in our neighborhoods is important."[114] Police administrators denied this. Chief Clarence Kelley, for instance, insisted that his men enforced the law equally in all neighborhoods,[115] perhaps another example of white delusions of racial transcendence. In the 1969 *Nation* article "Black Crimes, Black Victims," Robert Pearman condemned Kansas City's "overlooked problem in the policing of the ghetto—the deficiencies of investigation, public interest, public cooperation and prosecution. They are to be found in every major American city, running parallel with high crime rates, abortive prosecution and danger for the people who, by choice or circumstance, live within the community."[116]

Pearman wrote that the ghetto saw three times as many robberies and assaults as wealthier white areas. In 1968, for example, he found that 67 percent of homicide victims were black in a city only 20 percent African American, and that blacks were mostly killed by blacks. "To be a frequent victim is the price of living in the ghetto."[117] Pearman also pointed out

that theft aggravates the economic squalor in a ghetto by desta-
bilizing black entrepreneurship: "An embryo Negro business,
with shaky capital, trying to get started, can be wiped out by
a robbery…and such robberies are sure to come."[118] Replacing
merchandise and fixing window damage can cost thousands.

Black leaders decried black-on-black murder, along with the
social conditions and racist policies that encouraged it, for the
past century. They demanded proper law enforcement, protection, and prosecution. Convinced many white officers were
either apathetic or abusive, residents resisted speaking to the
authorities, something Representative Harold Holliday and
others also criticized, something that is still a problem. Many
residents and leaders demanded more black officers. Yet police
force demographics have never reflected the city population. In
2014, Kansas City was 55 percent white, but the police force
77 percent white; Kansas City, Kansas, was 40 percent white
with a 72 percent white police force; 45 percent compared
to 93 percent in Grandview; and 65 percent compared to 90
percent in Raytown.[119] The Kansas City Police Department did
not have a black police chief until 2011.

Researchers write in *Pulled Over* that blacks in Kansas City
are three times more likely to experience investigatory stops
(these are not stops for actual traffic violations), especially in
the white suburbs. They are twice as likely to not be told why
and five times more likely to be searched, but are less likely to
be found with anything illegal and act no more disrespectfully
than similarly treated whites.[120] One black Kansas Citian spoke
of being followed by police for fifteen minutes. "They followed
me all the way to the house.… I get out of the car…and they
said, 'Is this your car?' And I said, 'Yes'.… They ran the tags

[and] I walked on in the house.... They did it for about a couple weeks." Another described being handcuffed in a white neighborhood while his I.D. was checked to see if he was involved in a recent robbery. "He asked us where we lived and why we were over here. And he made us get out of the car.... I kept my composure.... I didn't wanna, you know, give him a reason to do anything else.... They put us in handcuffs. And we sat outside for about an hour, and then they just let us go."

Though some city officials stressed the need to learn lessons from Ferguson and Baltimore, and took positive steps, a common attitude seemed to be, as one article put it, "Kansas City is not Ferguson. Kansas City is not Baltimore."[121] Kansas City is different. Yet what the Kansas City Round Table on Access and Opportunity wrote in 2006 is no less true today: "Hopelessness, apathy, [and] resentment resulting from lack of progress are…all too obvious in Kansas City's urban core."[122]

In the 1920s, an African American killed another African American every single week in Kansas City, hugely out of proportion with white-on-white murder.[123] Today, the number of annual homicides has hovered around 100 for years. The 64130 zip code is called the "Murder Factory," the city itself "Killa City." At 21.3 homicides per 100,000 people, Kansas City had the fourth-highest murder rate in the United States in 2013, trailing Oakland, Baltimore, and Detroit.[124] Nearly 77 percent of murder victims are African American (whites 20 percent), as reported in 2015.[125] Suspects in 2014 were 49 percent black male and 15 percent white male.[126] Black organizations like the Ad Hoc Group Against Crime, founded by Alvin Brooks and others in 1977, are working to alleviate the problem—just like whites who despise and seek to silence Black Lives Matter demand. In 2014, the city saw its fewest homicides in decades, thanks to the No Violence Alliance, an anti-crime program.

The overwhelmingly white American media often neglect to talk about black victims. Eighty-six percent of television news directors and 91.3 percent of radio news directors are white.[127] About 4.7 percent of journalists in the nation's newsrooms are black.[128] Among other issues, this makes the 150,000 black children who go missing each year in the U.S. less visible. In October 2011, a white baby named Lisa Irwin vanished from her Kansas City home, and many readers will recall the national attention the case received. Missing black children from the area rarely receive comparable attention. Nationally, from 2005-2007, black children made up 19.5 percent of the missing youths reported on the news, even though 33.2 percent of missing child cases were black. Non-blacks made up 66.8 percent of the actual cases, but received 80.5 percent of media coverage.[129] There are also problems with media portrayals of suspects: black ones get disproportionate coverage. A 2015 study found blacks in New York City got 75 percent of television news coverage on crime, but their actual arrest rate was 51 percent; studies show this worsens anti-black sentiment.[130]

Welfare is a similar story. Because they are disproportionately poor, blacks are disproportionately on welfare (in Jackson County in 2009, 48 percent of blacks received food stamps, versus 11 percent of whites[131]). Yet it is a myth that most welfare recipients are black; they actually make up only 39 percent of all U.S. welfare recipients. The misperception that most welfare users are black is in part due to media storytelling. For example, the media mostly portrayed welfare recipients as white from 1950 to 1964. Yet from 1967-1992 they were portrayed as black in nearly 60 percent of news stories. In 1972 and 1973, nearly 75 percent of stories gave a black face to American welfare, helping increase white hatred of government aid.[132]

There is also a misconception that the majority of drug users are black. Actually, whites use illicit drugs at slightly higher rates, but blacks are three times more likely to be arrested. The war on drugs is mostly waged in poor black and brown neighborhoods, not middle-class or upper-class white ones. Kansas City blacks are nearly four times more likely to be arrested for drugs, being the main victims of a 736 percent increase in drug war arrests in Kansas City from 1980 to 2003, the third largest increase of any city. The black arrest rate went up 881 percent, the white arrest rate up 400 percent.[133] But nationally, "at least for the last twenty years...whites have engaged in drug offenses at rates higher than blacks.... An estimated 49% of whites and 42.9% of blacks age twelve or older have used illicit drugs" at some point, and "because the white population is more than six times greater than the black population, the absolute number of white drug offenders is far greater...."[134]

Likewise, whites commit most crimes (69 percent, versus blacks' 28 percent), according to the FBI's "Crime in the United States" 2012 report (Table 43). Whites led in charges of rape (65 percent), assault (63 percent), and burglary (67 percent), while blacks led in murder charges (49 percent, a lead of 1 percent) and robbery (55 percent). More minor categories were dominated by whites. The 2014 report (Expanded Homicide Tables 6 and 3) shows 82 percent of whites were killed by whites, 90 percent of blacks killed by blacks. Considering whites and blacks still live fairly segregated lives, this is not unexpected. Nor is the fact that disproportionate poverty causes black crime to remain way out of proportion to their low population (13 percent of Americans), as in Kansas City.

To some extent, white flight persists in Kansas City. Sometimes Johnson County and other places are not far enough for those wishing to find whiter areas. Historian James Loewen notes in *Sundown Towns: A Hidden Dimension of American Racism*: "Oak Grove, Missouri, has become a bedroom community for people working in Independence and even Kansas City who seek an all-white environment, even though it lies more than 40 miles east of Kansas City."[135] Gotham writes that white Kansas Citians seek out white schools for their children using racially coded inquiries about which schools are "safe" or "high-quality."[136] Schirmer makes the same observation.[137]

As in the past, racism of adults has infected some of Kansas City's children. In December 2011, a Lee's Summit North student was disciplined after starting a racist blog, which mentioned specific classmates and used "nigger" repeatedly. In what KCTV5 described as "one of the least inflammatory posts," the student wrote that blacks "are your typical trash of the world. They're pretty lazy and you'll want to shoot yourself after being in the presence of one after a certain amount of time."[138] At Shawnee Mission East High School, where the black population is 1.7 percent of the student body, black students complain of everyday slights, large and small: the feeling among whites that it is "trashy for a white girl to date a black guy"; jokes about slavery; the casual use of "nigger"; the equating of athleticism with "blackness." Black students launched the #ITooAmEast campaign after an East student started a web page that said, "Only thing I hate more than [Shawnee Mission South] are

Mexicans, niggers, and well [Shawnee Mission School District] niggers."[139]

Anti-black racism has sparked reverse racism. It is predictable that some blacks should distrust or hate whites (the police in particular). In 2012, two black teenagers drenched a Kansas City East High School student with gasoline and lit him on fire, allegedly saying, "This is what you deserve, white boy." That same year, a group of black men reportedly assaulted a white man in the street, using anti-white slurs.[140]

Overall, the racial disparities in Kansas City are jarring. According to the 2015 *State of Black Kansas City Equality Index*, published by UMKC for the Urban League of Greater Kansas City, the poverty rate for blacks in the greater metropolitan area is more than double that of whites (29.8 percent versus 12.6 percent). Black median income is just over half that of whites ($29,724 versus $54,044), and the home ownership rate is 65 percent that of whites. The median net worth for whites is nearly *eighteen times* higher: $6,314 for blacks, $110,500 for whites. The unemployment rate for blacks is double the unemployment rate for whites (recall from the Introduction that even blacks with college degrees are twice as likely to be unemployed than whites with college degrees). Those who resort to crime face longer sentences than whites. The average prison sentence for all offenses in Kansas City was 7.2 years for blacks, 5.5 years for whites.[141] One extreme case is that of black Kansas Citian Alvis J. Williams, currently serving *eighty years* for burglary. The average sentence for burglary in Missouri is 6.2 years.

Black Kansas Citians are more susceptible to a wide range of medical ailments for multiple reasons, from stress due to a discriminatory culture to lack of proper health care. The percentage of uninsured African Americans is more than double that of whites. The overall black death rate is only slightly higher than that of whites, but the black fetal death rate is more than double (7.4 fetal deaths versus 2.9 per 1,000 births). Obesity rates are a third higher for blacks, and the incidence of "HIV/AIDS among blacks is over 260 percent higher than that of whites."[142] Black students are much more likely to consider suicide. Black seniors are almost three times as likely to need Medicaid, requiring more care to keep them healthy.[143]

Our black students are slightly less likely to be taught by a highly qualified teacher or a teacher with a master's degree, and more likely to be taught by a teacher with a temporary or special assignment certificate. The average ACT score for black students is 14.5, 22.8 for white students. Post-high school education is 10 percent lower for blacks.[144] In 2014, 70 percent of KCMSD students scored below proficient in major subjects.[145] Only 12 percent of black Jackson County students scored proficient in English language arts (versus 35 percent of white students) and only 14 percent scored proficient in math (versus 49 percent).[146] In 2011-2012, the KCMSD suspended more than 20 percent of its black elementary students, double the percentage of white students suspended. Missouri as a whole suspended 14 percent of its black elementary students and 1.6 percent of its white students; for secondary schools, it was 27 percent compared to 7 percent. This gave Missouri the highest suspension rate of black elementary students in the nation, the largest racial gap in elementary student suspensions, and the fourth-largest racial gap in secondary school suspensions.[147]

Yet some conservative whites still insist "white privilege"— the notion that whites enjoy certain advantages in education, health care, the criminal justice system, housing, and employment—is a myth. They often claim this devalues their hard work and accomplishments. Not only is this an example of *argumentum ad consequentiam* (not believing *x* because one does not wish *x* to be true), it has a touch of irony. If a white person feels threatened by the notion that white privilege may have contributed to her success, one can only imagine how a black person feels her success is threatened by its reality—facing the uphill battle wrought by past and present discrimination.

It would serve many white Kansas Citians well to drive down Troost or Prospect to see where yesterday has brought us— boarded up homes and businesses; small shops with bars on the windows; a wealth of liquor stores, fast food joints, and thrift shops; decrepit buildings; an absence of grocery stores; pawn shops and gas stations; and payday loan providers. You may be shocked at how many of the latter you pass. These businesses are financed by major banks, and offer immediate loans with interest rates ranging from 400 to 1,000 percent. Payday loan providers prey on the desperately poor, and are overwhelmingly concentrated in black and Hispanic neighborhoods. Fifty-three percent of black Americans in 2011 lacked access to mainstream banking services, which makes payday loans tempting. Yet the devastating interest rates dig a family into an insurmountable financial hole and encourage more borrowing. Over $3 billion a year *in fees* is transferred from the poor to the banks.[148] Kansas Citians pay $26 million to loan providers each year.[149] Organizations like Communities Creating Opportunity are fighting to end this practice in Kansas City.

There is still much work to be done to end the exploitation and poverty that is so intimately linked with our racial history.

Progress will continue if we put on hold premature notions of racial transcendence, and study our dark history of racial hostility and the causes of poverty and crime with open minds. We whites need to abandon our myths of innate black laziness, aggression, and immorality, and seek out diverse neighbors and colleagues. Progress will continue, as always, with ordinary people working together to eradicate racism and poverty in their communities using all the tools of the past, from petitions and peaceful protests to strikes and civil disobedience. America desperately needs local and national policies that end exploitive banking and business practices; improve wages for workers; establish public work projects to end unemployment and rebuild our inner cities; lower or eliminate the cost of college; end the war on drugs, which focused on and imprisoned so many blacks; expand access to physical and mental health care; fund public schools equally; promote curricula that examine race relations beginning in elementary school; support diverse police forces that go through bias-reduction training and are armed with nonlethal weapons, while jailing abusive officers; consider conscious and subconscious biases during jury, judge, and lawyer selection; invest in public transportation, public housing, black businesses in impoverished areas, and so on.

Jonathan Kozol wrote in *The Shame of the Nation*, "No matter how complex the reasons that have brought us to the point at which we stand, we have, it seems, been traveling a long way to a place of ultimate surrender that does not look very different from the place where some of us began."[150]

Let's hope he is wrong. Let's hope we never surrender.

ENDNOTES

INTRODUCTION
1. Chris Harman, *A People's History of the World* (London: Verso, 2008), 252.
2. Ibid., 253.
3. Ibid., 249.
4. Ibid., 249.
5. James Loewen, *Lies My Teacher Told Me* (New York: Simon & Schuster, 2007).
6. Howard Zinn, *A People's History of the United States* (New York: HarperCollins, 2003), 35.
7. John Blassingame, *The Slave Community* (Oxford: Oxford University Press, 1979), 263.
8. Ibid., 82.
9. Ibid., 82, 84-85.
10. Ibid., 164.
11. James Loewen, *Sundown Towns* (New York: The New Press, 2005).
12. Ibid., 4.
13. Central Alabama Citizens Council, "Declaration of Segregation" handbill, Montgomery, Alabama, 10 February 1956; from Stewart Burns, ed. *Daybreak of Freedom: The Montgomery Bus Boycott* (Chapel Hill, N.C.: University of North Carolina Press, 1997), 154.
14. "Lynchings: By State and Race, 1882-1968," *University of Missouri-Kansas City.* Accessed February 15, 2014, http://law2.umkc. edu/faculty/projects/ftrials/shipp/lynchingsstate.html.

15. Colson Whitehead, "What We Don't See," *New York Times Magazine*, May 28, 2015, http://www.nytimes.com/2015/05/31/magazine/what-we-dont-see.html?_r=0.

16. Harvey Young, "The Black Body as Souvenir in American Lynching," *Theatre Journal* 57, no. 4 (2005): 639-657, doi: 10.1353/tj.2006.0054.

17. Associated Press, "Wealth Gap Widens Between Whites and Minorities," *Kansas City Star,* December 12, 2014.

18. Tim Wise, *Colorblind* (San Francisco: City Lights Books, 2010), 66.

19. Sophia Kerby, "The Top 10 Most Startling Facts About People of Color and Criminal Justice in the United States," *Center for American Progress*, March 13, 2012, http://www.americanprogress.org/issues/race/news/2012/03/13/11351/the-top-10-most-startling-facts-about-people-of-color-and-criminal-justice-in-the-united-states/.

20. John Swaine, Oliver Laughland, and Jamiles Lartey, "Black Americans Killed by Police Twice as Likely to be Unarmed as White People," *Guardian*, June 1, 2015, http://www.theguardian.com/us-news/2015/jun/01/black-americans-killed-by-police-analysis.

21. William Heffernan and John Kleinig, *From Social Justice to Criminal Justice* (Oxford: Oxford University Press, 2000), 28.

22. Wise, *Colorblind*, 78-79, 82.

23. Alison Hewitt, "A 'Black'-Sounding Name Makes People Imagine a Larger, More Dangerous Person, UCLA Study Shows," UCLA, October 7, 2015, http://newsroom.ucla.edu/releases/a-black-sounding-name-makes-people-imagine-a-larger-more-dangerous-person-ucla-study-shows.

24. Tim Wise, "What Whites Don't Know About Racism," *CNN.com*, November 25, 2015 and Tim Wise, *Dear White America* (San Francisco: City Light Books, 2012), 30-31.

25. Wise, *Colorblind*, 68.

26. Ibid., 98-99.

27. "Students of Color Still Receiving Unequal Education," *Center for American Progress,* August 22, 2012, http://www.american-progress.org/issues/education/news/2012/08/22/32862/students-of-color-still-receiving-unequal-education/.
28. Wise, *Colorblind,* 111.
29. Tierney Sneed, "Study: Black Students—Not Crime—Determine If Schools Get Security," *Talking Points Memo,* November 4, 2015, http://talkingpointsmemo.com/news/study-race-school-security.
30. Wise, *Colorblind,* 114-115, 122-123.
31. Ibid., 141-142.

CHAPTER ONE
1. "York," *PBS.org,* accessed February 15, 2014, http://www.pbs.org/lewisandclark/inside/york.html.
2. Meriwether Lewis and William Clark, "The Journals of Lewis and Clark," *Archive.org,* 2005, https:// archive.org/stream/thejournal-soflew08419gut/lcjnl10.txt.
3. Ibid.
4. Jonathan Earle and Diane Mutti Burke, *Bleeding Kansas, Bleeding Missouri: The Long Civil War on the Border* (Lawrence, KS: University Press of Kansas, 2013), 33.
5. Delia Gillis, *Kansas City* (Mount Pleasant, SC: Arcadia, 2007), 10.
6. Sonny Gibson, *Kansas City: Mecca of the New Negro* (Kansas City: 1997), 77.
7. William P. O'Brien, "Hiram Young: Black Entrepreneur on the Santa Fe Trail," *Wagon Tracks* 4, no. 1 (November 1989): http://www.santafetrail.org/the-trail/history/best-of-wagon-tracks/Hiram_Young.pdf.
8. K. David Hanzlick, *Rendering Assistance to Best Advantage: The Development of Women's Activism in Kansas City, 1870 to World War I,* doctoral dissertation (University of Missouri-Kansas City, 2013), https://mospace.umsystem.edu/xmlui/bitstream/handle/10355/35461/HanzlickRenAssBes.pdf?sequence=1, 65.

9. Gillis, *Kansas City,* 11.

10. Sherry Schirmer, *A City Divided: The Racial Landscape of Kansas City, 1900-1960* (Columbia, MO: University of Missouri Press, 2002), 27.

11. Charles Coulter, *Take Up the Black Man's Burden: Kansas City's African American Communities, 1865-1939* (Columbia: University of Missouri Press, 2006), 20.

12. Ken Klamm, "Blacks in Platte County," *Platte County Missouri Historical & Genealogical Society Bulletin* 59, no. 1 (January/February 2006), 9.

13. Gary Gene Fuenfhausen, "A Short History of the Institution of Slavery in Clay County, Missouri," accessed May 25, 2015, http://littledixie.net/slavery_in_clay_county.htm.

14. Diane Mutti Burke, *On Slavery's Border: Missouri's Small-Slaveholding Households, 1815-1865* (Athens: University of Georgia Press, 2010), 314.

15. Fuenfhausen, "Clay County," accessed May 25, 2015.

16. Lyle W. Dorsett, "Slaveholding in Jackson County, Missouri," *Missouri Historical Society Bulletin* 20 (October 1963): 25-27, 30.

17. Harrison Trexler, "The Value and Sale of the Missouri Slave," *Missouri Historical Review* 8 (October 1913): 71.

18. Dorsett, "Slaveholding," 30-31.

19. Fuenfhausen, "Clay County," accessed May 25, 2015.

20. Andrea Froese, "Slavery in Jackson County and Missouri," *Jackson County Historical Society Journal* 39, no. 3 (1999): 14.

21. Kristen Epps, *Bound Together: Masters and Slaves on the Kansas-Missouri Border, 1825-1865,* doctoral dissertation (University of Kansas, 2010), http://kuscholarworks.ku.edu/handle/1808/6441, 108, 106, 100.

22. Fuenfhausen, "Clay County," accessed May 25, 2015.

23. Epps, *Bound Together,* 57-67, 199.

24. Klamm, "Platte County," 9.

25. Epps, *Bound Together,* 101-102, 104-105.

26. Ibid., 154

27. Fuenfhausen, "Clay County," accessed May 25, 2015.

28. Ibid.

29. Klamm, "Platte County," 7.

30. Epps, *Bound Together*, 111.

31. John Blassingame, *Slave Testimony* (Baton Rouge: Louisiana State University Press, 1977), 599.

32. *The History of Jackson County, Missouri* (Kansas City: Union Historical Company, 1881), 297.

33. Gillis, *Kansas City*, 14.

34. Epps, *Bound Together*, 106-107.

35. "Missouri's Early Slave Laws," *Missouri Digital Heritage*, accessed February 15, 2014, http://www.sos.mo.gov/archives/education/aahi/earlyslavelaws/slavelaws.asp.

36. Van William Hutchinson, *Greater Kansas City and the Urban Crisis, 1830-1968*, doctoral dissertation (Kansas State University, 2013), http://krex.k-state.edu/dspace/bitstream/handle/2097/16896/ VanHutchison2013.pdf?sequence=1, 33.

37. Epps, *Bound Together*, 121.

38. Fuenfhausen, "Clay County," accessed May 25, 2015; "Map of White Supremacy Mob Violence," *Monroe Work Today*. Accessed January 21, 2016, http://www.monroeworktoday.org/explore/.

39. Klamm, "Platte County," 9.

40. Dorsett, "Slaveholding," 31, 34; Earle and Mutti Burke, *Bleeding*, 129.

41. Epps, *Bound Together*, 121, 161, 191-192, 117-119, 121-122, 161-162.

42. Peter Hinks, John McKivigan, and R. Williams, *Encyclopedia of Antislavery and Abolition* 1 (Westport, CT: Greenwood Publishing, 2007), 158.

43. Dorsett, "Slaveholding," 28.

44. William Young and Nathan Young, *Your Kansas City and Mine* (Kansas City: 1950), 8.

45. Dorsett, "Slaveholding," 28.

46. Ibid., 32.

47. Epps, *Bound Together*, 221-222; Earle and Mutti Burke, *Bleeding*, 164.

48. "A Brief History from 'A Walking Tour of Historic Parkville,'" *ParkvilleMO.gov*, accessed February 15, 2014, http://parkvillemo.gov/visitors/history/.

49. Hutchinson, *Urban Crisis*, 30.

50. For more see John Nichols, *The "S" Word: A Short History of an American Tradition…Socialism* (London: Verso, 2011).

51. Dorsett, "Slaveholding," 32-33.

52. Epps, *Bound Together*, 150-151.

53. Jeremy Prichard, "New England Emigrant Aid Company," *Civil War on the Western Border*, Kansas City Public Library, accessed February 17, 2014, http://www.civilwaronthewesternborder.org/content/new-england-emigrant-aid-company.

54. Epps, *Bound Together*, 172.

55. Jeremy Prichard, "Bogus Legislature," *Civil War on the Western Border*, Kansas City Public Library, accessed February 17, 2014, http://www.civilwaronthewesternborder.org/content/bogus-legislature.

56. Ibid.

57. Epps, *Bound Together*, 195.

58. Hanzlick, *Rendering Assistance*, 39.

59. Epps, *Bound Together*, 218-219.

60. Hutchinson, *Urban Crisis*, 38.

61. Rick Montgomery, "Foreword on the Civil War in Kansas City," *Civil War on the Western Border*, Kansas City Public Library, accessed February 17, 2014, http://www.civilwaronthewesternborder.org/essay/foreword-civil-war-kansas-city.

62. Hanzlick, *Rendering Assistance*, 32.

63. Montgomery, "Foreword."

64. Karl Marx, *Surveys from Exile* (London: Verso, 2010), 339, 341-342.

65. Ibid., 148.

66. Ibid.

67. Jeremy Neely, "A Most Cruel and Unjust War," *Civil War on the Western Border*, Kansas City Public Library, accessed February 17, 2014, http://www.civilwaronthewesternborder.org/essay/"-most-

cruel-and-unjust-war"-guerrilla-struggle-along-missouri-kansas-border.

68. Loewen, *Lies My Teacher Told Me*, 193.

69. "Quindaro Ruins," *Wycokck.org*, accessed February 15, 2014, http://www.wycokck.org/InternetDept. aspx?id=16256&banner=15284.

70. Dorsett, "Slaveholding," 36.

71. Mutti Burke, *On Slavery's Border*, 273.

72. United Daughters of the Confederacy, *Reminiscences of the Women of Missouri During the Sixties* (Jefferson City: Hugh Stephens Printing, 1920s), 255.

73. Rick Montgomery and Shirl Kasper, *Kansas City: An American Story* (Kansas City: Kansas City Star Books, 1999), 53.

74. Tony O'Bryan, "Collapse of the Union Women's Prison in Kansas City," *Civil War on the Western Border*, Kansas City Public Library, accessed February 17, 2014, http://www.civilwaron-thewesternborder.org/content/collapse-union-women's-prison-kansas-city.

75. Ibid.

76. Hanzlick, *Rendering Assistance*, 44.

77. Daughters of the Confederacy, *Reminiscences*, 263.

78. Terry Beckenbaugh, "Battle of Westport," *Civil War on the Western Border*, Kansas City Public Library, accessed February 17, 2014, http://www.civilwaronthewesternborder.org/content/battle-westport-0.

79. Catherine Watson, "Missouri's Bloody Civil War Battles," *Los Angeles Times,* April 10, 2011.

80. Neely, "Cruel," *Civil War on the Western Border.*

81. Epps, *Bound Together*, 244-245, 251.

82. Daughters of the Confederacy, *Reminiscences*, 255.

83. Mutti Burke, *On Slavery's Border,* 298.

84. Epps, *Bound Together*, 240-243.

85. "A Few Fascinating Missouri Civil War Facts," *Missouri Civil War Museum*, accessed February 17, 2014, http://www.mcwm. org/history_facts.html.

86. Epps, *Bound Together*, 283, 280.

87. Matthew Stanley, "1st Kansas Colored Volunteers," *Civil War on the Western Border*, Kansas City Public Library, accessed February 17, 2014, http://www.civilwaronthewesternborder.org/content/1st-kansas-colored-volunteers-later-79th-us-colored-in-fantry.

88. Epps, *Bound Together*, 265.

89. Ibid., 269.

90. Ibid., 272, 278, 281-282, 273; Earle and Mutti Burke, *Bleeding*, 16.

91. "United States Colored Troops in Missouri," *Missouri Digital Heritage*, accessed February 17, 2014, http://www.sos.mo.gov/archives/education/usct/usct_history.asp.

92. Diane Mutti Burke, "Slavery on the Western Border: Missouri's Slave System and its Collapse during the Civil War," *Civil War on the Western Border*, Kansas City Public Library, accessed March 18, 2014, http://www.civilwaronthewesternborder.org/essay/slavery-western-border-missouri's-slave-system-and-its-collapse-during-civil-war.

93. Epps, *Bound Together*, 234.

94. Fuenfhausen, "Clay County," accessed May 25, 2015.

95. Klamm, "Platte County," 10.

96. Fuenfhausen, "Clay County," accessed May 25, 2015; Earle and Mutti Burke, *Bleeding*, 163.

97. Dorsett, "Slaveholding," 36.

98. Fuenfhausen, "Clay County," accessed May 25, 2015.

CHAPTER TWO

1. U.S. Department of State, *Trafficking in Persons Report* (June 2013), 7.

2. Will Durant and Ariel Durant, *The Lessons of History* (New York: Simon & Schuster, 1968), 52.

3. Stephen Jay Gould, *The Mismeasure of Man* (New York: W. W. Norton & Company, 1996), 67, 85-87.

4. Loewen, *Lies*, 148-149. Loewen notes that in the twenty years after the Revolution (1780-1800) the number of free blacks increased from 2,000 to 20,000. Geography played a role in this event. Slavery grew weaker not just due to ideological changes, but also because tobacco cultivation declined and with it the profitability of slaveholding (for a brief moment, until cotton production exploded).

5. Alfred W. Blumrosen and Ruth G. Blumrosen, *Slave Nation: How Slavery United the Colonies and Sparked the American Revolution* (Naperville, Illinois: Sourcebooks, Inc., 2006).

6. Zinn, *A People's History*, 198.

7. Loewen, *Sundown Towns*, 27.

8. Zinn, *A People's History*, 200.

9. Loewen, *Sundown Towns*, 28-29.

10. "When Kansas City Celebrated Slavery's End," *Kansas City Times*, July 22, 1965.

11. Ibid.

12. Epps, *Bound Together*, 290.

13. Jennifer Laughlin, "Corvine Patterson," *Historical Journal of Wyandotte County* 2 (June 28, 1905): 319-320.

14. Suzanna M. Grenz, "The Exodusters of 1879: St. Louis and Kansas City Responses," *Missouri Historical Review* 73 (October 1978): 64.

15. Ibid., 65-66, 68.

16. Schirmer, *Divided*, 27.

17. Sherry L. Schirmer, "Historical Review of the Ethnic Communities in Kansas City," *Pan-educational Institute* (1976): 5.

18. Robert Athearn, *In Search of Canaan: Black Migration to Kansas, 1879-80* (Lawrence: The Regents Press of Kansas, 1978), 40.

19. Hanzlick, *Rendering Assistance*, 43.

20. Gibson, *Mecca*, 5.

21. Lorenzo Greene, Gary Kremer, and Antonio Holland, *Missouri's Black Heritage* (Columbia: University of Missouri, 1993), 98.

22. Coulter, *Burden*, 24-28; Rose M. Nolen, *Hoecakes, Hambone, and All That Jazz* (Columbia: University of Missouri Press, 2003), 59.

23. Gillis, *Kansas City*, 19.

24. A. Theodore Brown and Lyle W. Dorsett, *K.C.: A History of Kansas City, Missouri* (Boulder, Colorado: Pruett Publishing, 1978), 47.

25. Gillis, *Kansas City*, 25.

26. Nolen, *Hoecakes*, 83; Schirmer, "Ethnic Communities," 33.

27. Montgomery and Kasper, *Kansas City*, 185.

28. Gillis, *Kansas City*, 38.

29. Schirmer, *Divided*, 29.

30. Coulter, *Burden*, 26.

31. Coulter, *Burden*, 24-25.

32. Athearn, *Canaan*, 37, 200, 42; Earle and Mutti Burke, *Bleeding*, 165-166.

33. Gibson, *Mecca*, 15.

34. Hanzlick, *Rendering Assistance*, 46.

35. Schirmer, *Divided*, 29.

36. Loewen, *Sundown Towns*, 28.

37. Ibid., 178.

38. Ida Wells-Barnett. *A Red Record: Tabulated Statistics and Alleged Causes of Lynchings in the United States* (Chicago: Donohue and Henneberry, 1895).

39. Hanzlick, *Rendering Assistance*, 313.

40. Martha Hodes, *White Women, Black Men* (New Haven, CT: Yale University Press, 1999), 179.

41. Christopher Lovett, "A Public Burning: Race, Sex, and the Lynching of Fred Alexander," *Kansas History* 33, summer 2010, 98.

42. J. Silone Yates and A.H. Jones, "Kansas City Women's League," *The Woman's Era* 1, no. 1 (1894), http://womenwriters. library.emory.edu/abolition/content.php?level=div&id=er-a1_01.03.03&document=era1; Earle and Mutti Burke, *Bleeding*,

232-233; "Map of White Supremacy Mob Violence," *Monroe Work Today.*

43. David McCullough, *Truman* (New York: Simon & Shuster, 1992), 53.

44. Lovett, "A Public Burning," 98.

45. "Mob Once Hanged an Innocent Negro Here," *Kansas City Journal,* August 18, 1908.

46. Donald Bradley, "Region's History of Lynchings Overlooked," *Kansas City Star,* February 22, 2015.

47. "Lynchings: By State and Race, 1882-1968," *University of Missouri-Kansas City.* Accessed February 15, 2014, http://law2.umkc.edu/faculty/projects/ftrials/shipp/lynchingsstate.html.

48. Curtis, *Heritage,* 36.

49. Schirmer, *Divided,* 31.

50. Coulter, *Burden,* 181-184.

51. Schirmer, *Divided,* 32.

52. Coulter, *Burden,* 184.

53. Coulter, *Burden,* 185-186.

54. Ibid., 186.

55. Gibson, *Mecca,* 2.

56. Schirmer, *Divided,* 30.

57. William Curtis, *A Rich Heritage* (Traco Enterprises, 1985), 3.

58. Tanner Colby, *Some of My Best Friends Are Black* (New York: Penguin, 2012), 87.

59. Schirmer, *Divided,* 34-35.

60. Schirmer, "Ethnic Communities," 30.

61. Schirmer, *Divided,* 35.

62. Heather Scanlon, "Tour Through Hell's Half-Acre," *Squeezebox,* March 2, 2015, http://www.squeezeboxcity.com/tour-though-hells-half-acre/; Nolen, *Hoecakes,* 61.

63. Curtis, *Heritage,* 2.

64. Heather Scanlon, "From Slavery to Progressivism to…Racism: Kansas City from the 1860s-1900s," *Squeezebox,* February 6,

2015, http://www.squeezeboxcity.com/from-slavery-to-progressivism-to-racism-kansas-city-from-the-1860s-1900s/.

65. Loewen, *Sundown Towns*, 31.

66. Ibid., 31-32.

CHAPTER THREE

1. Colby, *Best Friends*, 86.

2. Kevin Gotham, *Race, Real Estate, and Uneven Development: The Kansas City Experience,1900-2000*(Albany: State University of New York Press, 2002), 36.

3. Coulter, *Burden*, 26.

4. Schirmer, *Divided*, 56.

5. Ibid., 56.

6. Coulter, *Burden*, 30.

7. Colby, *Best Friends*, 88.

8. Greene, *Black Heritage*, 114.

9. Montgomery and Kasper, *Kansas City*, 174.

10. Gary Kremer, "Just Like the Garden of Eden," in *Kansas City, America's Crossroads: Essays from the Missouri Historical Review, 1906-2006*, ed. Diane Mutti Burke and John Herron (Columbia: State Historical Society of Missouri, 2007), 255, 261.

11. Hanzlick, *Rendering Assistance*, 218.

12. Schirmer, *Divided*, 119.

13. Roy Wilkins, *Standing Fast* (New York: Da Capo Press, 1994), 63.

14. Schirmer, *Divided*, 42.

15. Coulter, *Burden*, 251.

16. Ibid., 51.

17. Schirmer, *Divided*, 43.

18. Brown and Dorsett, *K.C.*, 97.

19. Schirmer, *Divided*, 75.

20. Ibid., 151.

21. Hutchinson, *Urban Crisis*, 138.

22. Wilkins, *Standing Fast*, 64.

23. Hanzlick, *Rendering Assistance*, 319.

24. Schirmer, *Divided*, 42.
25. Colby, *Best Friends*, 88.
26. Montgomery and Kasper, *Kansas City*, 199.
27. Schirmer, *Divided*, 81.
28. Ibid., 115.
29. Greene, *Black Heritage*, 144.
30. Coulter, *Burden*, 252.
31. Lovett, "A Public Burning," 97-98.
32. Schirmer, *Divided*, 77.
33. Schirmer, *Divided*, 127-130, 140-141.
34. "Negro Hanged in Missouri," *The Evening Democrat* (Warren, PA), May 3, 1900.
35. Lovett, "A Public Burning," 94-115.
36. Susan Greenbaum, *The Afro-American Community in Kansas City, Kansas* (Kansas City, Kansas Department of Community Development, 1980), 65-66.
37. Ibid., 65-66.
38. "Mob of 1,000 Lynch Negro in Missouri, with Passengers on a Train as Witnesses," *New York Times*, August 8, 1925.
39. "Inquiry Ordered in Missouri Mob's Burning of Negro," *Albany Evening News,* November 29, 1933.
40. Ibid.
41. Coulter, *Burden*, 267.
42. Schirmer, *Divided*, 137-138, 158-160.
43. Hutchinson, *Urban Crisis*, 164.
44. Roy Wilkins, *Standing Fast* (New York: Da Capo Press, 1994), 65.
45. Hutchinson, *Urban Crisis*, 242.
46. Richard S. Kirkendall, *A History of Missouri: Volume V, 1919 to 1953* (Columbia: University of Missouri Press, 1986), 269.
47. Gotham, *Race*, 66.
48. Hutchinson, *Urban Crisis*, 132.
49. Kenneth Jackson, *The Ku Klux Klan in the City, 1915-1930* (New York: Oxford University Press, 1967), 163-164.
50. Wilkins, *Standing Fast*, 60.

51. Ibid., 61, 82.

52. Colby, *Best Friends*, 92.

53. Schirmer, *Divided*, 83.

54. Coulter, *Burden*, 262.

55. Colby, *Best Friends*, 96.

56. Schirmer, *Divided*, 123.

57. Ibid., 66-68.

58. Colby, *Best Friends*, 89.

59. Ibid., 89.

60. Coulter, *Burden*, 258.

61. Ibid., 261.

62. Schirmer, "Ethnic Communities," 26.

63. Nathan Pearson, *Goin' to Kansas City* (Champaign: University of Illinois Press, 1994), 91.

64. Brian Burnes, *Harry S. Truman: His Life and Times* (Kansas City: Kansas City Star Books, 2003), 78-82.

65. Pearson, *Kansas City*, 86.

66. Ibid., 84.

67. Schirmer, *Divided*, 166.

68. Brown and Dorsett, *K.C.*, 184.

69. Coulter, *Burden*, 57, 272.

70. Schirmer, "Ethnic Communities," 26.

71. Coulter, *Burden*, 57.

72. Ibid., 58.

73. Ibid., 269.

74. Ibid., 257; Nolen, *Hoecakes*, 84.

75. Brown and Dorsett, *K.C.*, 185.

76. Gotham, *Race*, 65.

77. Coulter, *Burden*, 255.

78. Wise, *Colorblind*, 69.

79. Pearson, *Kansas City*, 87-91.

80. "The Boss' Buddies," *University of Missouri-Kansas City Library*, accessed February 17, 2014, http://library.umkc.edu/spec-col/parisoftheplains/webexhibit/political/pol-02.htm.

81. Kremer, "Eden," 271.

82. Schirmer, *Divided,* 166, 162.

83. Ibid., 161.

84. Coulter, *Burden,* 277.

85. Ibid., 290.

86. Ibid., 276; Roger Horowitz, *Negro and White, Unite and Fight!* (Champaign: University of Illinois Press, 1997), 87.

87. Zinn, *A People's History,* 404.

88. Coulter, *Burden,* 287

89. Ibid., 287.

90. Gillis, *Kansas City,* 45.

91. Brown and Dorsett, *K.C.,* 201-202.

92. Kremer, "Eden," 271.

93. Young, *Your Kansas City,* 27.

94. Ibid., 27.

95. "The History of the Kansas City Call," *Black Archives of Mid-America,* accessed February 8, 2014, http://www.blackarchives.org/articles/history-kansas-city-call.

96. Schirmer, "Ethnic Communities," 11.

97. Ibid., 22.

98. "Kathryn Johnson, A Front Line Activist," *African American Registry,* accessed February 10, 2014, http://www.aaregistry.org/historic_events/view/kathryn-johnson-front-line-activist.

99. Young, *Your Kansas City,* 26.

100. Zinn, *A People's History,* 196.

101. James P. Cannon, "Trifling With the Negro Question," *Militant,* March 1, 1931, https://www.marxists.org/archive/cannon/works/1931/mar/negroes.htm.

102. Horowitz, *Negro and White,* 84; see 84-103.

103. Schirmer, *Divided,* 174.

104. Montgomery and Kasper, *Kansas City,* 129, 230.

105. Schirmer, *Divided,* 59-61.

106. Ibid., 62.

107. Montgomery and Kasper, *Kansas City,* 180.

108. Schirmer, *Divided,* 63.

109. Ibid., 63.

110. Montgomery and Kasper, *Kansas City*, 227.

111. Joe Louis Mattox, "Talkin' Bout 'The Third' And 'The Vine Part II,'" *Kansas City Call*, December 14-20, 2007.

112. Joe Louis Mattox, "Roy Wilkins, THE CALL and the NAACP," *Kansas City Call*, October 23-29, 2009.

CHAPTER FOUR

1. Colby, *Best Friends*, 77.

2. Kevin F. Gotham, "Missed Opportunities, Enduring Legacies: School Segregation and Desegregation in Kansas City, Missouri," *American Studies* 43, no. 2 (2002): 5.

3. Colby, *Best Friends*, 77.

4. Ibid.

5. Hutchinson, *Urban Crisis*, 267.

6. Colby, *Best Friends*, 75-76.

7. Greene, *Black Heritage*, 162.

8. Colby, *Best Friends*, 110.

9. Ibid., 122.

10. Ibid., 86.

11. Ibid., 71-76.

12. Ibid., 77.

13. Kevin F. Gotham, "A City Without Slums," *American Journal of Economics and Sociology* 60, no. 1 (January 2001): 307.

14. Gotham, *Race*, 88.

15. Ibid., 78-80.

16. Ibid., 80.

17. Suzanne Hogan, "Highway 71 and the Road to Compromise," *KCUR*, June 3, 2014, http://kcur.org/post/highway-71-and-road-compromise.

18. Gotham, *Race*, 88.

19. Alversia Pettigrew, *Memories of a Neck Child* (Independence, MO, 1996), 74.

20. Joe Louis Mattox, "Harry Truman's Hat Tip at 'The Top Hat' Changed My Life," *Jackson County Historical Society Journal* 46, no. 2 (Autumn 2005): 14-16.

21. Ibid., 101.
22. Ibid., 67.
23. Montgomery and Kasper, *Kansas City*, 274.
24. Brown and Dorsett, *K.C.*, 256.
25. Gotham, *Race*, 99-100.
26. Gotham, *Race*, 102.
27. Ibid.
28. Ibid., 103.
29. Ibid., 102.
30. Gotham, *Race*, 100-102.
31. Milton Katz and Susan Tucker, "A Pioneer in Civil Rights," *Kansas History* 18 (Winter 1995/1996): 236-237.
32. "Esther Brown," *Kansas Historical Society,* last modified January 2013, http://www.kshs.org/kansapedia/esther-brown/11991.
33. Katz and Tucker, "Pioneer," 238.
34. Ibid.
35. Ibid., 241.
36. Ibid., 235-247.
37. Ibid., 241.
38. Greene, *Black Heritage*, 168.
39. Young, *Your Kansas City*, 92.
40. Ibid., 92-93.
41. Ibid., 75.
42. Gotham, *Race*, 123.
43. Ibid., 126.
44. Ibid., 128.
45. Ibid., 152.
46. Ibid., 128.
47. Colby, *Best Friends*, 108.
48. Ibid., 108.
49. Gotham, *Race*, 127.
50. Ibid., 72.
51. Gotham, *Slums*, 307.
52. Brown and Dorsett, *K.C.*, 256.
53. Gotham, *Race*, 105-106.

54. Eric Juhnke, "A City Awakened: The Kansas City Race Riot of 1968," *Gateway Heritage* 20 (winter 1999-2000): 35.

55. "Kansas City, MO. et al. v. Williams et al.," *Rutgers School of Law*, accessed April 3, 2015, http://njlaw.rutgers.edu/collections/resource.org/fed_reporter/F2/205/205.F2d.47_1.html.

56. Joe Louis Mattox, "A Shout-Out for Kansas City's Parks and Boulevards," *Kansas City Call*, June 12-18, 2015.

57. Jason Roe, "Water Rights," *Kansas City Public Library*, accessed February 17, 2014, http://www.kclibrary.org/blog/week-kansas-city-history/water-rights.

58. Ibid.

59. Michael MacCambridge, *Lamar Hunt: A Life in Sports* (Kansas City: Andrews McMeel, 2012), 191.

60. Greene, *Black Heritage*, 235.

61. "2,500 Hear Martin L. King in Kansas City," *Kansas City Call*, April 18, 1957.

62. Martin Luther King, *The Papers of Martin Luther King, Jr.* 4 (Los Angeles: University of California Press, 2000), 178. See footnote 7 on page 169 for a note on the Kansas City speech.

63. Blaine O'Neill, "African Americans Campaign for Desegregation of Department Store Eating Facilities in Kansas City, Missouri, 1958-59," *Global Nonviolent Action Database*, December 9, 2010, http://nvdatabase.swarthmore.edu/content/african-amer-icans-campaign-desegregation-department-store-eating-facili-ties-kansas-city-miss.

64. Ibid.

65. Montgomery and Kasper, *Kansas City*, 291.

66. Brian Burnes and Glenn Rice, "Enforcing Equality: Kansas City Continues to Fight for Civil Rights," *Kansas City Star*, January 18, 2014.

67. Gillis, *Kansas City*, 94.

68. Brian Burnes and Glenn Rice, "Progress Marches On," *Kansas City Star*, January 19, 2015.

69. Gillis, *Kansas City*, 90.

70. Juhnke, "A City Awakened," 35.

71. Mike McGraw and Glenn Rice, "Unsolved Killing of Leon Jordan Echoes Civil Rights Era," *Kansas City Star,* September 9, 2010.

72. "Last Ride for Jim Crow," African-American Migration Experience, accessed November 1, 2014, http://www.inmotionaame.org/gallery/detail.cfm?migration=11&topic=3&id=601005&type= image&metadata=show&page=.

73. Burnes and Rice, "Equality," *Kansas City Star.*

74. Zinn, *A People's History*, 460.

75. "The Ten-Point Program," *Marxists.org,* accessed February 17, 2014, http://www.marxists.org/history/usa/workers/black-panthers/1966/10/15.htm.

76. "The Black Panther Party," *Marxists.org,* accessed February 17, 2014, http://www.marxists.org/history/usa/workers/black-panthers/.

77. Ibid.

78. Gaidi Faraj, *Unearthing the Underground: A Study of Radical Activism in the Black Panther Party and the Black Liberation Army*, doctoral dissertation (University of California, Berkeley, 2007), 165.

79. Ibid., 164-170.

80. Christopher Goffard, "Former Black Panther Patches Together Purpose in Africa Exile," *Los Angeles Times*, January 28, 2012, http://www.latimes.com/world/la-fg-black-panther-20120129-html-htmlstory.html.

81. Ibid.

82. Judson Jefferies, *On the Ground* (Jackson: University Press of Mississippi, 2010), 101.

83. "Black Panther Party: Kansas City and Beyond," *United African Alliance Community Center*, accessed February 17, 2014, http://www.uaacc.habari.co.tz/black_panther_party_in_kansas_ci.htm.

84. Gaidi Faraj, *Unearthing*, 172.

85. Jefferies, *Ground*, 106-108.

86. Gaidi Faraj, *Unearthing*, 154-155.

87. Goffard, "Former Black Panther," January 28, 2012.

88. Jefferies, *Ground,* 104.

89. Paul Alkebulan, *Survival Pending Revolution* (Tuscaloosa: University of Alabama Press, 2007), 75.

90. Jefferies, *Ground,* 105.

91. Alkebulan, *Survival,* 49.

92. Gaidi Faraj, *Unearthing,* 248-251.

93. Ibid., 175-176.

94. James McKinley, "A Black Panther's Mellow Exile," *New York Times,* November 23, 1997.

95. Gaidi Faraj, *Unearthing,* 176-177.

96. Ibid., 181.

97. Jefferies, *Ground,* 110.

98. Ibid., 109-113.

99. Martin Luther King, "Where Do We Go From Here?" (speech, 11th Annual Southern Christian Leadership Conference Convention, Atlanta, GA, August 16, 1967).

100. David Garrow, *Bearing the Cross* (New York: HarperCollins, 2004), 382.

101. Peter Dreier, "Martin Luther King Jr.: One of the Nation's Last Great Democratic Socialists," *Common Dreams,* January 18, 2016, http://www.commondreams.org/views/2016/01/18/martin-luther-king-jr-one-nations-great-democratic-socialists.

102. "Assassination Conspiracy Trial," *Martin Luther King, Jr. Center for Nonviolent Social Change,* accessed February 17, 2014, http://www.thekingcenter.org/assassination-conspiracy-trial.

103. "King v. Jowers Conspiracy Allegations," *U.S. Department of Justice,* accessed February 17, 2014, http://www.justice.gov/crt/about/crm/mlk/part6.php.

104. Zinn, *A People's History,* 462.

105. Marisol Bello and Judy Keen, "40 Years After the Riot, King's Vision 'Unfinished,'" *USA Today,* January 20, 2008.

106. John Swomley, "The Kansas City Riot Could Have Been Averted," *Focus Midwest* 6, July/August 1968, 11.

107. David Fly, "An Episcopal Priest's Reflections on the Kansas City Riot of 1968," *Missouri Historical Review* 100, no. 2 (2006): 106-107.
108. Juhnke, "A City Awakened," 36.
109. Swomley, "The Kansas City Riot," 7.
110. Ibid.
111. Ibid.
112. Ibid., 36.
113. Harry Ross, interviewed by Ron Horn, January 21, 1969, 2, http://library.umkc.edu/sites/default/files/images/spec-col/col-1968riot-interview-02-ross.pdf.
114. Ibid., 2-3.
115. Joel Rhodes, "It Finally Happened Here: The 1968 Riot in Kansas City, Missouri," *Missouri Historical Review* 91, April 1997, 300.
116. Male 1, interviewed by Robert Bechtel and Kenneth King, http://library.umkc.edu/sites/default/files/images/spec-col/col-1968riot-interview-01-anonymous-student-participants.pdf.
117. Male 2, interviewed by Robert Bechtel and Kenneth King, http://library.umkc.edu/sites/default/files/images/spec-col/col-1968riot-interview-01-anonymous-student-participants.pdf.
118. Swomley, "The Kansas City Riot," 8.
119. Fly, "Reflections," 107-110.
120. Juhnke, "A City Awakened," 37.
121. Rhodes, "It Finally Happened," 301.
122. Fly, "Reflections," 109.
123. Rhodes, "It Finally Happened," 303.
124. Swomley, "The Kansas City Riot," 9.
125. Juhnke, "A City Awakened," 39.
126. "Summary of Testimony from Sergeant Wilson," May 28, 1969, http://library.umkc.edu/sites/default/files/images/spec-col/col-1968riot-interview-04-wilson.pdf.
127. Rhodes, "It Finally Happened," 308.

128. Male 3, interviewed by Robert Bechtel and Kenneth King, http://library.umkc.edu/sites/default/files/images/spec-col/col-1968riot-interview-01-anonymous-student-participants.pdf.

129. Male 2, interviewed by Robert Bechtel and Kenneth King, http://library.umkc.edu/sites/default/files/images/spec-col/col-1968riot-interview-01-anonymous-student-participants.pdf.

130. Rhodes, "It Finally Happened," 310.

131. Bello and Keen, "40 Years," *USA Today*.

132. Fly, "Reflections," 110.

133. Ibid., 111.

134. Swomley, "The Kansas City Riot," 9.

135. Rhodes, "It Finally Happened," 310.

136. "Kansas City Riot Loss Set At Four Million," *Kansas City Call*, April 19-25, 1968.

137. "Citizens Join in Plea for End of Violence," *Kansas City Times*, April 12, 1968.

138. Male 1, interviewed by Robert Bechtel and Kenneth King, http://library.umkc.edu/sites/default/files/images/spec-col/col-1968riot-interview-01-anonymous-student-participants.pdf.

139. Swomley, "The Kansas City Riot," 9.

140. Kelley and Davis, "The Kansas City Cop," 45.

141. Rhodes, "It Finally Happened," 311.

142. Kelley and Davis, "The Kansas City Cop," 45.

143. Rhodes, "It Finally Happened," 312.

144. Swomley, "The Kansas City Riot," 9-10.

145. "Police Break 33 Doors At Byron Hotel," *Kansas City Call*, April 19-25, 1968.

146. Swomley, "The Kansas City Riot," 10.

147. Rhodes, "It Finally Happened," 312.

148. Lucile Bluford, "Answers Sought By Citizens," *Kansas City Call*, April 19-25, 1968.

149. "Rioting in City Takes Five Lives," *Kansas City Star*, April 11, 1968.

150. Swomley, "The Kansas City Riot," 10.

151. Ibid.

152. Juhnke, "A City Awakened," 41.

153. Harry Ross, interviewed by Ron Horn, January 21, 1969, 5, http://library.umkc.edu/sites/default/files/images/spec-col/col-1968riot-interview-02-ross.pdf.

154. Clarence Kelley and James Davis, "The Kansas City Cop," *Kansas City Magazine* 12, July 1987, 45.

155. Juhnke, "A City Awakened," 33.

156. Harry Ross, interviewed by Ron Horn, January 21, 1969, 5, http://library.umkc.edu/sites/default/files/images/spec-col/col-1968riot-interview-02-ross.pdf.

157. Paul Brink, "How A Liberal Looks At Kansas City Riots," *Kansas City Call*, April 19-25, 1968.

158. Swomley, "The Kansas City Riot," 10.

159. Juhnke, "A City Awakened," 40-41.

160. Ibid., 42.

161. Brown and Dorsett, *K.C.,* 267.

162. Juhnke, "A City Awakened," 43.

163. Gotham, *Race*, 125-126.

164. Calvin Trillin, "U.S. Journal: Kansas City--I Got Nothing against the Colored," *New Yorker* 44, May 11, 1968, 107.

165. Ibid., 109.

166. Bello and Keen, "40 Years," *USA Today*.

167. Keith Hinch, interviewed by Kenneth King, November 5, 1969, http://library.umkc.edu/sites/default/files/images/spec-col/col-1968riot-interview-03-hinch.pdf.

168. Jefferies, *Ground*, 100.

169. Male 3, interviewed by Robert Bechtel and Kenneth King, http://library.umkc.edu/sites/default/files/images/spec-col/col-1968riot-interview-01-anonymous-student-participants.pdf.

170. Melvin Lewis, "Has Progress Risen From Ashes of 1968 Riot Here?," *Kansas City Star*, April 9, 1973.

171. Trillin, "Kansas City," 110.

172. Ibid.

173. Susan White, "31st and Prospect Six Months Later," *Kansas City Town Squire* 1, November 8, 1968, 22-24.

CHAPTER FIVE

1. Gotham, *Race*, 137.
2. Montgomery and Kasper, *Kansas City*, 335.
3. Gotham, *Race*, 139.
4. Greene, *Black Heritage*, 225.
5. Gotham, *Race*, 146-147; Greene, *Black Heritage*, 217.
6. Burnes and Rice, "Equality," *Kansas City Star*.
7. Wise, *Colorblind*, 98.
8. Ibid., 98.
9. Ibid., 98-99.
10. Lynn Horsley, "Bank of America Accused of Bias in KC," *Kansas City Star*, October 2, 2014.
11. Julia Isaacs, "Economic Mobility of Families Across Generations," Brookings Institute, November 2007, http://www.brookings.edu/research/papers/2007/11/generations-isaacs.
12. "Leona P. Thurman, K.C.'s First Black Lawyer," African American Registry, accessed June 25, 2015, http://www.aaregistry.org/historic_events/view/leona-p-thurman-kcs-first-black-woman-lawyer.
13. Ibid.
14. Associated Press, "KC Black Mafia Once in Control," *Lawrence Journal-World*, July 30, 1971.
15. McGraw and Rice, "Unsolved Killing," Kansas City Star.
16. Mike McGraw and Glenn Rice, "'70s Slaying of KC Politician Leon Jordan a Mob Hit?," *Kansas City Star*, October 30, 2010.
17. Ibid.
18. Mike McGraw and Glenn Rice, "'Evidence Points to Mob's Associate's Involvement in Jordan Killing," *Kansas City Star*, October 31, 2010.
19. Greene, *Black Heritage,* 211.
20. Associated Press, "KC Black Leader is Slain," *Lawrence Journal-World*, April 9, 1979.
21. Mark Morris, "Parole Hearing for Killer in 1980 Hate Crime Reopens Old Wounds," *Kansas City Star*, April 23, 2013.

22. Alvin Sykes, "Investigating Anti-Civil Rights Cases: The Emmett Till Bill" (speech at the Crimes of the Civil Rights Era Conference, Boston, MA, April 27-28, 2007), accessed at http:// nuweb9.neu.edu/civilrights/wp-content/uploads/Sykes_The_ Emmett_Till_Bill.pdf.

23. Morris, "Parole," *Kansas City Star.*

24. Laura Ziegler, "The Life and Work of Kansas City Civil Rights Activist Alvin Sykes," *KCUR.org*, January 9, 2014, http://kcur. org/post/life-and-work-kansas-city-civil-rights-activist-alvin-sykes.

25. Greene, *Black Heritage,* 212.

26. Jeffery T. Ulmer, *Sociology of Crime, Law and Deviance Volume 2* (New York: Elsevier, 2000), 25.

27. Gillis, *Kansas City*, 107; Leon Rosenberg, *Dillard's: The First Fifty Years* (Fayetteville: University of Arkansas Press, 1988), 97.

28. Dave Newbart, "Dillard's--A Store That Just Doesn't Get It," *Phoenix New Times*, July 14, 1993.

29. "NAACP Releases 12th Annual Economic Reciprocity Report Detailing Corporate Diversity Progress," *NAACP.org*, accessed February 17, 2014, http://www.naacp.org/press/entry/naacp-re-leases-12th-annual-economic-reciprocity-report--detailing-cor-porate-diversity-progress/.

30. "Kansas City's First Black Mayor is No Neophyte," *Christian Science Monitor*, 1991, accessed February 17, 2014, http://www. csmonitor.com/1991/0404/akan.html/(page)/2.

31. Associated Press, "KC Teachers Continue Strike," *Lawrence Journal-World*, March 23, 1977.

32. Joshua Dunn, "The Sad History of Kansas City Public Schools," *History News Network*, accessed February 17, 2014, http://www. hnn.us/article/124967.

33. Ibid.

34. R. Shep Meinick, "The Two Billion Dollar Judge," *Claremont Institute*, July 13, 2009, http:// www.claremont.org/publications/ crb/id.1614/article_detail.asp.

35. Gotham, "Missed Opportunities," 26.

36. Gotham, "Missed Opportunities," 26.

37. Emilye Crosby, "School Desegregation and the Courts: Missouri v. Jenkins," review of Joshua Dunn, *Complex Justice*, H-Law, H-Net Reviews, July 2009, http://www.h-net.org/reviews/showrev.php?id=23877.

38. Ibid.

39. Paul Ciotti, "Policy Analysis: Money and School Performance," *Cato Institute*, accessed February 17, 2014, http://www.cato.org/pubs/pas/pa-298.html.

40. Dunn, "Sad History," *History News Network*.

41. Tanner Colby, "The Massive Liberal Failure on Race," *Slate Magazine*, February 3, 2014, http://www.slate.com/articles/life/history/features/2014/the_liberal_failure_on_race/how_the_left_s_embrace_of_busing_hurt_the_cause_of_integration.html.

42. "Effects of Poverty, Hunger, and Homelessness on Children and Youth," *American Psychological Association*, https://www.apa.org/pi/families/poverty.aspx?item=1; Josh Zumbrun, "SAT Scores and Income Inequality: How Wealthier Kids Rank Higher," *Wall Street Journal*, October 7, 2014.

43. Greene, *Black Heritage*, 217, 233; Montgomery and Kasper, *Kansas City*, 342.

44. Meinick, "Two Billion," *Claremont Institute*.

45. Crosby, "School Desegregation," H-Net.

46. Richard Hardy, Richard Dohm and David Leuthold, *Missouri Government and Politics* (Columbia: University of Missouri Press, 1995), 235.

47. Ciotti, "Money," *Cato Institute*.

48. "Suit Says Magnet Schools Bar Black Children," *New York Times*, August 3, 1989.

49. Mary Sanchez, "What I Learned from the Rev. Nelson 'Fuzzy' Thompson," *The Kansas City Star*, January 13, 2015.

50. Justice Clarence Thomas concurrence, *Missouri v. Jenkins* (93-1823), 515 U.S. 70 (1995), June 12, 1995, accessed at http://www.law.cornell.edu/supct/html/93-1823.ZC1.html.

51. Ciotti, "Money," *Cato Institute*.

52. Colby, "Liberal Failure," *Slate*.

53. Susan Saulny, "Board's Decision to Close 28 Kansas City Schools Follows Years of Inaction," *New York Times*, March 11, 2010.

54. Gwendolyn Grant, "Free at Last!," *Urban League of Greater Kansas City*, July 27, 2007, http://archive.is/thPXN#selection-647.0-651.385.

55. Gotham, "Missed Opportunities," 7.

56. Schirmer, *Divided*, 2.

57. Joe Robertson, "Failed Deal Between KC Schools, Academie Lafayette Reveals City's Issues with Race and Education," Kansas City Star, March 15, 2015.

58. Mark Smith, March 11, 2015 (8:49 a.m.), comment on "TKC Breaking and Exclusive News!!! Mainstream Media Fails to Report Overwhelming Community Opposition Stopped Kansas City Public Schools and Academie Lafayette Partnerships!!!," *Tony's Kansas City* (blog), March 11, 2015 (8:15 a.m.), http://www.tonyskansascity.com/2015/03/tkc-breaking-and-exclusive-news_11.html.

59. Anonymous, March 10, 2015 (4:52 p.m.), comment on "TKC Breaking News!!! Community Groups Stop Kansas City Public Schools Partnership with Academie Lafayette @ Southwest Campus!!!," *Tony's Kansas City* (blog), March 10, 2015 (2:57 p.m.), http://www.tonyskansascity.com/2015/03/tkc-breaking-news-community-groups-stop.html.

60. Anonymous, March 10, 2015 (7:47 p.m.), Ibid.

61. Jonathan Kozol, *The Shame of the Nation* (New York: Crown Publishers, 2005), 18.

62. "Civil Rights Project Reports Deepening Segregation and Challenges Educators and Political Leaders to Develop Positive Policies," *UCLA Civil Rights Project*, September 19, 2012, http://civilrightsproject.ucla. edu/news/press-releases/crp-press-releases-2012/civil-rights-project-reports-deepening-segregation-and-challenges-educators-and-political-leaders-to-develop-positive-policies.

63. Randy Miller, "Race Indeed Does Matter in the Classroom," *Huffington Post*, March 10, 2013, http://www.huffingtonpost.com/randy-miller/race-schools_b_2847603.html.

64. Gotham, "Missed Opportunities," 5.

65. "School Demographic Profile for Silver City Elementary School," *kckps.org*, October 2011, http://kckps.org/dera/demographics/silver_city.pdf.

66. Demographic information for the Metropolitan Avenue / S. 29th Street area, *Neighborhood Scout*, accessed February 17, 2014, http://www.neighborhoodscout.com/reports/10077412/#desc.

67. School profile handout, *Visitation School*, 2013.

68. "64113 Zip Code Detailed Profile," *City Data*, accessed February 17, 2014, http://www.city-data.com/zips/64113.html.

69. Kozol, *Shame*, 11.

70. John Logan and Brian Stults, "The Persistence of Segregation in the Metropolis: New Findings from the 2010 Census," census brief prepared for Project US2010, March 24, 2011, 6-7, http://www.s4.brown.edu/us2010/Data/Report/report2.pdf.

71. Judy L. Thomas, "Only a Matter of Time: Inside the American Extremist Movements," *Kansas City Star*, April 26, 2015.

72. Ishaan Tharoor, "In Facebook Photo, Suspected Charleston Shooter Wears Flags of Racist Regimes in Africa," *Washington Post*, June 18, 2015, http://www.washingtonpost.com/blogs/worldviews/wp/2015/06/18/in-facebook-photo-suspected-charleston-shooter-wears-flags-of-racist-regimes-in-africa/.

73. Travis Gettys, "Terrorist Targeted Historic SC Church on 193rd Anniversary of Thwarted Slave Revolt Planned by its Founder," *Raw Story*, June 18, 2015, http://www.rawstory.com/2015/06/terrorist-targeted-historic-sc-church-on-193rd-anniversary-of-thwarted-slave-revolt-planned-by-its-founder/.

74. Ralph Ellis, Ed Payne, Evan Perez, and Dana Ford, "Shooting Suspect in Custody After Charleston Church Massacre," *CNN*, June 18, 2015, http://www.cnn.com/2015/06/18/us/charleston-south-carolina-shooting/index.html.

75. "Fox's Steve Doocy: It's Extraordinary That Charleston Church Shooting is Being Called a Hate Crime," *Media Matters*, June 18, 2015, http://mediamatters.org/video/2015/06/18/foxs-steve-doocy-its-extraordinary-that-charles/204043.

76. Adam Johnson, "Dylann Roof's Manifesto Discovered by Online Activists, Lays Out 'Race War' Motiviation," *Alternet*, June 20, 2015, http://www.alternet.org/breaking-dylann-roofs-manifesto-discovered-online-activists-lays-out-race-war-motivation.

77. Anthea Butler, "Shooters of Color are Called 'Terrorists' and 'Thugs.' Why are White Shooters Called 'Mentally Ill'?" *Common Dreams*, June 19, 2015, http://www.commondreams.org/views/2015/06/19/shooters-color-are-called-terrorists-and-thugs-why-are-white-shooters-called.

78. Dara Lind, "Here's Why I'm Skeptical of Roland Fryer's New, Much-Hyped Study on Police Shootings," *Vox*, July 11, 2016, http://www.vox.com/2016/7/11/12149468/racism-police-shootings-data.

79. Glenn Rice, "Four Are Arrested in a Small Ferguson Protest Near the Country Club Plaza," *Kansas City Star*, November 28, 2014.

80. Cody Newill, "#Blacklivesmatter Protesters Arrested After Attempt to Block I-70 in Kansas City," *KCUR*, December 21, 2014, http://kcur.org/post/blacklivesmatter-protesters-arrested-after-attempt-block-i-70-kansas-city.

81. Mary Sanchez, "Kansas City Chose Community Over Chaos," *Kansas City Star*, August 14, 2014.

82. Donald Bradley, "Neo-Nazi Group Demonstration Draws Counter Protests in Kansas City," *Kansas City Star*, November 9, 2013.

83. Thomas, "Only a Matter of Time," *Kansas City Star*.

84. Associated Press, "KC District Changes Controversial Dress Code," *The Grio*, MSNBC, May 28, 2010, http://thegrio.com/2010/05/28/kc-district-changes-controversial-dress-code/.

85. Laura Ziegler, "New Lawsuit Alleges Racial Discrimination at Power & Light," *KCUR.org*, March 6, 2014, http://kcur.org/

post/new-lawsuit-alleges-racial-discrimination-power-and-light?-nopop=1.

86. Diane Stafford, "Class-Action Lawsuit Alleges Racial Discrimination at Power & Light," *Kansas City Star*, March 10, 2014.

87. Mike Hendricks, "Judge Tosses Lawsuit that Alleged Racial Discrimination at the Power & Light District," *Kansas City Star*, June 16, 2015.

88. "Report Details Plaza Disorder, Previous Incidents," *KCTV5*, April 12, 2010, http://www.kctv5.com/story/14782696/report-details-plaza-disorder-previous-incidents-4-12-2010.

89. Dave Eckert and Chris Oberholtz, "Police Use Pepper Spray to Break Up Plaza Fight Among Teens," *KCTV5*, September 15, 2013, http://www.kctv5.com/story/23436263/police-use-pepper-spray-to-break-up-plaza-fight-among-teens.

90. Katie Ferrell, "KCMO Police Arrest Juveniles Involved in Fights on the Plaza," *Fox4*, February 16, 2014, http://fox4kc.com/2014/02/16/kcmo-police-arrest-juveniles-involved-in-fights-on-the-plaza/.

91. Glenn E. Rice and Lynn Horsley, "Authorities Want to Kill 'Coffin' Trend After Teens Arrested on Country Club Plaza," *Kansas City Star*, April 6, 2015.

92. Colin Flaherty, "Kansas City Blues: Violent Black Mobs," *WorldNetDaily*, February 17, 2014, http://www.wnd.com/2014/02/kansas-city-dilemma-violent-black-mobs/.

93. Ibid.

94. eyholmess, April 6, 2015 (8:56 a.m.), comment on "Unruly Teens Arrested at Kansas City's Country Club Plaza After Jumping onto the Hoods of Cars," *Mass Appeal News*, April 6, 2015, http://www.massappealnews.com/2015/04/06/unruly-teens-arrested-at-kansas-citys-country-club-plaza-after-jumping-onto-the-hoods-of-cars/.

95. otherside65, April 6, 2015 (3:17 p.m.), Ibid.

96. Gunjack, April 6, 2015 (10:51 p.m.), Ibid.

97. Anonymous, May 16, 2013 (3:09 p.m.), comment on "'It's Only Going to Make a Lot of Black Kids Angry'—Kansas City

Moves to Save 'The Plaza' from Organized Blackness," *Stuff Black People Don't Like* (blog), May 16, 2013, http://stuffblackpeople-dontlike.blogspot.com/2013/05/its-only-going-to-make-lot-of-black.html.

98. rex freeway, May 16, 2013 (7:10 p.m.), Ibid.

99. Moondoggie, May 16, 2013 (7:18 p.m.), Ibid.

100. Anonymous, May 16, 2013 (7:29 p.m.), Ibid.

101. Anonymous, May 16, 2013 (7:36 p.m.), Ibid.

102. Wayne Hodges, "Racism in KC Bad for Business," *Examiner*, November 17, 2009; Lisa Gutierrez, "A Civics Lesson Gets Real," *Kansas City Star*, August 24, 2014; Associated Press, "Woman Who Miscarried After Arrest Sues Police," *NBC*, February 1, 2007; Associated Press, "Police Chief Wants K.C. Officer Fired," *Lawrence Journal-World*, June 28, 2007; Lisa Benson, "Man Files Formal Complaint Alleging Police Brutality," *KSHB*, December 21, 2010; Katie Banks, "ACLU Files Suit Claiming Young Boy's Rights Were Violated When He Was Handcuffed at KC Elementary School," *Fox4*, September 8, 2016.

103. Daniel Boothe and Mike McGraw, "Official Reports About the Shooting of Ryan Stokes Raise More Questions Than Answers," *Flatland*, July 30, 2015, http://www.flatlandkc.org/news-issues/official-police-story-shooting-ryan-stokes-raises-doubts-why/.

104. "Guilty Verdicts in Kansas City Hate-Crime Murder," *Crime Scene KC* (blog), *Kansas City Star*, May 8, 2008, http://blogs.kansascity.com/crime_scene/2008/05/guilty-verdicts.html.

105. Mark Morris, "Two Independence Residents are Sentenced in Hate Crime," *Kansas City Star*, January 23, 2013.

106. Sarah Netter, "Missouri Man Shocked at Being Labeled N-Word on Store Receipt," *ABC News*, October 22, 2008, http://abcnews.go.com/US/story?id=6088706.

107. "Hate Incidents," *Southern Poverty Law Center*, accessed May 22, 2015, https://www.splcenter.org/fighting-hate/hate-incidents?keyword=; "KC Man Arrested After Gunfire, Racial Taunts," *Kansas City Star*, January 2, 2009.

108. Mark Morris, "Parolee is Accused of Hate Crime in Platte County," *Kansas City Star*, March 7, 2013.

109. Amy Hawley, "Kansas City Fire Department Sued for Racism," *KSHB Kansas City 41*, February 19, 2014, http://www.kshb.com/news/local-news/kc-fire-dept-sued-for-racism.

110. Wise, "What Whites Don't Know."

111. "2014 Hate Crime Statistics," *FBI.gov*, accessed February 1, 2015, https://www.fbi.gov/about-us/cjis/ucr/hate-crime/2014/topic-pages/victims_final; J. Richard Cohen, "The FBI Has No Idea How Many Hate Crimes Happen in America Each Year," *Washington Post*, June 19, 2015.

112. "White Guy, Black Girl and Dinner. My First Taste of Racism," *CNN iReport*, October 18, 2009, http://ireport.cnn.com/docs/DOC-343043.

113. Sarah B. Heller, "Summer Jobs Reduce Violence Among Disadvantaged Youth," *Science* 346 (December 5, 2014): 1219-1223.

114. Wilkins, *Standing Fast*, 65; Brown and Dorsett, *K.C.*, 267.

115. Robert Pearman, "Black Crime, Black Victims," *Nation* 208 (April 21, 1969): 502.

116. Ibid., 501.

117. Ibid.

118. Ibid., 503.

119. Glenn Rice and Tony Rizzo, "Police Fall Short in Racial Diversity," *Kansas City Star*, August 24, 2014.

120. Charles Epp, Steven Maynard-Moody, and Donald Haider-Markel, *Pulled Over* (Chicago: University of Chicago Press, 2014), 155, 71, 61, 156, 86-88.

121. Diane Stafford, "Kansas City 'Peace Rally' Lauds Police-Community Cooperation," *Kansas City Star*, May 2, 2015.

122. "Report on Interviews with Planning Group Members," *Kansas City Round Table on Access and Opportunity*, April 19, 2006, http://www.aspeninstitute.org/sites/default/files/content/docs/rcc/KCRT_PLANNING_GROUP_-_REPORT_ON_INTERVIEWS.PDF.

123. Schirmer, *Divided*, 143, 141.

124. "KC Still Has a Deplorably High Murder Rate Ranking," *Kansas City Star*, December 2, 2014.

125. "Equality Index," *University of Missouri-Kansas City*, 24.

126. "Kansas City, Missouri Police Department Daily Homicide Analysis," *KCMO.org*, December 31, 2014, http://kcmo.gov/police/wp-content/uploads/sites/2/2013/10/DailyHomicide-Analysis2014-12-31.pdf.

127. Riva Gold, "Newsroom Diversity: A Casualty of Journalism's Financial Crisis," *Atlantic*, July 9, 2013.

128. "America's Newsrooms Fail to Match U.S. Diversity," *National Association of Black Journalists*, April 7, 2011, http://www.nabj.org/?page=ASNEsonDiversity.

129. Seong-Jae Min and John Feaster, "Missing Children in National News Coverage: Racial and Gender Representations of Missing Children Cases," *Communications Research Reports 27*, no. 3 (July-September 2010): 213.

130. Carimah Townes, "How News Outlets Help Convince You That Most Criminals Are Black," *Think Progress*, March 25, 2015; Melissa Carroll, "UH Study Finds News Media May Influence Racial Bias," *University of Houston*, May 28, 2015.

131. "Food Stamp Usage Across the Country," *New York Times*, November 28, 2009, http://www.nytimes.com/interactive/2009/11/28/us/20091128-foodstamps.html?_r=1&.

132. Shelley Irving and Tracy Loveless, "Dynamics of Economic Well-Being," *U.S. Census Bureau*, May 2015; Martin Gilens, *Why Americans Hate Welfare: Race, Media and the Politics of Antipoverty Policy* (Chicago: University of Chicago Press, 1999), 123.

133. Katherine Beckett, "Race and Drug Law Enforcement in Seattle," *ACLU*, September 2008, https://www.aclu.org/files/assets/race20and20drug20law20enforcement20in20seattle_20081.pdf; Ryan S. King, "Disparity by Geography," *Sentencing Project*, May 2008, http://www.sentencingproject.org/wp-content/uploads/2016/01/Disparity-by-Geography-The-War-on-Drugs-in-Americas-Cities.pdf.

134. "National Survey on Drug Use and Health Report: Substance Use and Mental Disorders in the Kansas City MSA," Substance Abuse and Mental Health Services Adminitration, 2012; Jamie Fellner, "Race, Drugs, and Law Enforcement in the United States," *Human Rights Watch*, June 19, 2009.

135. Loewen, *Sundown Towns*, 389.

136. Gotham, *Race*, 149-150.

137. Schirmer, *Divided*, 3.

138. DeAnn Smith and Heather Staggers, "Lee's Summit North Student Disciplined for Racist Blog," *KCTV5*, December 16, 2011.

139. Julia Poe, "Is East Racist?," *Harbinger*, accessed May 22, 2015, http://smeharbinger.net/is-east-racist.

140. "Hate Incidents," *Southern Poverty Law Center*, accessed May 22, 2015, http://www.splcenter.org/get-informed/hate-incidents?year=&state=MO.

141. "Equality Index," *University of Missouri-Kansas City*, 8-11, 24.

142. Ibid., 14.

143. Ibid., 13-17.

144. Ibid., 19.

145. "Steady March Toward Accreditation," *Kansas City Star*, March 2, 2015.

146. Lewis Diuguid, "Urban League Report Shows Blacks and Latinos Continue to Lag Behind Whites in Kansas City Area," *Kansas City Star*, February 13, 2015.

147. Joe Robertson, "Missouri's Suspension Rate of Black Elementary Students Highest in the Nation," *Kansas City Star*, February 23, 2015.

148. Nicholas Bianchi, "Profiting from Poverty," *National People's Action*, January 2012, http://npa-us.org/files/images/profiting_from_poverty_npa_payday_loan_report_jan_2012_0.pdf.

149. *We Are Superman: The Transformation of 31st and Troost*, directed by Kevin Bryce (2012; Kansas City, MO).

150. Kozol, *Shame*, 10.

BIBLIOGRAPHY

"2014 Hate Crime Statistics." *FBI.gov.* Accessed February 1, 2014. https://www.fbi.gov/about-us/cjis/ucr/hate-crime/2014/topic-pages/victims_final.

"2,500 Hear Martin L. King in Kansas City." *Kansas City Call,* April 18, 1957.

"64113 Zip Code Detailed Profile." *City Data.* Accessed February 17, 2014. http://www.city-data.com/zips/64113.html.

Alkebulan, Paul. *Survival Pending Revolution.* Tuscaloosa: University of Alabama Press, 2007.

"America's Newsrooms Fail to Match U.S. Diversity." *National Association of Black Journalists.* April 7, 2011. http://www.nabj.org/?page=ASNEsonDiversity.

"Assassination Conspiracy Trial." *Martin Luther King, Jr. Center for Nonviolent Social Change.* Accessed February 17, 2014. http://www.thekingcenter.org/assassination-conspiracy-trial.

Associated Press. "KC Black Leader is Slain." *Lawrence Journal-World,* April 9, 1979.

Associated Press. "KC Black Mafia Once in Control." *Lawrence Journal-World,* July 30, 1971.

Associated Press. "KC District Changes Controversial Dress Code." *The Grio, MSNBC,* May 28, 2010. http://thegrio.com/2010/05/28/kc-district-changes-controversial-dress-code/.

Associated Press. "KC Teachers Continue Strike." *Lawrence Journal-World,* March 23, 1977.

Associated Press. "Wealth Gap Widens Between Whites and Minorities." *Kansas City Star,* December 12, 2014.

Athearn, Robert. *In Search of Canaan: Black Migration to Kansas, 1879-80.* Lawrence: The Regents Press of Kansas, 1978.

Beckenbaugh, Terry. "Battle of Westport." *Civil War on the Western Border.* Kansas City Public Library. Accessed February 17, 2014. http://www.civilwaronthewesternborder.org/content/battle-westport-0.

Bello, Marisol and Judy Keen. "40 Years After the Riot, King's Vision 'Unfinished.'" *USA Today*, January 20, 2008.

Bianchi, Nicholas. "Profiting from Poverty." *National People's Action.* January 2012. http://npa-us.org/files/images/profiting_from_poverty_npa_payday_loan_report_jan_2012_0.pdf.

"Black Panther Party: Kansas City and Beyond." *United African Alliance Community Center.* Accessed February 17, 2014. http://www.uaacc.habari.co.tz/black_panther_party_in_kansas_ci.htm.

"The Black Panther Party." *Marxists.org.* Accessed February 17, 2014. http://www.marxists.org/ history/usa/workers/black-panthers/.

Blassingame, John. *The Slave Community.* Oxford: Oxford University Press, 1979.

Blassingame, John. *Slave Testimony.* Baton Rouge: Louisiana State University Press, 1977.

Bluford, Lucile. "Answers Sought By Citizens." *Kansas City Call*, April 19-25, 1968.

Blumrosen, Alfred W. and Ruth G. Blumrosen. *Slave Nation: How Slavery United the Colonies and Sparked the American Revolution.* Naperville, Illinois: Sourcebooks, Inc., 2006.

"The Boss' Buddies." *University of Missouri-Kansas City Library.* Accessed February 17, 2014. http://library.umkc.edu/spec-col/parisoftheplains/webexhibit/political/pol-02.htm.

Bradley, Donald. "Neo-Nazi Group Demonstration Draws Counter Protests in Kansas City." *Kansas City Star,* November 9, 2013.

Bradley, Donald. "Region's History of Lynchings Overlooked." *Kansas City Star*, February 22, 2015.

"A Brief History from 'A Walking Tour of Historic Parkville.'" *ParkvilleMO.gov.*   Accessed   February 15, 2014. http://parkvillemo.gov/visitors/history/.

Brink, Paul. "How A Liberal Looks At Kansas City Riots." *Kansas City Call*, April 19-25, 1968.

Brown, A. Theodore and Lyle W. Dorsett. *K.C: A History of Kansas City, Missouri.* Boulder, Colorado: Pruett Publishing, 1978.

Burnes, Brian. *Harry S. Truman: His Life and Times.* Kansas City: Kansas City Star Books, 2003.

Burnes, Brian and Glenn Rice. "Enforcing Equality: Kansas City Continues to Fight for Civil Rights." *Kansas City Star,* January 18, 2014.

Burnes, Brian and Glenn Rice. "Progress Marches On." *Kansas City Star*, January 19, 2015.

Butler, Anthea. "Shooters of Color are Called 'Terrorists' and 'Thugs.' Why are White Shooters Called 'Mentally Ill'?" *Common Dreams*, June 19, 2015. http://www.commondreams.org/views/2015/06/19/shooters-color-are-called-terrorists-and-thugs-why-are-white-shooters-called.

Central Alabama Citizens Council. "Declaration of Segregation" handbill. Montgomery, Alabama. 10 February 1956. In *Daybreak of Freedom: The Montgomery Bus Boycott*, edited by Stewart Burns, 154. Chapel Hill, N.C.: University of North Carolina Press, 1997.

Ciotti, Paul. "Policy Analysis: Money and School Performance." *Cato Institute.* Accessed February 17, 2014. http://www.cato.org/pubs/pas/pa-298.html.

"Citizens Join in Plea for End of Violence." *Kansas City Times*, April 12, 1968.

"Civil Rights Project Reports Deepening Segregation and Challenges Educators and Political Leaders to Develop Positive Policies." *UCLA Civil Rights Project.* September 19, 2012. http://civilrightsproject.ucla.edu/news/press-releases/crp-press-releases-2012/civil-rights-project-reports-deepening-

segregation-and-challenges-educators-and-political-leaders-to-
develop-positive-policies.

Cohen, J. Richard. "The FBI Has No Idea How Many Hate Crimes
Happen in America Each Year." *Washington Post*, June 19,
2015, http://www.washingtonpost.com/posteverything/
wp/2015/06/19/there-are-260000-hate-crimes-in-america-
each-year-why-does-the-fbi-think-there-are-only-6000/.

Coulter, Charles. *Take Up the Black Man's Burden: Kansas City's African
American Communities, 1865-1939*. Columbia: University of
Missouri Press, 2006.

Colby, Tanner. "The Massive Liberal Failure on Race." *Slate Magazine*.
February 3, 2014. http://www.slate.com/articles/life/history/
features/2014/the_liberal_failure_on_race/how_the_left_s_
embrace_of_busing_hurt_the_cause_of_integration.html.

Colby, Tanner. *Some of My Best Friends Are Black*. New York: Penguin,
2012.

Crosby, Emilye. "School Desegregation and the Courts: Missouri
v. Jenkins." Review of Joshua Dunn, *Complex Justice*. H-Net
Reviews, July 2009. http://www.h-net.org/reviews/showrev.
php?id=23877.

Curtis, William J. *A Rich Heritage: A Black History of Independence,
Missouri*. Traco Enterprises, 1985.

Demographic information for the Metropolitan Avenue / S. 29th Street
area. *Neighborhood Scout*. Accessed February 17, 2014. http://
www.neighborhoodscout.com/reports/ 10077412/#desc.

Diuguid, Lewis. "Urban League Report Shows Blacks and Latinos
Continue to Lag Behind Whites in Kansas City Area." *Kansas
City Star*, February 13, 2015.

Dorsett, Lyle W. "Slaveholding in Jackson County, Missouri." *Missouri
Historical Society Bulletin* 20 (October 1963): 25-27, 30.

Dreier, Peter. "Martin Luther King Jr.: One of the Nation's Great
Democratic Socialists." *Common Dreams*, January 18, 2016.
http://www.commondreams.org/views/2016/01/18/martin-
luther-king-jr-one-nations-great-democratic-socialists.

Dunn, Joshua. "The Sad History of Kansas City Public Schools." *History News Network.* Accessed February 17, 2014. http://www.hnn.us/article/124967.

Durant, Will and Ariel Durant. *The Lessons of History.* New York: Simon & Schuster, 1968.

Earle, Jonathan and Diane Mutti Burke. *Bleeding Kansas, Bleeding Missouri.* Lawrence, KS: University Press of Kansas, 2013.

Eckert, Dave and Chris Oberholtz. "Police Use Pepper Spray to Break Up Plaza Fight Among Teens." *KCTV5,* September 15, 2013. http://www.kctv5.com/story/23436263/police-use-pepper-spray-to-break-up-plaza-fight-among-teens.

"Effects of Poverty, Hunger, and Homelessness on Children and Youth." *American Psychological Association.* Accessed March 17, 2014. https://www.apa.org/pi/families/poverty.aspx?item=1.

El Nasser, Haya. "Cities Moving Beyond Segregation." *USA Today,* December 7, 2011. http://usatoday30.usatoday.com/news/nation/story/2011-12-06/segregation-kansas-city/51694850/1.

Ellis, Ralph, Ed Payne, Evan Perez, and Dana Ford. "Shooting Suspect in Custody After Charleston Church Massacre." *CNN,* June 18, 2015. http://www.cnn.com/2015/06/18/us/charleston-south-carolina-shooting/index.html.

Epp, Charles, Steven Maynard-Moody, and Donald Haider-Markel. *Pulled Over.* Chicago: University of Chicago Press, 2014.

Epps, Kristen. *Bound Together: Masters and Slaves on the Kansas-Missouri Border, 1825-1865.* Doctoral dissertation, University of Kansas, 2010. http://kuscholarworks.ku.edu/handle/1808/6441.

"Esther Brown." *Kansas Historical Society.* Last modified January 2013. http://www.kshs.org/ kansapedia/esther-brown/11991.

Faraj, Gaidi. *Unearthing the Underground: A Study of Radical Activism in the Black Panther Party and the Black Liberation Army.* Doctoral dissertation, University of California, Berkeley, 2007.

Fellner, Jamie. "Race, Drugs, and Law Enforcement in the United States." *Human Rights Watch,* June 19, 2009. http://www.

hrw.org/news/2009/06/19/race-drugs-and-law-enforcement-united-states.

Ferrell, Katie. "KCMO Police Arrest Juveniles Involved in Fights on the Plaza." *Fox4*, February 16, 2014. http://fox4kc.com/2014/02/16/kcmo-police-arrest-juveniles-involved-in-fights-on-the-plaza/.

"A Few Fascinating Missouri Civil War Facts." *Missouri Civil War Museum*. Accessed February 17, 2014. http://www.mcwm.org/history_facts.html.

Flaherty, Colin. "Kansas City Blues: Violent Black Mobs." *WorldNetDaily*, February 17, 2014. http://www.wnd.com/2014/02/kansas-city-dilemma-violent-black-mobs/.

Fly, David. "An Episcopal Priest's Reflections on the Kansas City Riot of 1968." *Missouri Historical Review* 100, no. 2 (2006): 106-107.

"Fox's Steve Doocy: It's Extraordinary That Charleston Church Shooting is Being Called a Hate Crime." *Media Matters*, June 18, 2015. http://mediamatters.org/video/2015/06/18/foxs-steve-doocy-its-extraordinary-that-charles/204043.

Froese, Andrea. "Slavery in Jackson County and Missouri." *Jackson County Historical Society Journal* 39, no. 3 (1999): 14.

Fuenfhausen, Gary Gene. "A Short History of the Institution of Slavery in Clay County, Missouri." Accessed May 25, 2015. http://littledixie.net/slavery_in_clay_county.htm.

Garrow, David. *Bearing the Cross*. New York: HarperCollins, 2004.

Gettys, Travis. "Terrorist Targeted Historic SC Church on 193rd Anniversary of Thwarted Slave Revolt Planned by its Founder." *Raw Story*, June 18, 2015. http://www.rawstory.com/2015/06/terrorist-targeted-historic-sc-church-on-193rd-anniversary-of-thwarted-slave-revolt-planned-by-its-founder/.

Gibson, Sonny. *Kansas City: Mecca of the New Negro*. Kansas City: 1997.

Gilens, Martin. *Why Americans Hate Welfare: Race, Media and the Politics of Antipoverty Policy*. Chicago: University of Chicago Press, 1999.

Gillis, Delia. *Kansas City.* Mount Pleasant, SC: Arcadia, 2007.

Gold, Riva. "Newsroom Diversity: A Casualty of Journalism's Financial Crisis." *Atlantic*, July 9, 2013. http://www.theatlantic.com/national/archive/2013/07/newsroom-diversity-a-casualty-of-journalisms-financial-crisis/277622/.

Gotham, Kevin F. "A City Without Slums." *American Journal of Economics and Sociology* 60, no. 1 (January 2001): 307.

Gotham, Kevin F. "Missed Opportunities, Enduring Legacies: School Segregation and Desegregation in Kansas City, Missouri." *American Studies* 43, no. 2 (2002): 5.

Gotham, Kevin F. *Race, Real Estate, and Uneven Development: The Kansas City Experience, 1900-2000.* Albany: State University of New York Press, 2002.

Gould, Stephen Jay. *The Mismeasure of Man.* New York: W. W. Norton & Company, 1996.

Grant, Gwendolyn. "Free at Last!" *Urban League of Greater Kansas City*, July 27, 2007. http://archive.is/thPXN#selection-647.0-651.385.

Greenbaum, Susan. *The Afro-American Community in Kansas City, Kansas.* Kansas City, Kansas Department of Community Development, 1980.

Greene, Lorenzo, Gary Kremer, and Antonio Holland. *Missouri's Black Heritage.* Columbia: University of Missouri, 1993.

Grenz, Suzanna M. "The Exodusters of 1879: St. Louis and Kansas City Responses." *Missouri Historical Review* 73 (October 1978): 64.

"Guilty Verdicts in Kansas City Hate-Crime Murder." *Crime Scene KC* (blog), *Kansas City Star*, May 8, 2008. http://blogs.kansascity.com/crime_scene/2008/05/guilty-verdicts.html.

Gutierrez, Lisa. "A Civics Lesson Gets Real." *Kansas City Star*, August 24, 2014.

Hanzlick, K. David. *Rendering Assistance to Best Advantage: The Development of Women's Activism in Kansas City, 1870 to World War I.* Doctoral dissertation, University of Missouri-Kansas

City, 2013. https://mospace.umsystem.edu/xmlui/bitstream/ handle/ 10355/35461/HanzlickRenAssBes.pdf?sequence=1.

Hardy, Richard, Richard Dohm and David Leuthold. *Missouri Government and Politics*. Columbia: University of Missouri Press, 1995.

Harman, Chris. *How Marxism Works*. London: Bookmarks, 1986.

Harman, Chris. *A People's History of the World*. London: Verso, 2008.

"Hate Incidents." *Southern Poverty Law Center*. Accessed May 22, 2015. http:// www.splcenter.org/get-informed/hate-incidents?year=&state=MO.

Hawley, Amy. "Kansas City Fire Department Sued for Racism." *KSHB Kansas City 41*, February 19, 2014. http://www.kshb. com/news/local-news/kc-fire-dept-sued-for-racism.

Heffernan, William and John Kleinig. *From Social Justice to Criminal Justice*. Oxford: Oxford University Press, 2000.

Hendricks, Mike. "Judge Tosses Lawsuit that Alleged Racial Discrimination at the Power & Light District." *Kansas City Star*, June 16, 2015.

Hinch, Keith. Interviewed by Kenneth King. November 5, 1969. http://library.umkc.edu/sites/default/files/images/spec-col/col-1968riot-interview-03-hinch.pdf.

Hinks, Peter, John McKivigan, and R. Williams. *Encyclopedia of Antislavery and Abolition* 1. Westport, CT: Greenwood Publishing, 2007.

The History of Jackson County, Missouri. Kansas City: Union Historical Company, 1881.

"The History of the Kansas City Call." *Black Archives of Mid-America*. Accessed February 8, 2014. http://www.blackarchives.org/ articles/history-kansas-city-call.

Hodes, Martha. *White Women, Black Men*. New Haven, CT: Yale University Press, 1999.

Hodges, Wayne. "Racism in KC Bad for Business." *Examiner*, November 17, 2009. http://www.examiner.com/article/racism-kc-bad-for-business.

Hogan, Suzanne. "Highway 71 and the Road to Compromise." *KCUR*, June 3, 2014. http://kcur.org/post/highway-71-and-road-compromise.

Horsley, Lynn. "Bank of America Accused of Bias in KC." *Kansas City Star*, October 2, 2014.

Hutchinson, Van William. *Greater Kansas City and the Urban Crisis, 1830-1968.* Doctoral dissertation, Kansas State University, 2013. http://krex.k-state.edu/dspace/bitstream/handle/2097/16896/ VanHutchison2013.pdf?sequence=1.

"Inquiry Ordered in Missouri Mob's Burning of Negro." *Albany Evening News,* November 29, 1933.

Isaacs, Julia. "Economic Mobility of Families Across Generations." Brookings Institute, November 2007. http://www.brookings.edu/research/papers/2007/11/generations-isaacs.

Jackson, Kenneth. *The Ku Klux Klan in the City, 1915-1930.* New York: Oxford University Press, 1967.

Jefferies, Judson. *On the Ground.* Jackson: University Press of Mississippi, 2010.

Johnson, Adam. "Dylann Roof's Manifesto Discovered by Online Activists, Lays Out 'Race War' Motiviation." *Alternet*, June 20, 2015. http://www.alternet.org/breaking-dylann-roofs-manifesto-discovered-online-activists-lays-out-race-war-motivation.

Juhnke, Eric. "A City Awakened: The Kansas City Race Riot of 1968." *Gateway Heritage* 20 (winter 1999-2000): 35.

"Kansas City's First Black Mayor is No Neophyte." *Christian Science Monitor*, 1991. http://www.csmonitor.com/1991/0404/akan.html/(page)/2.

"Kansas City, Missouri Police Department Daily Homicide Analysis." *KCMO.org.* December 31, 2014. http://kcmo.gov/police/wp-content/uploads/sites/2/2013/10/DailyHomicideAnalysis2014-12-31.pdf.

"Kansas City, MO. et al. v. Williams et al." *Rutgers School of Law.* Accessed April 3, 2015. http://njlaw.rutgers.edu/collections/resource.org/fed_reporter/F2/205/205.F2d.47_1.html.

"Kansas City Riot Loss Set At Four Million." *Kansas City Call,* April 19-25, 1968.

"KC Still Has a Deplorably High Murder Rate Ranking." *Kansas City Star,* December 2, 2014.

"Kathryn Johnson, A Front Line Activist." *African American Registry.* Accessed February 10, 2014. http://www.aaregistry.org/ historic_events/view/kathryn-johnson-front-line-activist.

Katz, Milton and Susan Tucker. "A Pioneer in Civil Rights." *Kansas History* 18 (Winter 1995/1996): 236-237.

Kelley, Clarence and James Davis. "The Kansas City Cop." *Kansas City Magazine* 12, July 1987, 45.

Kerby, Sophia. "The Top 10 Most Startling Facts About People of Color and Criminal Justice in the United States." *Center for American Progress.* March 13, 2012. http://www.americanprogress. org/issues/race/news/2012/03/13/11351/the-top-10-most-startling-facts-about-people-of-color-and-criminal-justice-in-the-united-states/.

King, Martin Luther. *The Papers of Martin Luther King, Jr.* 4. Los Angeles: University of California Press, 2000.

King, Martin Luther. "Where Do We Go From Here?" Speech at the 11th Annual Southern Christian Leadership Conference Convention, Atlanta, GA, August 16, 1967.

"King v. Jowers Conspiracy Allegations." *U.S. Department of Justice.* Accessed February 17, 2014. http://www.justice.gov/crt/about/ crm/mlk/part6.php.

Kirkendall, Richard S. *A History of Missouri: Volume V, 1919 to 1953.* Columbia: University of Missouri Press, 1986.

Klamm, Ken. "Blacks in Platte County." *Platte County Missouri Historical & Genealogical Society Bulletin* 59, no. 1 (January/ February 2006): 9.

Knafo, Saki. "When it Comes to Illegal Drug Use, White America Does the Crime, Black America Gets the Time." *Huffington Post,* September 17, 2013. http:// www.huffingtonpost. com/2013/09/17/racial-disparity-drug-use_n_3941346.html.

Kozol, Jonathan. *The Shame of the Nation: The Restoration of Apartheid Schooling in America*. New York: Crown Publishers, 2005.

Kremer, Gary. "Just Like the Garden of Eden." In *Kansas City, America's Crossroads: Essays from the Missouri Historical Review, 1906-2006*, edited by Diane Mutti Burke and John Herron. Columbia: State Historical Society of Missouri, 2007.

"Last Ride for Jim Crow." African-American Migration Experience. Accessed November 1, 2014. http://www.inmotionaame.org/gallery/detail.cfm?migration=11&topic=3&id=601005&type=image&metadata=show&page=.

Laughlin, Jennifer. "Corvine Patterson." *Historical Journal of Wyandotte County* 2 (June 28, 1905): 319-320.

"Leona P. Thurman, K.C.'s First Black Lawyer." African American Registry. Accessed June 25, 2015. http://www.aaregistry.org/historic_events/view/leona-p-thurman-kcs-first-black-woman-lawyer.

Lewis, Melvin. "Has Progress Risen From Ashes of 1968 Riot Here?" *Kansas City Star*, April 9, 1973.

Lewis, Meriwether and William Clark. "The Journals of Lewis and Clark." *Archive.org*, 2005. https:// archive.org/stream/thejournalsoflew08419gut/lcjnl10.txt.

Loewen, James. *Lies My Teacher Told Me*. New York: Simon & Schuster, 2007.

Loewen, James. *Sundown Towns: A Hidden Dimension of American Racism*. New York: The New Press, 2005.

Logan, John and Brian Stults. "The Persistence of Segregation in the Metropolis: New Findings from the 2010 Census." Census brief prepared for Project US2010. March 24, 2011, 6-7. http://www.s4.brown.edu/us2010/Data/Report/report2.pdf.

Lovett, Christopher. "A Public Burning: Race, Sex, and the Lynching of Fred Alexander." *Kansas History* 33 (summer 2010): 94-115.

"Lynchings: By State and Race, 1882-1968." *University of Missouri-Kansas City*. Accessed February 15, 2014. http://law2.umkc.edu/faculty/projects/ftrials/shipp/lynchingsstate.html.

MacCambridge, Michael. *Lamar Hunt: A Life in Sports.* Kansas City: Andrews McMeel, 2012.

Males 1, 2, and 3. Interviewed by Robert Bechtel and Kenneth King. http://library.umkc.edu/ sites/default/files/images/spec-col/col-1968riot-interview-01-anonymous-student-participants.pdf.

Marx, Karl. *Surveys from Exile.* London: Verso, 2010.

Mattox, Joe Louis. "Harry Truman's Hat Tip at 'The Top Hat' Changed My Life." *Jackson County Historical Society Journal* 46, no. 2 (Autumn 2005): 12-18.

Mattox, Joe Louis. "Roy Wilkins, THE CALL and the NAACP." *Kansas City Call*, October 23-29, 2009.

Mattox, Joe Louis. "Talkin' Bout 'The Third' and 'The Vine Part II.'" *Kansas City Call*, December 14-20, 2007.

McCullough, David. *Truman.* New York: Simon & Shuster, 1992.

McGraw, Mike and Glenn Rice. "'70s Slaying of KC Politician Leon Jordan a Mob Hit?" *Kansas City Star,* October 30, 2010.

McGraw, Mike and Glenn Rice. "Evidence Points to Mob's Associate's Involvement in Jordan Killing." *Kansas City Star,* October 31, 2010.

McGraw, Mike and Glenn Rice. "Unsolved Killing of Leon Jordan Echoes Civil Rights Era." *Kansas City Star,* September 9, 2010.

McKinley, James. "A Black Panther's Mellow Exile." *New York Times*, November 23, 1997.

Meinick, R. Shep. "The Two Billion Dollar Judge." *Claremont Institute.* July 13, 2009. http://www.claremont.org/publications/crb/id.1614/article_detail.asp.

Miller, Randy. "Race Indeed Does Matter in the Classroom." *Huffington Post.* March 10, 2013. http://www.huffingtonpost.com/randy-miller/race-schools_b_2847603.html.

Min, Seong-Jae and John Feaster. "Missing Children in National News Coverage: Racial and Gender Representations of Missing Children Cases." *Communications Research Reports* 27, no. 3 (July-September 2010): 213.

"Missouri's Early Slave Laws." *Missouri Digital Heritage.* Accessed February 15, 2014. http://www.sos.mo.gov/archives/education/aahi/earlyslavelaws/slavelaws.asp.

"Mob of 1,000 Lynch Negro in Missouri, with Passengers on a Train as Witnesses." *New York Times,* August 8, 1925.

"Mob Once Hanged an Innocent Negro Here," *Kansas City Journal,* August 18, 1908.

Montgomery, Rick and Shirl Kasper. *Kansas City: An American Story.* Kansas City: Kansas City Star Books, 1999.

Montgomery, Rick. "Foreword on the Civil War in Kansas City." *Civil War on the Western Border.* Kansas City Public Library. Accessed February 17, 2014. http://www. civilwaronthewesternborder. org/essay/foreword-civil-war-kansas-city.

Morris, Mark. "Parolee is Accused of Hate Crime in Platte County." *Kansas City Star,* March 7, 2013.

Morris, Mark. "Parole Hearing for Killer in 1980 Hate Crime Reopens Old Wounds." *Kansas City Star,* April 23, 2013.

Morris, Mark. "Two Independence Residents are Sentenced in Hate Crime." *Kansas City Star,* January 23, 2013.

Mutti Burke, Diane. *On Slavery's Border: Missouri's Small-Slaveholding Households, 1815-1865.* Athens: University of Georgia Press, 2010.

Mutti Burke, Diane. "Slavery on the Western Border: Missouri's Slave System and its Collapse during the Civil War." *Civil War on the Western Border,* Kansas City Public Library. Accessed March 18, 2014. http://www.civilwaronthewesternborder.org/essay/slavery-western-border-missouri's-slave-system-and-its-collapse-during-civil-war.

"NAACP Releases 12th Annual Economic Reciprocity Report Detailing Corporate Diversity Progress." *NAACP.org.* Accessed February 17, 2014. http://www.naacp.org/press/ entry/naacp-releases-12th-annual-economic-reciprocity-report--detailing-corporate-diversity-progress/.

Neely, Jeremy. "A Most Cruel and Unjust War." *Civil War on the Western Border.* Kansas City Public Library. Accessed February

17, 2014. http://www. civilwaronthewesternborder.org/essay/"-most-cruel-and-unjust-war"-guerrilla-struggle-along-missouri-kansas-border.

"Negro Hanged in Missouri." *The Evening Democrat* (Warren, PA), May 3, 1900.

Netter, Sarah. "Missouri Man Shocked at Being Labeled N-Word on Store Receipt." *ABC News*. October 22, 2008, http://abcnews. go.com/US/story?id=6088706.

Newbart, Dave. "Dillard's—A Store That Just Doesn't Get It." *Phoenix New Times,* July 14, 1993.

Newill, Cody. "#Blacklivesmatter Protesters Arrested After Attempt to Block I-70 in Kansas City." *KCUR*, December 21, 2014. http://kcur.org/post/blacklivesmatter-protesters-arrested-after-attempt-block-i-70-kansas-city.

Noland, Brian. "In Working Toward Justice, Minorities are Underrepresented Among the Nation's Lawyers." *Kansas City Star*, February 6, 2015.

Nolen, Rose. *Hoecakes, Hambone, and All That Jazz*. Columbia: University of Missouri Press, 2003.

O'Brien, William P. "Hiram Young: Black Entrepreneur on the Santa Fe Trail." *Wagon Tracks* 4, no. 1 (November 1989): http://www. santafetrail.org/the-trail/history/best-of-wagon-tracks/Hiram_Young.pdf.

O'Bryan, Tony. "Collapse of the Union Women's Prison in Kansas City." *Civil War on the Western Border*. Kansas City Public Library. Accessed February 17, 2014. http://www. civilwaronthewesternborder.org/content/collapse-union-women's-prison-kansas-city.

O'Neill, Blaine. "African Americans Campaign for Desegregation of Department Store Eating Facilities in Kansas City, Missouri, 1958-59." *Global Nonviolent Action Database*. December 9, 2010. http://nvdatabase.swarthmore.edu/content/african-americans-campaign-desegregation-department-store-eating-facilities-kansas-city-miss.

Pearman, Robert. "Black Crime, Black Victims." *Nation* 208 (April 21, 1969): 502.

Pearson, Nathan. *Goin' to Kansas City.* Champaign: University of Illinois Press, 1994.

Pettigrew, Alversia. *Memories of a Neck Child.* Independence, MO, 1996.

Poe, Julia. "Is East Racist?" *Harbinger.* Accessed May 22, 2015. http:// smeharbinger.net/is-east-racist.

"Police Break 33 Doors At Byron Hotel." *Kansas City Call*, April 19-25, 1968.

Prichard, Jeremy. "Bogus Legislature." *Civil War on the Western Border.* Kansas City Public Library. Accessed February 17, 2014. http://www.civilwaronthewesternborder.org/ content/ bogus-legislature.

Prichard, Jeremy. "New England Emigrant Aid Company." *Civil War on the Western Border.* Kansas City Public Library. Accessed February 17, 2014. http://www. civilwaronthewesternborder. org/content/new-england-emigrant-aid-company.

"Quindaro Ruins." *Wycokck. org.* Accessed February 15, 2014. http://www.wycokck.org InternetDeptaspx?id=16256&banner=15284.

"Raytown, Missouri (MO) Income, Earnings, and Wages Data." *City Data.* 2009. http://www.city-data.com/income/income-Raytown-Missouri.html.

"Report Details Plaza Disorder, Previous Incidents." *KCTV5*, April 12, 2010. http:// www.kctv5.com/story/14782696/report-details-plaza-disorder-previous-incidents-4-12-2010.

"Report on Interviews with Planning Group Members." *Kansas City Round Table on Access and Opportunity*, April 19, 2006. http://www.aspeninstitute.org/sites/default/files/content/ docs/rcc/KCRT_PLANNING_GROUP_-_REPORT_ON_ INTERVIEWS.PDF.

Rhodes, Joel. "It Finally Happened Here: The 1968 Riot in Kansas City, Missouri." *Missouri Historical Review* 91 (April 1997): 300.

Rice, Glenn. "Four Are Arrested in a Small Ferguson Protest Near the Country Club Plaza." *Kansas City Star*, November 28, 2014.

Rice, Glenn and Lynn Horsley. "Authorities Want to Kill 'Coffin' Trend After Teens Arrested on Country Club Plaza." *Kansas City Star*, April 6, 2015.

Rice, Glenn and Tony Rizzo. "Police Fall Short in Racial Diversity." *Kansas City Star*, August 24, 2014.

"Rioting in City Takes Five Lives." *Kansas City Star*, April 11, 1968.

Rizzo, Tony. "Inmate, Experts are Baffled by Burglary Term of 80 Years." *Kansas City Star*, April 18, 2015.

Robertson, Joe. "Failed Deal Between KC Schools, Academie Lafayette Reveals City's Issues with Race and Education." *Kansas City Star*, March 15, 2015.

Robertson, Joe. "Missouri's Suspension Rate of Black Elementary Students Highest in the Nation." *Kansas City Star*, February 23, 2015.

Roe, Jason. "Water Rights." *Kansas City Public Library*. Accessed February 17, 2014. http://www.kclibrary.org/blog/week-kansas-city-history/water-rights.

Rosenberg, Leon. *Dillard's: The First Fifty Years*. Fayetteville: University of Arkansas Press, 1988.

Ross, Harry. Interviewed by Ron Horn. January 21, 1969. http://library.umkc.edu/sites/default/files/images/spec-col/col-1968riot-interview-02-ross.pdf.

Sanchez, Mary. "Kansas City Chose Community Over Chaos." Kansas City Star, August 14, 2014.

Sanchez, Mary. "What I Learned from the Rev. Nelson 'Fuzzy' Thompson." *Kansas City Star*, January 13, 2015.

Saulny, Susan. "Board's Decision to Close 28 Kansas City Schools Follows Years of Inaction." *New York Times,* March 11, 2010.

Scanlon, Heather. "From Slavery to Progressivism to…Racism: Kansas City from the 1860s-1900s." *Squeezebox,* February 6, 2015. http://www.squeezeboxcity.com/from-slavery-to-progressivism-to-racism-kansas-city-from-the-1860s-1900s/.

Scanlon, Heather. "Tour Through Hell's Half-Acre." *Squeezebox*, March 2, 2015. http://www.squeezeboxcity.com/tour-though-hells-half-acre/.

Schirmer, Sherry L. *A City Divided: The Racial Landscape of Kansas City, 1900-1960*. Columbia, MO: University of Missouri Press, 2002.

Schirmer, Sherry L. "Historical Review of the Ethnic Communities in Kansas City." *Pan-educational Institute*, 1976.

"School Demographic Profile for Silver City Elementary School." *Kckps.org*. October 2011. http://kckps.org/dera/demographics/silver_city.pdf.

School profile handout. *Visitation School*. 2013.

Smith, DeAnn and Heather Staggers. "Lee's Summit North Student Disciplined for Racist Blog." *KCTV5*, December 16, 2011. http://www.kctv5.com/story/16343301/lees-summit-student-under-scrutiny-for-racist-blog.

Stafford, Diane. "Class-Action Lawsuit Alleges Racial Discrimination at Power & Light." *Kansas City Star*, March 10, 2014.

Stafford, Diane. "Kansas City 'Peace Rally' Lauds Police-Community Cooperation." *Kansas City Star*, May 2, 2015.

Stanley, Matthew. "1st Kansas Colored Volunteers." *Civil War on the Western Border*. Kansas City Public Library. Accessed February 17, 2014. http://www.civilwaronthewesternborder.org/content/1st-kansas-colored-volunteers-later-79th-us-colored-infantry.

"The State of Black Kansas City 2015 Equality Index." *University of Missouri-Kansas City*, 2015. http://iamempoweredkc.org/assets/2015/2015-Equality-Index-State-of-Black-Kansas-City-abridged.pdf.

"Steady March Toward Accreditation." *Kansas City Star*, March 2, 2015.

Stern, Kimberly W. "Long Considered KC's Racial Dividing Line, Troost Avenue is Diversifying." *Kansas City Star*, April 29, 2014.

"Students of Color Still Receiving Unequal Education." *Center for American Progress*. August 22, 2012. http://www.

americanprogress.org/issues/education/news/2012/08/22/
32862/students-of-color-still-receiving-unequal-education/.

"Suit Says Magnet Schools Bar Black Children." *New York Times*,
August 3, 1989.

"Summary of Testimony from Sergeant Wilson." May 28, 1969.
http://library.umkc.edu/ sites/default/files/images/spec-col/col-
1968riot-interview-04-wilson.pdf.

Swaine, John, Oliver Laughland, and Jamiles Lartey. "Black Americans
Killed by Police Twice as Likely to be Unarmed as White
People." *Guardian*, June 1, 2015. http://www.theguardian.
com/us-news/2015/jun/01/black-americans-killed-by-police-
analysis.

Swomley, John. "The Kansas City Riot Could Have Been Averted."
Focus Midwest 6 (July/August 1968): 11.

Sykes, Alvin. "Investigating Anti-Civil Rights Cases: The Emmett Till
Bill." Speech at the Crimes of the Civil Rights Era Conference.
Boston, MA, April 27-28, 2007. http://nuweb9.neu.edu/
civilrights/wp-content/uploads/Sykes_The_Emmett_Till_Bill.
pdf.

"The Ten-Point Program." *Marxists.org*. Accessed February 17,
2014. http://www.marxists.org/history/usa/workers/black-
panthers/1966/10/15.htm.

Tharoor, Ishaan. "In Facebook Photo, Suspected Charleston Shooter
Wears Flags of Racist Regimes in Africa." *Washington Post*, June
18, 2015. http://www.washingtonpost.com/ blogs/worldviews/
wp/2015/06/18/in-facebook-photo-suspected-charleston-
shooter-wears-flags-of-racist-regimes-in-africa/.

Thomas, Clarence. Concurrence, *Missouri v. Jenkins (93-1823), 515
U.S. 70 (1995)*. June 12, 1995. http://www.law.cornell.edu/
supct/html/93-1823.ZC1.html.

Thomas, Judy L. "Only a Matter of Time: Inside the American
Extremist Movements." *Kansas City Star*, April 26, 2015.

Townes, Carimah. "How News Outlets Help Convince You That
Most Criminals Are Black." *Think Progress*, March 25, 2015.

http://thinkprogress.org/justice/2015/03/25/3638635/dont-let-mainstream-media-fool-you/.

"Trayvon Martin's Unpunished Shooting Death Among 100+ Extrajudicial Killings of Unarmed Blacks." *Democracy Now.* July 17, 2013. http://www.democracynow.org/2013/7/17/ trayvon_martins_ unpunished_shooting_death_among.

Trillin, Calvin. "U.S. Journal: Kansas City—I Got Nothing against the Colored." *New Yorker* 44, May 11, 1968, 107.

Trexler, Harrison. "The Value and Sale of the Missouri Slave." *Missouri Historical Review* 8 (October 1913): 71.

United Daughters of the Confederacy. *Reminiscences of the Women of Missouri During the Sixties.* Jefferson City: Hugh Stephens Printing, 1920.

"United States Colored Troops in Missouri." *Missouri Digital Heritage.* Accessed February 17, 2014. http://www.sos.mo.gov/archives/ education/usct/usct_history.asp.

United States Department of State, *Trafficking in Persons Report.* June 2013.

Watson, Catherine. "Missouri's Bloody Civil War Battles." *Los Angeles Times,* April 10, 2011.

We Are Superman: The Transformation of 31ˢᵗ and Troost. Directed by Kevin Bryce. 2012. Kansas City, MO.

Wells-Barnett, Ida. *A Red Record: Tabulated Statistics and Alleged Causes of Lynchings in the United States.* Chicago: Donohue and Henneberry, 1895.

"When Kansas City Celebrated Slavery's End." *Kansas City Times,* July 22, 1965.

"White Guy, Black Girl and Dinner. My First Taste of Racism." *CNN iReport,* October 18, 2009. http://ireport.cnn.com/docs/DOC-343043.

White, Susan. "31st and Prospect Six Months Later." *Kansas City Town Squire* 1, November 8, 1968, 22-24.

Whitehead, Colson. "What We Don't See." *New York Times Magazine,* May 28, 2015. http://www.nytimes.com/2015/05/31/ magazine/what-we-dont-see.html?_r=0.

Wilkins, Roy. *Standing Fast.* New York: Da Capo Press, 1994.

Wise, Tim. *Colorblind.* San Francisco: City Lights Books, 2010.

Wise, Tim. *Dear White America.* San Francisco: City Light Books, 2012.

Wise, Tim. "What Whites Don't Know About Racism." *CNN.com.* November 25, 2015.

Yates, J. Silone and Jones, A.H. "Kansas City Women's League." *The Woman's Era* 1, no. 1 (1894).http://womenwriters.library.emory. edu/abolition/content.php?level=div&id=era1_01.03.03 &document=era1.

Young, Harvey. "The Black Body as Souvenir in American Lynching." *Theatre Journal* 57, no. 4 (2005): 639-657. doi: 10.1353/ tj.2006.0054.

Young, William and Young Jr., Nathan. *Your Kansas City and Mine.* Kansas City: 1950.

Youth Ambassadors. *I'm Not No One.* Kansas City: AlphaGraphics, 2014.

"York." *PBS.org.* Accessed February 15, 2014. http://www.pbs.org/ lewisandclark/inside/ york.html.

Ziegler, Laura. "Another Suit Filed Alleging Discrimination at Power & Light." *KCUR.org.* March 10, 2014. http://kcur.org/post/ another-suit-filed-alleging-discrimination-power-light-district.

Ziegler, Laura. "New Lawsuit Alleges Racial Discrimination at Power and Light." *KCUR.org.* March 6, 2014. http://kcur. org/post/new-lawsuit-alleges-racial-discrimination-power-and-light?nopop=1.

Ziegler, Laura. "The Life and Work of Kansas City Civil Rights Activist Alvin Sykes." *KCUR.org.* January 9, 2014. http://kcur. org/post/life-and-work-kansas-city-civil-rights-activist-alvin-sykes.

Zinn, Howard. *A People's History of the United States.* New York: HarperCollins, 2003.

ACKNOWLEDGMENTS

I would like to extend a special thanks to Charles Coulter, Alvin Brooks, Jason Roe, Diane Mutti Burke, and Joe Louis Mattox for reading my early manuscript and offering their invaluable insights. Thanks, also, to the staff at the Kansas City Public Library for providing easy access to historical documents in the Missouri Valley Special Collections Archive. Finally, my thanks to Doug Weaver, Anne Stanton, and Heather Shaw at Mission Point Press, for bringing this book to life.

INDEX

Photo by Becker Griffin

Garrett S. Griffin was born in Kansas City. He studied at Missouri State University and earned a graduate degree in history education at Rockhurst University. After a couple years working with special needs students, he is now a political writer. He lives in Grandview, Missouri.

www.ingramcontent.com/pod-product-compliance
Lightning Source LLC
Chambersburg PA
CBHW021355090426
42742CB00009B/855